SUCCESSFUL
FOCUS
GROUPS

OTHER RECENT VOLUMES IN THE
SAGE FOCUS EDITIONS

SUCCESSFUL FOCUS GROUPS

Advancing the State of the Art

David L. Morgan
editor

SAGE PUBLICATIONS
International Educational and Professional Publisher
Newbury Park   London   New Delhi

For information address:

SAGE Publications, Inc.
2455 Teller Road
Newbury Park, California 91320

SAGE Publications Ltd.
6 Bonhill Street
London EC2A 4PU
United Kingdom

SAGE Publications India Pvt. Ltd.
M-32 Market
Greater Kailash I
New Delhi 110 048 India

Printed in the United States of America

Library of Congress Cataloging-in-Publication Data

Morgan, David L.
    Successful focus groups : advancing the state of the art / David
L. Morgan.
        p. cm.—(Sage focus edition : 156)
    Includes bibliographical references and index.
    ISBN 0-8039-4873-5 (cl.)—ISBN 0-8039-4874-3 (pb)
    1. Focused group interviewing. 2. Social sciences—Research—
Methodology. I. Title.
H61.28.M68   1993
300'.72—dc20   93-6872

93 94 95 96 97 10 9 8 7 6 5 4 3 2 1

Sage Production Editor: Astrid Virding

Contents

Preface

Like many other edited collections, this book had its beginnings at a conference. Still, those of us who have contributed to it would like to think that it has a special origin. One reason is that we organized the conference specifically for the purpose of bringing together the work that now forms the chapters of this book. Another reason is that our meetings consisted almost entirely of focus group-like discussions rather than paper presentations. The range of issues that we discussed was wide indeed, and we used the insights that we gained from those discussions both to guide the outline for the overall book and to inform the individual chapters. Since that original meeting, we have worked long and hard on our goal of producing a book that not only demonstrates current trends in focus group research but also advances the state of the art in our emerging field.

A distinctive contributor to the success of this project was our original meeting place, the Menucha Conference Center near Portland, Oregon. *Menucha* is a Hebrew word, meaning "a peaceful place," and that peaceful environment helped to stimulate many exciting exchanges. At the start, few of us had ever even met one another, but over the course of a long weekend, we became newfound colleagues. The spirit that we developed was nurtured by the beauty of our surroundings, so in the final chapter and elsewhere the reader will find references to the Menucha Conference.

In addition to the good people who run Menucha, we also owe a major acknowledgment to our funding sources: the American Sociological Association (based on a grant to the ASA from the National Science Foundation) and a matching grant from Portland State University's Faculty Development Program. Lest anyone think that this was a lavish affair, however, I would also like to thank the conference participants, who defrayed many of their personal expenses to make our gathering possible.

Among the many individuals who contributed to this project, I would like to single out two for special mention. First, my graduate assistant and colleague Steve March. In addition to being a man of all work during the conference itself, Steve accompanied me on our first scouting trip to Menucha, and it was he who pointed out that no one would sit in such an inspiring setting and listen to a bunch of papers! Second, I would like to thank our editor at Sage, Mitch Allen, who was at Menucha. Even if he has never done a focus group in his life, Mitch did give us a great deal of valuable advice on how to put together a book.

Any project as complex as putting on a conference and producing a book produces a great deal of indebtedness. I owe special thanks to: my wife, Susan Wladaver-Morgan, who provided advice, support, and last-minute copy editing; the secretaries at the Institute on Aging, Lucy Sacharkiw and Sue Reggiani, who helped with everything from meal arrangements to mailings; and my graduate assistant Richard White who toiled over endless details so that this book could finally arrive in your hands.

— DAVID L. MORGAN

Introduction

Just 5 years ago, few social scientists had heard of focus groups, yet now they are the subject of widespread interest. The field has grown by recruiting both bright new investigators, who use focus groups as their primary data-gathering tool, and more experienced researchers, who are applying their existing expertise to this less explored technique. This book brings together the work of the leading social science researchers in focus groups and group interviews to meet the needs of both these sets of readers. Our goals are to help those who are relatively new to this method to do the best possible research with focus groups and to encourage those with more experience to join us in developing this rapidly growing method.

Although the chapters in this book cover a wide variety of specific topics, all the authors share an interest in advancing focus groups as a social science research method. It was this interest that led to the Menucha Conference that was the origin of this book. There was a clear consensus among us that increased attention to methodological issues was vital to the future of focus groups. Therefore, in deciding on the topics that we wanted to cover in this book, we set ourselves the long-term goal of achieving a level of sophistication that would give focus groups a permanent place within the range of social science research methods. We also agreed that improving current research procedures was just as important as methodological innovation. To this end, these chapters balance discussions of methodological issues with practical demonstrations of how these issues apply to real-world research projects.

The authors take two related routes to achieving our stated objective of advancing the state of the art in focus group research. On the one hand, we share our expertise and experience to meet the practical needs of an increasingly large group of social scientists who are interested in focus groups. On the other hand, we develop a vision of the future to lay a foundation for more advanced applications of focus groups within social science research.

Although this is not a book for absolute beginners, the material in these chapters should be immediately accessible to anyone who has read one of the several basic books on focus groups for social scientists or an equivalent book from the marketing literature. Yes, the authors do take a sophisticated approach to their topics, but even those who are relatively new to focus groups should have little difficulty assimilating the materials because of the many practical examples included.

Layout of the Book

Part I examines a series of basic principles that are relevant to all focus group research, regardless of the type of focus group one is doing. In the first chapter, Richard Krueger and I discuss not just "when to do focus groups and why," but also when not to do them and why not to do them. As part of the maturing of our field, we need to recognize that focus groups have some very real limitations, and we need to avoid the temptation to apply them to every possible topic under the sun. At the same time, there is no reason that we should be shy about our virtues, so we extol the advantages of focus groups and explode some myths about them. We end the chapter with our own consideration of the strengths of focus groups, showing how the unique advantages of focus groups can help one decide when to use them.

The second chapter, by James Frey and Andrea Fontana called "The Group Interview in Social Research," is the only one that is reprinted from a previous publication. These authors place focus groups within the larger realm of types of group interviews. Too often, it seems that focus groups are virtually the only form of group interview, but Frey and Fontana show that various forms of group interviews have been used quite widely, even if they have not been so widely acknowledged. One way that our field can grow is not only by considering other possible ways of doing things but also by realizing that we have some unquestioned assumptions about what we do and why we do it a particular way. By comparing focus groups with other forms of group interviews, Frey and Fontana offer us an excellent opportunity to challenge our presuppositions.

In Chapter 3, John Knodel takes up issues of design and analysis from a practical point of view. This emphasis on applying design principles in research projects using focus groups is rapidly becoming one of the hallmarks of our field. Knodel's discussion of design issues is especially strong for studies that use the researcher's theoretical interests to break the total set of participants into separate subsets. This strategy of comparing and contrasting groups that represent different perspectives is a powerful example of focus group research design. Importantly, Knodel shows how this initial design decision carries through into the analysis as well as in the collection of the data. In addition, his practical orientation to these issues will provide readers with many useful suggestions.

In Chapter 4, Terrance Albrecht, Gerianne Johnson, and Joseph Walther bring a fresh perspective to focus groups by considering them from the point of view of communication researchers. Among the topics they consider are validity issues, influence processes, and comparisons to nominal groups and Delphi groups. Of particular interest is their discussion of fantasy themes as a way both to stimulate group communication and to analyze the shared discourse in groups. They end with a series of recommendations that summarize the applicability of principles from communications research to focus groups. By offering a combination of new ideas and innovative approaches to familiar problems, this chapter provides a strong demonstration of the value of interdisciplinary contacts for the growth of our field.

In the fifth chapter, Richard Krueger reviews the wide range of factors that affect the quality of focus groups. Like many of us, he is concerned that the rapid growth of interest in focus groups will lead to problems of quality control. By providing a thorough summary of the different factors that can affect the quality of research, he paints an accurate picture of the complexities of focus groups. But Krueger is no exponent of doom and gloom; instead, he uses each of his 10 factors to point out specific things that focus group researchers should be doing to ensure the quality of the work that we do. His approach thus emphasizes a major theme that runs through all of the chapters in Part I: We need to be aware of the implicit choices that we are making as we design, conduct, and analyze our focus groups. To get good results, we need to make smart choices, and these four chapters provide a valuable guide to making such choices.

Part II contains four chapters that consider ways of combining focus groups with other methods. Certainly the best known use of focus groups in combination with other methods has been as a preliminary step in the development of survey instruments. Unfortunately, despite the widespread popularity of this practice, relatively little has been written about what is involved in the actual execution of focus groups for the development of survey instruments. By remedying this omission, the first two chapters in this section are important steps toward a systematic body of knowledge on this intersection of qualitative and quantitative methods.

In Chapter 6, Theodore Fuller, John Edwards, Sairudee Vorakitphokatorn, and Santhat Sermsri describe the insights that they gained by using focus groups to develop a survey on the effects of crowding in Bangkok, Thailand. As they note, their major concepts were already in place, based on research in the United States, but they needed to translate more than just the language to make their questions appropriate in a different cultural context. They found that their focus groups were particularly valuable for validating the relevancy of their existing concepts, formulating new hypotheses, and pointing the research team toward the best way of communicating with the target audience for their survey.

In Chapter 7, Kerth O'Brien presents her development of a questionnaire on the responses of gay and bisexual men to the HIV/AIDS epidemic. Once again, the formulation of the questions is central to this process to, as she puts it, help the investigator to ask the right questions and to ask them in the right way. In addition, O'Brien shows how focus groups provided insights into issues of sample location and recruitment as well as establishing the credibility of the researcher and the project. All of these issues are important when working with vulnerable and understudied populations, and this chapter is particularly notable for showing how focus groups can help survey researchers to resolve these problems.

These preliminary uses of focus groups in the development of surveys differ from the truly triangulated combination of these two methods that Brent Wolff, John Knodel, and Werasit Sittitrai take up in Chapter 8. They report on a study that simultaneously used focus groups and surveys to investigate how changes in family size were linked to the well-being of villagers in rural Thailand. The authors show how focus groups can contribute to a multimethod approach by confirming and illustrating findings, clarifying and elaborating on unexpected or contradictory results, and uncovering new explanatory categories that were not foreseen at the start of the project. Overall, they show how a carefully designed combination of methods can produce results that clearly are more than the sum of the separate parts.

Chapter 9 by Benjamin Crabtree, Kim Yanoshik, William Miller, and Patrick O'Connor concludes Part II by moving away from surveys to consider the combination of group and individual interviews. If the three preceding chapters represent long overdue descriptions of increasingly common practices, this one explores subjects that have been, to this point, largely overlooked. Based on their experiences with each technique, Crabtree et al. point out a number of factors that can influence the choice between individual and group interviews: time and money, depth versus breadth, interview dynamics, communication context, analysis and sampling issues, method as intervention, and logistics. The portrait that emerges is a classic summary of the relative advantages and disadvantages of each technique. Although, as the authors note in their conclusion, we still need to do more research that directly compares group and individual interviews, the lessons that they have learned from their experiences are an important first step toward a greater understanding of the complementary nature of these two forms of interviewing.

In contrast to Part II, the chapters in Part III take up issues that apply to projects that rely solely on focus groups. Chapter 10, by Raymond Padilla, begins this section by discussing ways that focus groups can help to implement the kind of participatory research advocated by Paulo Freire. What he terms *dialogical research* actually involves two different dialogues: that among the research participants and that between the participants and the researchers. It is the dialogue between the researchers and the participants that defines this form of research, and the goal is to direct everyone's efforts to meeting the participants' needs. In addition to presenting the role of focus groups in this process, Padilla forcefully reminds us that our purposes must define our methods. Thus this chapter not only demonstrates the variety of uses for focus groups but also challenges our thinking about how we use focus groups for our own research goals.

In Chapter 11, Richard Zeller presents three principles for conducting groups that involve sensitive topics: capitalizing on reactivity, using self-disclosure, and legitimizing participants' responses. In doing so, he nicely illustrates how to apply basic knowledge from such fields as research methodology, communication studies, and social psychology to resolving specific issues in focus group research. Because Zeller uses standard principles from the social sciences as the foundation for developing his strategies, the many concrete examples from his own research on sexuality also have immediate relevance for those working with other sensitive topics. Overall, this chapter provides an excellent illustration of the linkage between the fundamental knowledge base of the social sciences and practical strategies for designing focus group research projects.

Robin Jarrett's chapter considers the complexities of doing focus groups with low-income, minority women. Many of the issues she discusses (access, rapport, etc.) will be familiar to most qualitative researchers, but these issues often receive too little attention in focus group research. We need to think carefully about all the procedures in our research projects and not just concentrate on those golden minutes within the groups themselves. As Jarrett demonstrates, these procedural issues can be vital when working with hard-to-reach groups. Still, as she points out, many of the general principles of focus group research will apply to our roles as researchers with such groups, as well as to the kinds of discussions that happen in these groups. As her own research so ably demonstrates, our work with groups that lie outside the stereotypic mainstream requires a balance between the generalities that we can apply to most groups and a sensitivity to the specific issues that apply to specialized populations.

In Chapter 13, Thomas Plaut, Suzanne Landis, and June Trevor present their work with community-based health care in the last chapter in this section. Their application of focus groups is an admirable example of how to use the participants' own perspectives in designing a large-scale, long-term intervention. They also show (as does O'Brien in Chapter 7), that the kinds of contacts that occur in focus groups are not just a source of data but also a way for researchers to show that they take the participants' views seriously and thus to build the kind of trust that long-term relationships require. The programs that these authors have created demonstrate that effective community-based interventions must do more than meet the needs of the community; they must come from the community, and focus groups are a powerful means of facilitating this process.

The final section of the book consists only of Chapter 14, my report on a series of focus groups at the Menucha Conference that envisioned "future directions for focus groups." In our groups, we discussed four areas that we considered vital to our future as a field: doing more research on focus groups, creating more links to other disciplines, developing focus groups for various purposes, and working on technology issues. Because these general themes connect with the more detailed presentations in the earlier chapters, this concluding chapter provides a useful summary of the larger issues that we are dealing with as a field. This dual attention to both practical and abstract issues also illustrates our two broad approaches to creating successful focus groups: helping researchers to find the solutions that are already within reach and encouraging innovative work that will expand the boundaries of our field.

—DAVID L. MORGAN

PART I

Basic Principles

1

When to Use Focus Groups and Why

DAVID L. MORGAN
RICHARD A. KRUEGER

Too often, decision making about focus groups is governed by myths. Other chapters in this volume address the myths that surround the technical issues of how to do focus groups (see also Morgan, 1992). In this chapter, we will first tackle the mythology surrounding the appropriate uses for focus groups, then point out some reasons *not* to use focus groups, and finish with some of our views about when focus groups are most likely to have advantages over other research methods. Our goal is to give the reader a better basis for making decisions about when and why to use focus groups for a particular purpose.

Social science and evaluation research are still at a stage at which most of our knowledge about focus groups comes from personal experience rather than systematic investigation. Even so, the past several years have seen a rapid expansion in the range of experiences that we have been able to draw on. Until quite recently, much of our knowledge about focus groups came from marketing researchers. Now we know much more about how to apply focus groups in our own areas of interest. This chapter is a step toward systematizing our experience to guide future work. As those of us with social science and evaluation research backgrounds have expanded our experience with using focus groups, we have learned that too many of the "rules" derived from other fields turned out to be undependable when applied to our own needs and goals. The reasons why marketers use focus groups are not the same as the reasons why evaluation researchers use focus groups. And the reasons why evaluators use focus groups are not the same as the reasons why academic researchers use focus groups.

In our view, having the ability to draw on the experiences of researchers from a number of different domains helps us all. And that is the reason for our collaboration on this chapter. Krueger represents experience with focus groups in program development and evaluation. Morgan represents experience with focus groups in academically oriented qualitative research. Together, our goal is to compare and summarize our experiences to guide others. At the same time, we are mindful that if we had limited ourselves to following only the advice that was available when we each began doing focus groups, we would never have discovered many of the possibilities we will be discussing here. So we encourage our readers to learn from our experiences but not to feel bound by them.

Some Common Myths About Focus Groups

Reaching intelligent decisions about when to use focus groups requires that we go beyond the mythology that has guided too much of past practice. There are myths about both the advantages and disadvantages of focus groups. We have been too hasty in assuming that focus groups are appropriate for some purposes and too slow in applying them to other purposes. We will thus question myths about both when to use focus groups and when not to. In each case, we will get at the assumptions behind the myth, so that the reader can make a well-reasoned decision about how these issues apply to any particular research project.

Focus Groups Are Cheap and Quick

Focus groups often *appear* to be done cheaply because the research team donates a large amount of labor or the labor is paid for from another source. If a volunteer or staff member can moderate the groups, analyze the data, and prepare the report, then actual monetary outlays can be minimized. If it is necessary to hire professionals to do these tasks, however, total project costs can easily exceed $1000 per group and may even fall into the range of $3000 to $4000 per group.

Focus groups can only be done quickly in very unusual circumstances. Although the group itself may last only 1 or 2 hours, it takes time to create an effective set of questions, locate the appropriate participants, and make sense of the data they provide. Recruitment and analysis are especially likely to be expensive and time-consuming, unless the participants are already at hand and the project goals are very limited and direct.

The myth that focus groups can be done cheaply and quickly has lead to many inappropriate uses of focus groups, based more on expediency than on the appropriateness of the method for the purposes at hand. The reality is that focus groups require planning, effort, and resources, just like every other research method. And, just like every other research method, making a realistic assessment of time and money issues at the beginning of a project is a good way to avoid problems later on.

**Focus Groups Require Moderators
With Highly Developed Professional Skills**

Those of us who work in evaluation and qualitative social science had to confront this myth early on, due to the lack of trained moderators in our fields. In reality, it may be more than merely feasible to find a good moderator from within the research team, it may in fact be preferable to do so. This is particularly true when there is a real need for a moderator who has a detailed familiarity with either the project goals or the participants' points of view. For example, when the research project's goals are in a continual state of evolution, someone who is directly involved in the project can do a better job of steering the discussion in useful directions. Or when the participants are part of a distinctive cultural group, someone with the appropriate sensitivity may be a more effective moderator than someone who merely has professional credentials.

Worrying about the skills a professional moderator would bring to a project often gets the project heading in the wrong direction right from the beginning. Instead, the first-order goals should be to define what the purposes of the project are and who the participants in the groups should be. Then one can confront the real issue: What kind of moderator will it take to get useful data from these participants?

Too much emphasis on the moderator's skills also diverts attention from the fact that the outcome of a research project depends on more than just the ability to lead a group. Most important, if the research team lacks the requisite analysis skills, then the quality of the group discussions hardly matters. Even as mundane a matter as recruitment may override the importance of the moderator's contributions, if it proves impossible to provide enough participants in the appropriate categories. The lesson is that a successful focus group project requires a variety of skills and often depends on the input of several different members of a qualified research team. Just because the moderator's role is a distinctive aspect of focus groups, we must not lose sight of the other contributions that are also necessary.

In demythologizing professional moderators, it is just as important, however, not to create a new myth that anyone can moderate a focus group. The moderator is the instrument in a focus group interview. If the moderator, as the data-collection instrument, is not prepared, not attentive or not skillful, then the results will be just as bad as in a poorly prepared survey questionnaire. Consequently, on-the-job-training will not be appropriate in many projects. On balance, when seeking alternatives to professional moderators, the key is to find someone who has experience working with groups (not necessarily *leading* groups) and who is also capable of working with both the research team and the participants in this particular project.

Focus Groups Must Consist of Strangers

This is a good example of a useful rule of thumb that has become an overly rigid restriction on when to use focus groups. Limiting ourselves to groups composed of strangers would make it exceedingly difficult to conduct focus groups in organizations, communities, and other ongoing social settings. For social scientists and evaluators, our need to work in such settings means that we often do encounter problems with prior acquaintance, but we resolve this issue by adjusting our uses of the method, rather than walking away from the problem.

The most obvious design strategy is to rely on a skilled moderator to meet the challenges posed by such groups. Another way to minimize problems with group composition is through extra effort in selecting and ordering the questions in the interview guide. Expanding the number of groups will also help with the goal of seeing beyond the narrow set of concerns that may dominate a particular set of acquaintances. These additional efforts are easily justifiable when such groups are often the only way to address a particular research question.

People Will Not Talk About
Sensitive Topics in Focus Groups

This myth seems to be based on commonsense imaginings of what people might be willing to discuss in groups. In actual experience, people readily talk about a wide range of personal and emotional topics.

A good example is Knodel et al.'s (1987) work on family size and birth control issues in rural Thailand. Of course, research involving sensitive topics does require careful planning, and Zeller (in this volume) discusses a number of techniques for creating a safe atmosphere for self-disclosure.

Practical experience also points to a very different problem: the overdisclosure of sensitive information. This can happen when the momentum in a group leads participants to reveal details of their personal lives that they would ordinarily keep private. Too often, there is a certain thrill in the open discussion of taboo topics. If the moderator does not pull back from the initial disclosure of oversensitive information, other participants may well come forth with even more personal revelations. When these discussions are tape recorded, an additional ethical issue is posed.

Once again, however, we need to guard against creating a new myth: We are not claiming that people will talk about anything and everything in focus groups. The reality is that researchers who work with sensitive topics must make plans to both encourage appropriate self-disclosures and discourage disclosures that go beyond the legitimate aims of the research.

Focus Groups Tend to Produce Conformity

This myth is another instance of a confusion between focus groups and other kinds of groups. In particular, conformity as a problem was highlighted by social psychologists working with group decision making, but focus groups almost never push groups to make decisions. Similarly, nominal group research methods often seek consensual solutions among group members, but focus groups almost never push participants to reach a consensus.

Instead of such conformity-producing goals as making decisions or reaching consensus, focus groups emphasize the goal of finding out as much as possible about participants' experiences and feelings on a given topic. A good moderator will strive to create an open and permissive atmosphere in which each person feels free to share her or his point of view. When there is some fear that pressures toward conformity may limit discussion, the opening instructions to the group can emphasize that you want to hear about a range of different experiences and feelings, and subsequent questions and probes can follow up on this theme by asking for other points of view. When participants see that the researchers are genuinely interested in learning as much as possible about their experiences and feelings, then conformity is seldom a problem.

**Focus Groups Are a Natural Means
of Collecting Data**

Rather than arguing about whether focus groups are natural, it is best to consider where they fit within a range of data-gathering techniques. In terms of research methods, focus groups use more natural settings than some techniques (surveys) and less natural settings than others (participant observation). Furthermore, as Frey and Fontana (in this volume) point out, focus groups use more natural settings than some group interviews (laboratory studies of group dynamics) and less natural settings than others (field observations of ongoing groups). Even within focus groups, there is a range of naturalness, from video taping in specially designed facilities that have observers and one-way mirrors to home-based conversations among neighbors.

It is important not to confuse the use of *natural settings* with the larger goal of conducting *naturalistic inquiries* (Lincoln & Guba, 1985). In nearly all focus group projects, the goal is to collect concentrated discussions on topics of interest to the researcher, but the discussion of these topics may or may not feel natural to the participants. Thus in assessing the naturalness of a set of focus groups, the match between the researchers' topics of interest and the participants' topics of ordinary conversation is often more important than the characteristics of the research setting.

**Focus Groups Should Not Be Used
for Decision Making**

This myth is most common in marketing research, where there is a heavy reliance on sample surveys as inputs to decision making. It is hardly surprising that research projects involving consumer products devote large amounts of resources to generalizing their results to large populations, given that the costs of making inappropriate decisions may be quite high. The issues are very different, however, when resources are more limited, or when decisions have less costly consequences.

To determine whether focus groups are adequate for making a decision, the researcher should begin by asking how difficult it would be to obtain "better" information. When monetary resources are scarce, the choice may be between making decisions based on focus groups versus no data at all. Even when resources do allow a choice between focus groups and other methods, the appropriate question is whether other methods provide enough improvement in the data to justify a greater expenditure of money or effort. We also need to consider the consequences of a wrong decision. If a mistake is not costly or is easily reversed, then extensive data collection procedures of any form may be a poor investment. Overall, we need to replace a knee-jerk rejection of focus groups as a basis for decision making with a careful specification of when they can provide useful information in a cost-effective manner.

Focus Groups Must Be Validated
by Other Methods

This is part of a general myth that relegates all qualitative methods to a preliminary, exploratory role that prepares the way for "real research." This myth has been applied to focus groups with particular force in marketing research, with its already-noted emphasis on survey research as a basis for decision making.

One response to claims that the findings of focus groups and other qualitative methods need to be validated by quantitative methods is to present situations in which qualitative methods have a distinct advantage. An obvious case is projects that are directed at specific contexts, as is often the case in evaluation research. When the research topic involves understanding the success or failure of a particular program in a specific setting, focus groups may well be the most efficient and effective tool for uncovering the reasons behind this outcome. Thus when one's goal is specification rather than generalization, focus groups and other qualitative methods are likely to be preferred over quantitative methods.

The goal of learning why a particular project succeeded or failed also highlights a larger point. Regardless of the setting, projects that are trying to answer how-and-why questions need to use very different methods than projects that are trying to answer what-and-how-many questions (Yin, 1989). When the goal is to generate theories or explanations, focus groups and other qualitative methods are the appropriate tools.

At the same time that we attack the myth that focus groups must be backed up by other methods, we still want to advocate the goal of improving our research efforts through a judicious combination of methods. There are many situations in which such combinations will yield data that are more useful than either method taken alone. Thus there is nothing wrong with the already classic use of focus groups in the early stages of large survey research projects, so long as it does not "ghettoize" focus groups by limiting them to preliminary exploration. Another promising combination is the pairing of individual and group interviews within qualitative studies, but this is an area in which there has been surprisingly little research (see Crabtree et al., this volume). All in all, there is every sign that combinations of methods that celebrate the contributions of focus groups will be continuing sources of new insights into when and why to use focus groups.

When Not *to Use Focus Groups*

The great advantage of expanding our methodological tool kit is that new techniques allow us to do a better job of matching our tools to our needs. There is an old proverb that when your only tool is a hammer, all problems will appear to be nails. Seen in this light, focus groups are not just a different way of doing things we have been doing all along, they may also lead us to change the very way that we think about the problems that interest us.

The downside of new methods is captured in a different hammer proverb: "When you give a small child a hammer, he [*sic*] will discover that a lot of things need pounding" (Kaplan, 1964). As a result, focus groups will be used to "pound" so many things that a few of them are guaranteed to get broken. As responsible researchers, it is our duty to consider situations that extend focus groups beyond their actual range of utility.

In presenting the list below, we have tried to avoid problems that can occur with any research method. For example, one should not undertake research when one has too little control over the research situation. For focus groups, this often involves sponsors, supervisors, or other influentials who want to handpick the participants; this selection bias, whether direct or inadvertent, can severely jeopardize the results of the focus group process. Similarly, many of the caveats that apply to qualitative research in general also apply to focus groups. In particular, most qualitative research is based on trust and open communication, so it makes no sense to attempt focus groups unless the researchers are respectful, tolerant, and considerate of the target audience.

Do Not Use Focus Groups When the Primary Intent Is Something Other Than Research

The primary purpose of projects that rely on focus groups is to collect qualitative data to answer research questions. Unfortunately, there is a constituency that wants to apply the term *focus groups* to other purposes, such as resolving conflicts, building consensus, increasing communication, changing attitudes, and making decisions. The issue is not whether these are legitimate purposes for groups—it is whether groups with such purposes are in any real sense focus groups. Work groups make decisions in committees and increase consensus and communication during team-building sessions and retreats. Support groups and group therapy can reorganize individuals' lives. And the ability of groups to change opinions and behaviors is one of the most basic findings in social science (Lewin, 1951). What sets these various groups apart from focus groups is the fact that they are done for purposes other than collecting data. Of course, this difference in purpose typically means that these groups will be conducted very differently from focus groups, and their results will be used in very different ways.

Given that the primary purpose of focus groups is to collect qualitative data, the fact that they are groups means that they may also serve other purposes as secondary functions. These secondary roles must, however, be clear from the beginning. This is particularly true when one is working for outside agencies and organizations, where there may be a very broad sense of what "research" is. In that case, the researcher must be completely clear about the purposes that the sponsor expects the focus groups to serve, and must be equally clear in presenting focus groups as data-collection devices for answering research questions. When the *sponsors* are pursuing some other goal, such as conveying a sense of listening or an impression of responsiveness, there undoubtedly is another tool that is better suited to their needs.

Do Not Use Focus Groups When a Group Discussion Is Not an Appropriate Forum

The basic goal in conducting focus groups is to hear from the participants about on the topics of interest to the researcher. This means that focus groups are not a viable option unless we can compose and conduct groups in ways that allow participants to voice their views. This issue first arises when determining who the participants in the groups will be. Composing groups that make some participants unwilling to express themselves defeats the purpose of the research. This is most likely to occur when the group is not homogeneous in regard to the research topic, as when both employees and supervisors are interviewed about work-group issues. Even in relatively homogeneous groups, free expression can be squelched by demanding that each group reach a consensus. This limiting of participants' self-expression also occurs in projects that emphasize the researcher's point of view, rather than the participants'. In focus groups, our goal should be to listen to the participants' points of view, and groups that limit the participants' opportunity to present their own feelings, opinions, and experiences are counter to this goal.

Ethical concerns are other obvious reasons why a group discussion could be a poor choice. As we noted earlier in our discussion of underdisclosure and overdisclosure, focus groups clearly can be conducted on sensitive topics (witness their popularity in AIDS research). Such research must, however, be extremely careful in regard to ethical issues, and insufficient attention to these issues is a sure way to dampen the open discussion that is at the very heart of focus groups. A major concern here is the protection of confidentiality from other members within the group. Although the research can reasonably ensure confidentiality of the official research data, the researcher cannot ensure that information will not be disclosed by other participants in the focus group. Strategies such as asking people not to disclose what they have heard in the group can backfire.

A different problem in generating a group discussion involves the sheer mechanics of assembling and conducting groups composed of certain types of participants. In this case, the participants are quite willing to discuss the topic at hand, but bringing the individuals together to do so poses insurmountable obstacles. It is difficult to assemble groups of widely dispersed participants, especially those with transportation difficulties (see Crabtree et al., this volume). It also is difficult to conduct groups with participants who have problems with the social aspects of participating in groups, especially those with extreme mental or behavioral disturbances. Overall, it is simply not possible to interview every type of person, and some of the problems that affect interviewing as a general means of data collection are magnified in groups.

**Do Not Use Focus Groups When the Topic
Is Not Appropriate for the Participants**

The match between the researchers' topics of interest and the participants' ability to discuss those topics is essential for successful focus
groups. To assess this match during the planning stages, ask the basic
question, "How easy will it be to generate a free-flowing and productive
conversation on this topic?"

A mismatch with the researchers' interests occurs most often when
participants have too little involvement in the topic. Evaluators and
social scientists seldom gain much by asking participants to report on
things that are beyond their experience. The classic example is in
comparisons of users and nonusers of some service, when it is like
pulling teeth to get the latter to come up with anything to say about their
lack of experience. Similar problems occur when the participants do
have relevant experiences, but the researchers go after them at the
wrong level of specificity by seeking either too big a picture or too
detailed a picture.

Interestingly, a different mismatch with the researchers' interests can
occur when the participants' involvement with the topic is too high. This
situation may lead participants into efforts at self-promotion or an obligation to know the answers. Over-involvement is especially common among
expert informants who may have thought about an issue so much that they
no longer know what they don't know. Avoid the strike it rich temptation
of concentrating on a single, highly knowledgeable segment.

Another problem with inappropriate topics occurs when we assemble
the appropriate groups, but then ask inappropriate questions. Certain
types of questions yield little benefit, but participants like to talk about
them anyway. This happens when focus group participants want to talk
about solution strategies even before they have identified the nature of
the problem. Indeed, some solutions are best left in the hands of experts.
For example, lay participants may not have the requisite experience,
training, or insight to plan a particular event or program; however, they
can tell us a great deal about their previous experiences with similar
events or programs. Thus an appropriate set of questions will concentrate on the areas for which a particular set of participants can contribute
to the overall goals of the project.

The best match between researchers' and participants' interests happens
when they each share the same goals: Producing useful information. When

such a goal is not self-evident, careful attention to design issues can help to create a viable discussion. One solution is to work with a variety of questions within each group. This process allows the researcher to seek out the topics that are of interest to participants; it is especially useful for locating the level of specificity at which participants can comfortably and productively discuss the issues. A complementary strategy is to work with a variety of different groups. Comparisons across different categories of participants provide useful data on how good the match is between the research topic and the interests of each segment. This is particularly useful in assessing the validity of the views expressed by over-involved experts.

Do Not Use Focus Groups When
Statistical Data Are Required

This final warning should fall under the heading of things that are so obvious that they do not need to be said. The key problem is that focus group samples are usually both unrepresentative and dangerously small. Even so, those who request focus groups often specifically ask for statistical results. For example, they may want to know what percent of the population fits into various categories. In these situations, focus groups might be helpful in ensuring that an eventual survey instrument is valid, but the statistical projections should not be made based solely on focus group results.

Another source of the temptation to create statistical data comes from the ease of polling participants in groups, or otherwise seeking "votes" on various subjects. This can be a useful technique for sparking further discussion, or simply for determining how much consensus is present in a group. But such "data" are of little value for characterizing the actual beliefs of any population.

Both of these situations differ from the legitimate kind of quantification involved in applying content analysis techniques to focus groups. The key difference is that content analysis is used for the explicit purpose of characterizing what is in a particular set of transcripts. Even here, however, the temptation is still strong to treat the numerical results as representing something more than what was said in these groups. The bottom line is that some kind of counting may occasionally be useful in either conducting or analyzing focus groups, but one must always keep the fundamentally qualitative purposes of focus groups firmly in mind.

The Advantages of Focus Groups

In this final section, we consider some of the situations for which focus group may be a particularly desirable research method. At some level, the decision to use focus groups in a research project is a decision *not* to use a good many other possible research methods. In making such a decision, it is helpful to know what the advantages of focus groups are. Although most existing treatments of focus groups (including our own) contain statements about the most likely uses for focus groups, these are usually pitched at a high level of generality. Indeed, more often than not, these statements describe situations in which any of several different qualitative methods could be appropriate.

Clearly, the thing that distinguishes focus groups is the presence of group interaction in response to researchers' questions. In this section, we present several types of goals that should lead researchers to give special consideration to focus groups because of the advantages provided by interaction among participants.

**Consider Focus Groups When There Is
a Power Differential Between
Participants and Decision Makers**

Those who hold positions of power and influence often need to gain feedback from those with no power. Normal channels of communication are sometimes not available and, when frustration is excessive, these situations can be explosive. The interaction that focus groups bring is useful in these situations because it allows groups of peers to express their perspective. Having the security of being among others who share many of their feelings and experiences, the participants possess a basis for sharing their views.

Thus focus group interviews, when conducted in a nonthreatening and permissive environment, are especially useful when working with categories of people who have historically had limited power and influence. This includes people of color as well as those with limited income or lower literacy skill. Of course, conducting research in the presence of a power imbalance often involves an ethical dimension, and the sponsors of such research should be informed of the risks associated with first empowering people to express their views and then ignoring these views.

**Consider Focus Groups When There Is
a Gap Between Professionals and
Their Target Audiences**

A gap between professionals and the target group can be due to such factors as language, culture, and region; furthermore, the professionals involved may be decision makers, academics, and administrators, for example. Many professional disciplines are facing crises because their language and logic are too different and removed from the people they are trying to serve. Physicians, professors, teachers, architects, business executives, attorneys, and others have all developed ways of thinking about reality that may be substantially different from the people they are trying to reach.

Because the interactions in focus groups provide a clear view of how others think and talk, they are a powerful means of exposing professionals to the reality of the customer, student, or client. In addition, because the professionals work with the research team to set the questions for the discussions, they can get immediate and vivid feedback about how others respond to their ideas. The advantages that focus groups provide for bridging such gaps help to explain their popularity in such otherwise diverse applications as showing manufacturers how consumers respond to their products, helping survey researchers find appropriate questionnaire topics and wording, and providing public health workers with new insights into promoting healthy behavior.

**Consider Focus Groups When Investigating
Complex Behavior and Motivations**

It can be dangerous to oversimplify human motivation. By comparing the different points of view that participants exchange during the interactions in focus groups, researchers can examine motivation with a degree of complexity that is typically not available with other methods. When the goal is to modify behavior that depends on complex information flow or a mix of attitudes, knowledge, and past experiences, then focus groups can provide the researcher with a tool that is uniquely suited to the task. Of course, the goal of understanding complex behavior often requires more than one way of finding out about that behavior, so focus groups for this purpose will typically be used along with observation, secondary data, and other sources.

One of the most common examples of using focus groups to understand complex motivations is when people do not have easily accessible ways of talking about a research topic. Normally, people are not in touch with or able to articulate their motivations, feelings, attitudes, and opinions. Many of the behaviors we might wish to understand are not matters of conscious importance to research participants. At the beginning of a focus group, such participants will not be immediately able to express all their feelings or motivations on a topic. As they hear others talk, however, they can easily identify the degree to which what they are hearing fits their situation. By comparing and contrasting, they can become more explicit about their own views. In addition, as they do express their own feelings and experiences, they may find that answering questions from the moderator and other participants makes them aware of things that they had not thought about before. Thus in contrast to surveys in which one is frequently warned against asking about a topic if people do not have prior opinions, the interaction in focus groups often creates a cuing phenomenon that has the potential for extracting more information than other methods.

But we should not assume that focus groups will always reveal deep motivational insights. They can also show that people may be less logical, less thoughtful, and less organized than we expected. By sharing their experiences with similar others, participants often feel free to admit things like, "I really just didn't think about it. I just did it." In these circumstances, listening to focus groups can be a good antidote to the overrational view that researchers and other professionals sometimes impose on their fellow human beings.

Consider Focus Groups to Learn More
About the Degree of Consensus on a Topic

Often a major part of our research goal is to learn more about the range of opinions or experiences that people have. Focus groups have a strong advantage here because the interaction in the group can provide an explicit basis for exploring this issue. Of course, the degree of consensus in the group can only become open to observation if the researchers make it clear that they want to hear a range of opinions, so one should never mistake the failure to disagree for the actual presence of consensus.

One of the things that frequently becomes clear in such discussions is that each individual may have several different opinions about the subject. This is visible in statements of qualified agreement, such as "I agree with you, so long as . . . ." It also shows up when apparent disagreements are resolved by uncovering the presence or absence of some particular set of circumstances. This is the familiar realization that how one feels or what one does depends on the particular circumstances. The advantage of focus groups is that the exchanges among the participants help them to clarify for themselves just what it is that their opinion or behavior depends on. We, as researchers, can thus gain insights into both the range of opinions they have and the sets of circumstances that will lead to one response rather than another.

**Consider Focus Groups When You Need
a Friendly Research Method That Is
Respectful and Not Condescending
to Your Target Audience**

Focus groups have a unique niche for obtaining information as tensions between opposing parties begin to rise. Surveys and other means of obtaining information may be ineffective because neither party trusts the other's intentions. By creating and sustaining an atmosphere that promotes meaningful interaction, focus groups convey a humane sensitivity, a willingness to listen without being defensive, and a respect for opposing views that is unique and beneficial in these emotionally charged environments. Naturally, when the tensions are excessive, it is unlikely that focus groups or any other procedure will work adequately.

Even in situations that are not fraught with conflict, the friendliness of focus groups can be a major advantage. This friendliness extends to both the participants, who typically enjoy their interactions together, and to the end users of the research, who believe that they get a much better understanding of others' points of view through listening to their discussions. From the researcher's point of view, a successful focus groups project can help to forge a human connection between those who commission a project and those who serve as the subjects of their investigations. And, whether this helps to reduce tensions in troubled settings or simply makes people feel good about their experiences in the research process, it is a valuable end in itself.

Taken together, the points we discussed hardly constitute an exhaustive list of the advantages of focus groups or even of the advantages that flow from the opportunity to observe group interaction. Still, they provide useful answers to our original questions of when and why to use focus groups. Before concluding, however, we would like to return to the point that any decision to use focus groups necessarily comes at the expense of other methods that are, at least implicitly, rejected. One of the things that this chapter obviously does not include is a handy table or diagram that depicts which situations are or are not appropriate for focus groups. Such devices clearly have their advantages for showing beginners, especially graduate students, the applications and strengths of different methods. On the downside, however, such summaries give a misleading impression of the clarity and specificity of our decisions about which research methods to use. For seasoned researchers, the critical choice of which method to use is often based on what we know we can do well. This means that if you know you can get a good enough answer to your research question by using focus groups, then that is preferable to an inept application of a technically superior method. Generally, poorly done research, of any type, is worse than useless when it leads us to trust false results.

We also have another, and more important, reason for foregoing any summary listing of the circumstances in which one should or should not use focus groups: This would limit our ability to improvise, to be responsive to a particular situation, and to adapt and create a generation of new and better research procedures. Instead, we need to approach the possibility of innovating by assessing the risks that one runs by moving outside the received wisdom. In some situations, it is safer to take more risks and try out unproven approaches; in others the need for a high-quality answer is so great that it is crucial to stick to proven procedures. When innovation is indeed possible, we wholeheartedly encourage it.

Throughout, we have been careful not to assert that there is one right way to apply focus groups. Others may indeed have found ways to get around some of the limitations we have noted. Or they may have capitalized on advantages that we have overlooked. As each of the present authors has learned, however, anyone who proposes new uses for focus groups accepts a certain burden of proof for demonstrating the practical value of these approaches. So we will look forward to the possibility of being proven wrong about any of the lessons that we have gleaned from our own experiences, but we, and the rest of the field, will insist that new approaches be backed by solid evidence of their effectiveness.

2

The Group Interview in Social Research

JAMES H. FREY
ANDREA FONTANA

Introduction

Discussions of strategies for conducting social research normally focus
on two types of data gathering: observation and interviews. In the first
case, the researcher assumes one of several roles as a participant
observer watching and listening as events unfold and members interact
in a setting that is familiar or natural to the persons being observed. In
the second case, the researcher asks probing or directed questions that
reflect earlier observation or theoretical orientation. In both strategies
the individual respondent or participant is the source of data. We
suggest that social investigation can be enhanced by employing the
group interview technique in which several participants in a social
context can be interviewed simultaneously. This technique is not meant
to replace the individual interview, but rather group interviewing will

AUTHORS' NOTE: Reprinted by permission from *The Social Science Journal,* Volume
28, Number 2, pages 175-187. Copyright ©1991 by JAI Press. This is a revised version
of an article presented at the Annual Meeting of the Pacific Sociological Association,
Sparks, Nevada, April 1989. The authors would like to thank Peter Adler, Karen Peterson,
Eldon Snyder, Elmer Spreitzer, Francesca M. Cancian, and three anonymous reviewers
for their insightful comments on earlier drafts.

provide data on group interaction, on realities as defined in a group context, and on interpretations of events that reflect group input. The use of the group interview is not limited to sociologists and anthropologists who are normally associated with the use of qualitative techniques such as participant observation or fieldwork. Political scientists, for example, might use the group interview to assess perceptions of candidates, reactions to political advertising and images, patterns of decision making, views of political and policy issues, or interpretations of questions being prepared for a voter survey. Historians will find the group interview helpful when trying to reconstruct an event or classify the role of a historical figure in that particular event. Policy studies researchers will find the group interview especially helpful in determining the reaction and perception of an affected population to a policy change. Finally, economists interested in marketing and consumer behavior are already making use of group interviews in a variety of ways (e.g., product evaluation and consumer survey pretest). Those who study work environments, job satisfaction, morale, or work behavior can utilize the group interview effectively in their research. Thus the group interview can be of value to social scientists, regardless of discipline. A caveat is in order before proceeding. *Group* is an ambiguous term that could refer to a dyad as well as to a large assembly of respondents. We suspect that the literature has tended to reify methodological techniques and treat these "ideal types" as "real" while in fact ignoring or excluding how the actual interviewing takes place (we would like to thank an anonymous reviewer for this point). How many of us have referred to and reported interviews as one on one, totally glossing over the fact that others, friends, family, colleagues, fellow inmates, gang members, team members, fellow workers, and many more, were present and contributed in some fashion to the interview? The caveat in this chapter is that we are not rediscovering the group interview but merely helping it "come out of the closet." The available formats for group interviews will be discussed after a brief review of the use of these interviews in social science.

The Group Interview in Social Science

The use of group interviews dates back to 1926 when Emory Bogardus tested his social distance scale (Bogardus, 1926). Robert Merton and his colleagues also used the group interview in studies of the social effects of mass communication (Merton, Fiske, & Kendall, 1956). Later Merton adapted the focused interview style to individuals and discovered the role of psuedogemeinshaft in the manipulation of group members (Merton, 1987). Harriet Zuckerman (1972) also adapted this focused technique to interviews of Nobel laureates. David L. Morgan and Margaret T. Spanish (1984) and Morgan (1988) have demonstrated the effectiveness of the focus group technique in their studies of health issues.

James D. Thompson and Nicholas J. Demerath (1952) report on experiences with the group interview in their research on management problems in the military. Wendell French, Edward Gross, and Herman Resnick (1986) implemented the group interview technique in a study of faculty reactions to proposed budget cuts in a major university system. In his study of prisons, John Irwin (1970) used group interviews to validate data from one-to-one interviews on criminal careers. James H. Frey and Donald Carns (1988) used group interviews in their study of job satisfaction among casino card dealers. Finally, group interviews of older workers reentering the labor force were used by Frey and Andrea Fontana (1988) to obtain information on motivation to return to work and on the meaning of work to these respondents.

Finally, even though there is some tradition in sociology for the use of the group interview in research, there is almost no reference to it as a data-gathering technique in the literature on field research. Furthermore, classic ethnographic accounts such as the study of street corner groups and gangs by Elliot Liebow (1967) and William F. Whyte (1981) do not make reference to either formal or informal group interviews (Bernard, 1988; Spradley, 1979). We feel that the group interview can be a valuable component of a fieldwork strategy that includes the use of several data-gathering techniques.

The anthropological literature reveals the same pattern—no reference to group interviews. It is possible that field researchers have judged the group interview technique to be inappropriate and invalid. As a result, they have either discarded it as a viable strategy or not utilized it at all because tradition dictates against the use of any field technique other than observation and one-on-one interviews. However, since many field settings naturally lend themselves to the formation of informal and spontaneous groups as well as to formal group organization, we suspect that many field researchers conducted group interviews but did not report these interviews as a component of a field strategy. For example, Bronislaw Malinowski's diaries contain accounts of his conversations with groups of native Trobriand Islanders, but reports of his research do not explicitly include results from these "interviews" (Malinowski, 1967).

It is obvious that field ethnographers must have encountered respondents in a group setting. Group interviews can take place during any phase of the field investigation process. The discussion that follows will review the conditions or purposes under which group interviews can usefully be conducted.

Purposes

Exploratory

Field research is often utilized for the initial or exploratory phase of a research project. In this phase the researcher is typically looking at a social context that is unfamiliar or new. These studies can be used to satisfy a researcher's curiosity, to arrive at a better understanding of a social context, to test the feasibility of a more complex study, to develop methodological techniques, to identify nuances of a research setting that could impact the investigation, to identify key informants, to add precision to a research problem, and to serve as a source of grounded theory (Babbie, 1989).

Herbert Blumer (1969) recommends bringing together several knowledgeable observers who are familiar with the social situation under investigation into a discussion or resource group. This group "is more valuable many times over than any representative sample" (Blumer, 1969, p. 41). The group discussion will serve to revise or solidify the researcher's image of the reality of a social setting.

Pretest

An extension of the exploratory purpose of a group interview is the use of these groups in pilot testing or pretests. That is, these groups can be used to test various questionnaire items for readability, comprehension, wording, order effects, and response variation. In this case the interview is very structured with specific questions asked. Several risk-perception and risk-assessment scales were tested with a group interview in a study of the impact of a nuclear waste repository (Desvousges & Frey, 1989). Marketing studies frequently use groups to try out items that might be used in questionnaires on consumer preferences or product orientations (Calder, 1977). Less structured interviews are conducted if the goal is to generate hypotheses or respond to scenarios. In this case the interview is open-ended and the setting can be less formal. It is this application that is most relevant to field research. The researcher can float ideas or thoughts about a social context to spontaneous groups that form in natural field settings (e.g., a street corner or neighborhood tavern) or in a more formal setting (e.g., school or conference room) that is located in the field setting. Of course, group interviews can be used in a posttest context where representatives of the population under study are asked to interpret certain results.

Triangulation

While exploratory and pretest interviews open the way to further research, triangulation aims at providing a larger data base (Denzin, 1989), further decoding and interpretation of data, and additional methodological rigor. Group interview would lend itself very well to the use of multiple data-gathering techniques as well as to the use of "indefinite triangulation" (Cicourel, 1974). Group interview would avail the researcher of the opinions of a large number of subjects in a relatively easy-to-access fashion; it thus would complement any other method being used. It would, on one side, "triangulate" the data of formal methodological techniques by adding to them the human element of the voices of multiple subjects; it would, on the other hand, with the cross-referenced multiple opinions stemming from its group nature, lend methodological rigor to the one-on-one interpretive nature of field interviews and ethnographic reports.

Finally, group interviews would be helpful in the process of "indefinite triangulation." By allowing opinions to bounce back and forth and be modified by the group, rather than being the definitive statement of a single respondent, group interviews would allow us to elaborate statements made and to realize the indexical nature of many statements made by respondents, a technique particularly favored by ethnomethodologists (Cicourel, 1974).

Phenomenology

Group interviews do not have to be provisional or superficial. They can be used as the sole technique for gathering data and then be used for exploratory purposes. According to Leonard Schatzman and Anselm Strauss (1973) the group interview or "multiple respondent" interviews are effective in settings where the relationships among respondents are complex and views are diverse. They go on to say:

> In addition, this form of information gathering provides an especially nice situation for revealing variations in perspective and attitude and a ready means, through subtle pitting of one against the other, for distinguishing between shared and variable perspectives. The pitting process hardly needs manipulation since the hosts themselves, by speech and gesture, will naturally "correct" each other's rendering or "reality." By contrast, in the one-to-one interview the pitting is more calculated, and probably is without any immediate corrective for the respondent. (Schatzman & Strauss, 1973, p. 82)

The one-to-one interviews have certain advantages, but researchers can utilize the opportunity to conduct group interviews, either in formal or natural settings, in order to obtain opinion or attitude at another level, (i.e., group consensus or disagreement on reality). Norman Denzin (1989) indicates that groups create their own structure and meaning and a group interview provides access to their level of meaning, in addition to clarifying arguments and revealing diversity in views and opinion.

John Lofland and Lyn H. Lofland (1984) suggest group interviews as a supplement to the traditional face-to-face individual interview particularly where the topic is benign and not embarrassing. This type of interview technique can stimulate recall and opinion elaboration. It can also serve to assist the respondent to re-evaluate a previous position or statement that is in need of "amplification, qualification, amendment or contradiction" (Lofland & Lofland, 1984, p. 14). In other words, the group interview could be a source of validation, (e.g., interviewing together respondents who have previously been interviewed separately), for previously gathered data via one-on-one interviewing or it could bring the researcher closer to the "truth" by the addition of embellishing interpretive data.

In a discussion of the use of group interviews in marketing research Bobby J. Calder (1977) asserted that this technique is an excellent vehicle to establish what Alfred Schutz (1967) called "intersubjectivity" or ordinary descriptions of reality shared by actors. In a group setting actors are able to obtain feedback on their views of reality; they can respond to other or differing views; and the researcher can vicariously experience a reality in the same manner as the respondent through interaction and unstructured interviewing. In the field, the researcher normally has a personal relationship with those being observed. The nature of the relationship enables the researcher to share the experience of the observed. When this experience is expressed in the group setting and it adds a dimension to the knowledge of everyday life that the researcher might have overlooked or missed if data gathering had been limited to one-on-one interviews. Finally, it is possible that accounts of reality formation are more likely to be stimulated and to be expressed in greater depth when shared in a group interview format. This possibility should make the utilization of the group as a data-gathering vehicle even more attractive to field workers with a phenomenological research purpose.

Recently, a new trend in field research has emerged, related to the general cultural phenomenon of postmodernism. While postmodernism is too wide and diffuse an approach to be succinctly defined here, its relevance to the social sciences is emerging (Dickens & Fontana, 1992; Geertz, 1988; Van Maanen, 1988). Basically, the postmodernist approach in sociology questions the control over the discipline of established paradigms and scrutinizes closely the often self-validating assumptions that underlie these paradigms. Thus postmodernist ethnographers wish to study everyday life accounts by remaining as faithful as possible to the perceptions of the members of the (sub)culture being examined. Specifically, postmodernist ethnographers have been concerned with the overly "authoritative" voice of the ethnographer and with the fact that much of what is reported in field interviews, among other ethnographic procedures, is but the subjective interpretation of the ethnographer (Denzin, 1988; Marcus & Fischer, 1986). Postmodernist ethnographers have been suggesting, among other points, that (1) ethnographic accounts be more polyphonic and thus present more of the accounts of the subject studies; and (2) that the role of the ethnographer be "minimized" in the report, to diminish authorial bias and influence.

While group interviews would not eliminate the subjective, interpretive nature of the data, it would help reduce it. Group interviews would be helpful on the two points suggested above. Accounts would be more "polyphonic," as in a collective interview situation; more subjects would participate; and thus a broader spectrum of respondents' opinions would be reported. The interviewer's influence on the interviewee, while not eliminated, would be diffused by the very fact of being in a group rather than in a one-on-one situation.

Dimensions of Group Interviews

The nature of the interview can vary by several dimensions, the most significant of which are the role of the interviewer, the extent to which the questions are preplanned or structured, the purpose of the interview (phenomenological, exploratory, pretest) and the nature of the setting of the interview (i.e., naturally occurring group meeting or a setting formally arranged by researcher). Each is discussed below.

Role of Interviewer

There are essentially two styles that can be assumed by the interviewer. The first calls for a rather passive, nondirective approach where the interviewer-observer only asks enough questions or probes on a limited basis or offers reinforcement to keep a discussion going. In this case the interview may be exploratory or phenomenological where unstructured questioning is employed. This type of interviewing is more plausible in a setting that is informal or naturally occurring. The other side of the interviewer's role is directive or active. In this situation the interviewer is very involved with the direction of the interview either as an active and empathetic participant in the interview or as someone who exercises considerable control over the direction of the interview by administering a structured and ordered set of items or by constantly keeping the group on track. This role is more readily implemented in formal, nonnatural settings.

Question Structure

The purpose of the interview will dictate the question format. In exploratory and phenomenological groups, unstructured, open-end questions are normally implemented. This permits greater flexibility in response patterns and probe tactics. Unstructured questioning is easily implemented in field settings where naturally occurring groups form on a spontaneous basis. However, formally arranged settings, either in the field or at another location, can also be the site of the administration of an unstructured questionnaire guide. In other words, setting is not a limitation to the unstructured interview. The preplanned structured interview can be administered in formal settings quite easily, but is difficult to implement in informal, spontaneous settings. The pretest

Table 2.1 Purposes of Group Interviews

Exploratory	Develop familiarity, test methodological techniques, understand setting, formulate hypotheses, identify informal respondents
Pretest	Test questionnaire items, assess product or advertising reactions, try ideas or interpretations on relevant group
Triangulation	Uses multiple methods to enhance validity
Phenomenological	Determine meanings on another level beyond one-to-one, elaboration, learn polyphonic accounts

purpose lends itself more readily to structured interviewing; exploratory and phenomenological do not.

Purpose of Interview

The distinctions among purposes have been described earlier. Exploratory group interviews can be conducted in either informal, natural settings or in formal, arranged settings. Pretest interviews are best conducted in formal settings arranged by the interviewer who is actively administering a structured interview schedule. Phenomenological interviews can be conducted in naturally occurring settings provided the group can maintain itself for a lengthy time period and distractions can be monitored.

Setting of the Interview

Marketing research has institutionalized a tradition of group interviewing called the focus group, which takes place in a formal, prearranged setting, usually a room for 8-12 persons sitting around a conference table while being observed via a one-way mirror or being audio and/or video taped. The interviewer is usually directive by administering a structured or partially structured question format for pretest or exploratory purposes. This experience would be difficult, but not impossible, to duplicate in a field setting. It is possible that a field researcher could arrange for a group interview in a setting that is natural to a field location. The back room of a tavern, the lounge of a public agency, or the home of a key informant represent potential locations where exploratory and phenomenological interviews could take place.

The most frequently occurring opportunity for a group interview in the field will probably be the situation where two or more members of the population under study will gather in a spontaneous manner at a familiar field location such as a street corner, a coffee shop, a tavern, a park, a work setting, or a playground. Stephen Lyng and David Snow report success with group interviews of skydivers at a natural setting where these participants gathered after jumps:

> These informal gatherings (bars and restaurants) proved to be a rich source of data, since it was here that jumpers most often expressed their feelings and ideas about their sport. (Lyng & Snow, 1986, p. 163)

We feel that these informal group gatherings provide an excellent occasion for the interviewer to engage the group, probably in an initially directive way, but evolving to a passive, enabling role, with questions. These would usually be unstructured in format. The normal reaction of a field worker is to simply observe the group interaction and to listen to the dialogue. We recommend that, where and when the field worker deems it appropriate, the group be approached with questions. The key is to be able to recognize when these situations occur and how to best manage them when they do.

These dimensions are reflected in the various types of group interviews that have been implemented in research. Some of these types are applicable to field research, others are not.

Types of Group Interviews

Focus Group

The focus group interview has been adopted as a major data-gathering technique by market researchers who are interested in the appeal of advertising strategies or in consumer product preferences (Axelrod, 1975). This technique has also been used by social scientists as an aid to questionnaire development (Desvousges & Frey, 1989) and as part of program evaluation (Krueger, 1988). The focus group developed in response to dissatisfaction with polling techniques and as an extension of the group therapy methods employed by psychiatrists (Bellenger, Barnhardt, & Goldstucker, 1976). A focus group interview is a qualitative

Table 2.2   Group Interview Dimensions

Interviewer Role	Directive	Nondirective
Question Format	Structured	Unstructured
Purpose	Exploratory, pretest	Phenomenological
Setting	Formal	Natural

research technique that includes 8-10 persons brought to a centralized location to respond to questions on a topic of particular interest to a sponsor or client (Greenbaum, 1988). The interview is led by a "moderator" who keeps the respondents "focused" on a particular topic. The focus group is generally conducted for applied purposes and, therefore, would be classified as a pretest vehicle. It is ordinarily conducted in a setting formally established for the interview; the moderator is directive, and the interview questions are purposive and usually somewhat structured. Merton and his associates (1956) implemented a version of this technique. Some researchers advocate focus groups (Morgan, 1988), but we propose that the focus group is just one form of group interview that is feasible for use in field research. The focus group interview has limited usefulness as a field technique, although it might be utilized by a field worker in a natural setting that allowed for separation or isolation from the other ongoing activity of the field context.

Brainstorming

This technique is most often used to generate new ideas. The interviewer simply tosses out an idea or thought, and the group members respond to each other as the idea is evaluated. It is conducted in formal or natural settings, the purpose is largely exploratory, the interviewer's role is passive, and there is no structure to the questioning. This approach could be used in the field, but without some interviewer control a high rate of trivial or unusable data can be a problem. In addition, responses tend to be insightful but superficial. Brainstorming may be a good field strategy for initial stages of a group interview, or it may be a technique to determine if a naturally occurring group has a potential for a more structured, but still informal, group interview.

Nominal and Delphi Groups

Techniques of group interviewing where the participants are physically isolated but their observations are shared through a coordinator have almost no place in fieldwork, but they can be of value to researchers with other purposes in mind. In each case there is high task orientation; interaction among members is minimized or nonexistent; the researcher plays a dominant, assertive role; interpersonal dynamics are minimized; and questioning is normally structured. The Delphi technique, which relies on mail questionnaires, is especially time-consuming. Neither is able to fulfill phenomenological purposes but can be used for pretest and exploratory research. However, both techniques have been used effectively in decision-making studies and in policy formation deliberations. The Delphi technique is especially useful in studies that require the participation of a geographically dispersed population such as managers or executives of international corporations.

Natural and Formal Field Interview

Group interviews in the field can take place in two ways. First, the field worker can interview groups as they spontaneously form in a natural location in the field setting. Instead of simply observing these groups and inquiring about the content of the interaction in a one-to-one interview with each participant, the interviewer can enter the group and pose questions. This may be done once observation is no longer productive and the interviewer has established rapport. By virtue of entering the group and asking the questions the field worker has altered the "natural" status of the group. Yet, that might be a sufficient price to pay in return for the additional data that can be generated as a result of a multiple-interview opportunity. The informal, natural group interview is an excellent technique for exploratory queries on interpretations of previously gathered data, and it can be a validity check on information gathered in a one-to-one interview. Informal interviews can be a way to check for bias in data collected in other ways (Moeller, Mescher, More, & Shafter, 1980). Additional phenomenological insight is a possibility but, more often than not, the setting may not be conducive for an in-depth, probing interview that requires conflict and emotion to be expressed. The phenomenological purpose may better be articulated in the formal group interview where the field worker is able to arrange for a group of respondents to meet in a location within the field setting that can accommodate several persons and that is free of distractions. In this setting the researcher is freer to ask probing questions, to allow interpersonal dynamics to play out to their fullest extent, and to become an empathetic observer. This type of interview also makes it possible for the interviewer to play a more directive role and it certainly will solidify and legitimate the researcher's role in the field setting.

Advantages and Disadvantages

Group interviewing is a research technique that takes advantage of group dynamics to produce new and additional data. In addition to the respondent-interviewer relationship, the evolving relations among group members can be a stimulus to elaboration and expression. An additional phenomenological dimension is added to the interpretation and understanding of an event, activity, or behavioral pattern that has taken place in the field. In fact, group interviews can be a source of validation for events observed and for individual interview data.

Group interviews are also less costly than the more traditional face-to-face variety simply because more persons are interviewed in the same time frame. Group interviews are efficient in the sense that the interviewer-respondent relation can be prolonged or is less likely to be bogged down because the group members will stimulate each other. There is nothing more frustrating to an interviewer than to be a victim of a recalcitrant respondent. The group interview is an excellent mechanism for bringing the researcher closer to even more respondents, it is flexible, and it permits considerable probing (Wells, 1979). The group interview can provide some insight for the field worker, into the nature of relationships in the field (e.g., power differential or friendship patterns) that might otherwise not have been discernible through observation or interviews. The group interview process is, in itself, revealing on this account (Goldman, 1962). The nonverbal actions of the respondents plus the substance of the relations of group members can tell the field researcher a great deal about social relations that exist beyond the group. Thus the group interview can provide a greater depth of understanding about the field context and about relations of the members of a particular setting. Not only do group interviews take advantage of group dynamics, provide insight into social relationships in the field,

Table 2.3 Type of Group Interviews and Dimension

Type	Setting	Role of Interviewer	Question Format
Focus group	Formal-preset	Directive	Structured
Brainstorming	Formal or informal	Nondirective	Very unstructured
Nominal/Delphi	Formal	Directive	Structured
Field, natural	Informal, spontaneous	Moderately nondirective	Very unstructured
Field, formal	Preset, but in field	Somewhat directive	Semistructured

reduce distance between researcher and the social context, and reduce total cost, but this type of interview can stimulate new ideas, identify language or symbols not previously acknowledged, serve as a testing ground for hypotheses or analytic suggestions, and expand the depth and variation in response or description of relevant social events.

Plans to implement the group interview technique call for nothing different in strategies for entering the field and establishing rapport. These strategies are the same for one-to-one interviews or group interviews. The requirements of objectivity, reliability, and validity are also the same. In fact, these may be enhanced by the utilization of a group interview technique. The only factor that is different is that the field worker be sensitive to natural groupings and be able to take advantage of these whether they occur in spontaneous settings or are arranged for a location familiar to field respondents.

There are some problems with group interviews. First, group interviews require different skills than do individual interviews. The field worker must be sensitive to group dynamics such as how the opinions of one member can sway others or to how relations outside the group influence response patterns within the group or how size effects response patterns. This is especially crucial since the group members will probably know each other and will have already established a patterned relationship. Only a few researchers will have the sensitivity to group processes that will make them eligible to conduct group interviews since social scientists are not routinely "trained" in interviewing in their graduate school experience.

On a more practical side, locations conducive to group interviews may not exist, natural groupings may not develop, and if they do form, the researcher may not be permitted access to the group, particularly if that group has established a history of getting together. It may be very difficult, for example, for a researcher to be accepted into a regular poker-playing group or a group that meets at coffee break. In addition, group responses can be affected by the size of the group, by the group members' view of the purpose of the interview, and by the differences in background of the members. In fact, group interviews, particularly the natural and focus groups, may experience the pressure to conformity (Isenberg, 1986); individuals may be stifled rather than stimulated by the group; there may be a higher ratio of interpersonal conflict in interacting groups, and this could drain the response energy of the group; the production of irrelevant data may be high; posturing by members of the group could create a level of false information or awareness of the research problem; and the outcome of the interview could very possibly be biased by the interviewer's role in the group.

If the group interview is employed, some of the flexibility in the observer role is compromised. The covert role is virtually impossible to implement, and the peripheral member role may be all that is possible since the role of interviewer requires some coordinating and directing (Adler & Adler, 1987). Thus the field researcher who implements group interviews will need to employ a more active membership role if intense phenomenological interviewing is required, but the less active role facilitates organizing informal spontaneous group interviews.

Conclusion

The group interview is a tool that social researchers should consider utilizing, particularly as a strategy to obtain phenomenological data in natural settings. The sole purpose of this technique is not limited to exploratory inquiry or to the development of procedures and questionnaire items for subsequent quantitative studies. It is a technique that can stand alone as a procedure for obtaining data on any social context that is being studied in an ethnographic manner. Finally, we do not propose that the group interview be a substitute for the traditional one-on-one interview. Rather, the group interview should be considered for use along with other techniques of interviewing and observation.

3

The Design and Analysis of Focus Group Studies

A Practical Approach

JOHN KNODEL

Practitioners of modern social science research are increasingly recognizing the value of focus group methodology to collect qualitative data either for its own right or to be used in conjunction with quantitative data. There is already a substantial literature on how to conduct focus groups, based largely on marketing research experience (e.g., Greenbaum, 1987). Far less has been written about how to design focus group studies and analyze their results, especially within the framework of social science research (but see Morgan, 1988; Stewart & Shamdasani, 1990). This chapter provides a practical approach to design and analysis.

Designing a Focus Group Study

As with other approaches to studying social phenomena, designing a focus group study requires careful thought and reflection. Given that focus groups can be used for a variety of purposes within social science research, the design of a focus group study will depend on its purpose. At one extreme, maximum flexibility may be desired; the number of groups to be held and even the precise characteristics of the populations to be targeted are decided in a stepwise fashion as the fieldwork progresses. Such a flexible approach allows the fieldwork to stop once few new insights appear to emerge from additional sessions. This very flexible approach is probably most suitable when the research is of a very exploratory nature and when it is useful to digest the content of each successive focus group session before deciding if another is needed with any particular target group. This may be the case with pilot studies of a particular topic. Likewise, if focus groups are being used to help formulate questions and response categories for a structured questionnaire, only a few sessions may be necessary; decisions on precisely how many and with whom are contingent on the utility of the sessions as they are held.

At the other extreme, when qualitative information is needed on issues about which the researchers have substantial background knowledge and a reasonable grasp of the issues they wish to examine and extensive analysis of the data is anticipated, a detailed design, set in advance, is likely to be more appropriate. Much of the discussion that follows relates to this latter type of design and assumes that the project will involve several subsets of the population, although many of the points are relevant even if the study concerns a single population segment. The discussion is illustrated with examples taken primarily from research on aging but could just as well have used examples from any other area of social science interest.

Setting Objectives and Formulating Discussion Guidelines

The first step in designing a focus group study should be to define and clarify the concepts that are to be investigated. In general, it is advisable to keep the number of broad concepts examined in a focus group moderate so that each can be examined in detail. The general concepts to be explored need to be formulated as a set of discussion guidelines that can be used by the moderator during the focus group sessions. The basic idea of the guidelines is to lay out a set of issues for the group to discuss. It is important to bear in mind that the moderator will mostly be improvising comments and questions within the framework set by the guidelines. By keeping the questions open-ended, the moderator can stimulate useful trains of thought in the participants that were not anticipated.

Guidelines should be kept relatively brief. Remember that the objective of a focus group is an in-depth examination of the concepts being covered. If there are particular aspects of a topic that you want to ensure are probed, this can be noted in the guidelines without formulating separate questions. This way the moderator can bring them up in a more natural manner. Presumably many of these points will come up spontaneously in the course of the discussion. If there are too many concepts and associated questions, there will be insufficient time to cover them before the participants become fatigued.

An example of a set of guidelines intended to guide a discussion of the position and support systems of elderly in a developing country is provided in Table 3.1. Note that the guidelines tend to be general in nature, be open-ended, and seek to find what is going on without specifically asking directly about the situation of the individual participants. However, participants are likely to share their personal experience voluntarily to support their opinions. Such personal information can also be useful, as it helps ground the discussion in reality and can serve as a concrete referent when asking about what is typical or common. Note also that guidelines need not be as detailed as shown in Table 3.1. If a less structured discussion is desired, a simple list of topics might even suffice, provided the moderator is well versed in the nature of the issues and thus will know when and what to probe. However, if comparisons are to be made across differently defined subgroups, relatively detailed guidelines such as those shown can help ensure that similar points are discussed across groups.

If the focus groups are part of a project involving other data collection (e.g., a survey or cases studies) consideration must be given to how the focus group data fit into the overall research plan. This is crucial because they may affect which population subgroups you wish to target for the discussions, what the differences between them are, and how many focus group sessions need to be organized.

Targeting the Participants

Given a clear idea of the concepts that are to be investigated, the next critical step in designing a focus group study is to decide on the characteristics of the individuals who are to be targeted for sessions. When there is interest in comparing views of people with differing

Table 3.1   Example of Focus Group Guidelines for a Study of Support and Exchange Systems Involving the Elderly

TOPIC 1. Support of Elderly

1.1 Where do elderly prefer to live in relation to their children?
[Probe: coresident, in own house but nearby children]

1.2 What assistance do elderly expect to receive from children?
[Probe: daily activities, work, help when sick, remittances]

1.3 In reality, can the elderly depend on children for assistance and care or do they need to depend on themselves? Why?

1.4 How can the elderly help ensure that they will get support and care from children?
[Probe: withholding inheritance, providing higher education]

1.5 Does the assistance and care received by elderly from children differ according to the characteristics of the elderly person?
[Probe: wealth, work status, health]

1.6 Does the assistance and care received by elderly from children differ according to the characteristics of the child?
[Probe: sex, marital status, residence, occupation, education]

1.7 What help do elderly generally receive from sources other than children?
[Probe: How about elderly with no children?]

TOPIC 2. Economic Role of the Elderly

2.1 Do most elderly work in this community?
[Probe: type of work]

2.2 Do elderly work because they want to or because they have to?
[Probe: relation to economic status]

TOPIC 3. Role of Elderly in the Family

3.1 How do elderly who live with children contribute to the household?
[Probe: household chores, child care, expenses]

3.2 How do the elderly help children who live away?

TOPIC 4. Respect

4.1 How do people show respect for the elderly?
[Probe: in general, from adult children]

4.2 Does the respect shown the elderly at the present time differ from the past? How? Why?
[Probe: role of educational gap between generations]

backgrounds or attitudes toward the topic of discussion, the usual approach is to hold discussions with separate groups, each homogeneous within itself but differing in terms of particular characteristics specified as the selection criteria. These separate focus group sessions will deal with the same topics and have a similar or identical set of discussion guidelines. A comparison between attitudes in the different sets of groups can then be done during the analysis phase. Note that consideration of participant characteristics is done for several purposes and that it is necessary when designing a focus group study to specify characteristics according to the purpose served. Two broad types of group definition characteristics can be distinguished: those that differentiate groups from each other (*break characteristics*) and those that are common to all groups (*control characteristics*).

Break Characteristics. In focus group studies within the social sciences, designs will often incorporate different subsets with potentially contrasting views or experiences concerning the issues under investigation. Break characteristics define how these subsets are differentiated. For example, a study of support systems of the elderly might want to compare views of elderly parents and those of adult children in both rural and urban areas. In this case there are two break variables: Generation (elderly versus adult children) and type of area (rural versus urban). Together the two break variables define four different population subsets for which separate focus group sessions would be held: rural elderly, urban elderly, rural adult children, urban adult children. Note that incorporating break characteristics into a design is useful not only for contrasting views between subgroups but also for establishing which views are common. Indeed, as discussed below, the analyst is often able to be more confident in drawing conclusions about the latter than the former.

Control Characteristics. Even when focus group sessions are held with different subsets of the population, it is often important to ensure that the groups all share some common characteristics. Control characteristics may be uniform characteristics or may specify a common composition for each group. For example, all groups might be limited to a particular region in the country, to people within the midrange of socioeconomic levels, and to individuals affiliated with the predominant religion. In this example, all groups share some set of *uniform control characteristics*. In addition, one or more *common composition control characteristics* may be specified for each group. For example, you may wish to have the views of both men and women represented in each group, and thus gender would be a characteristic explicitly taken into consideration when forming groups. However, rather than using gender to differentiate the groups, both men and women would be recruited for each group.

Note that what may be a control characteristic in one study may be a break characteristic in another. Note also that some focus group studies may involve only one population subset. For example, a study might focus only on the elderly in a particular city and all groups would be composed of this particular population subset (with or without some specified composition within each group). In this case, there are no break characteristics specified. Instead, the group definition characteristics are the same for all groups and can thus all be considered as uniform control characteristics.

Holding separate sessions with homogeneous but contrasting groups is believed to produce information in greater depth than would be the case with heterogeneous groups, because it will be easier for participants sharing similar key characteristics to identify with each other's experiences. Although there is little systematic methodological research to test this assumption, it is at least the intuitive rationale behind the conventional practice of maintaining some degree of intragroup homogeneity. Thus, in addition to permitting comparisons among different types of groups, defining separate groups in terms of break characteristics helps avoid mixing persons who may have sharp differences in opinion or behavior associated with the topics under study. For example, adult children may speak more frankly about the difficulties of caring for elderly parents if no elderly are present. Likewise, the elderly may be more open about their perceptions of lack of respect shown by younger individuals if no members of the younger generation are present.

In addition to break characteristics that have direct substantive relevance for the particular topic, groups are often separated by social status, even if social status is not expected to be related to the phenomenon under study. The reason for this is the assumption that if participants within a group differ sharply in social status, those who perceive themselves as inferior may be deferential toward the others and feel inhibited to speak their minds. Thus socioeconomic status is commonly incorporated into the design as a break variable. An alternative is to limit the study to persons with similar status (i.e., define some level of socioeconomic status as a uniform control characteristic). Likewise, in some cultures or with respect to some topics, mixing men and women in the same group may inhibit frank discussion, and thus it may be necessary to introduce gender as a break variable.

In sum, the choice of break or control characteristics incorporated in any particular study should be based on both substantive considerations specific to the topic under investigation and on considerations concerning the facilitation of frank group discussion. Thus for reasons related to the substantive nature of the issues being investigated, a study of adolescent sexuality would use a set of characteristics different from that used for a study of support systems of the elderly, regardless of the cultural context. However, whether groups in either or both studies would best be separated according to gender or socioeconomic status would depend on the particular cultural context of the population in which the study is being conducted.

Determining the Number of Sessions

A variety of considerations, both practical and substantive, must be taken into account when deciding on the number of focus group sessions to be held. On the practical side, obviously budget and time constraints are critical. In estimating the costs, consideration needs to be given to all phases, including transcription (and translation if conducted in a language foreign to the analyst) as well as the cost of the time used for analysis. Consideration also needs to be given to the time frame of the study. Transcription (and translation) take considerable time if done carefully. Time needed for analysis can also be substantial and is more or less proportional to the number of pages of transcript generated (and to the detail and care of the analysis).

Practical constraints on the number of groups that can be held limits the number of break characteristics that can be incorporated in any particular study design to differentiate groups. Based on theoretical considerations, differentiation should be made along the lines of only the most important break characteristics. Other important characteristics can be dealt with by using uniform control characteristics to focus the study on a particular subset of the population, thus eliminating variation with respect to these characteristics and facilitating discussion and interpretation of results. Generally, the incorporation of break characteristics should be kept to as low a level as is consistent with examining the major differences between subgroups in the population. Otherwise the cost in both money and time increase substantially.

In terms of substantively related considerations, the number of sessions depends on the complexity of the design as defined by the number of break characteristics incorporated in the study. Typically, at least one group needs to be conducted for each combination of break variables used to define a group, although for some studies interest may be in only selected combinations. Moreover, at least several groups are needed for each different combination of break characteristics that the researcher wishes to use as the basis of comparisons when analyzing the data. If only one session is held for a particular type of group, it is not possible to determine if unique patterns emerging from that group are related to the defining characteristics or are simply flukes related to the particular session. Note, however, that during the analysis phase, it is unrealistic to make comparisons between every unique combination of break variables. This point is discussed below.

Table 3.2 indicates how a set of characteristics might be incorporated into a focus group study design of support and exchange systems affecting the elderly in Thailand. Because there are four break characteristics, each with two dimensions, the design shown in Table 3.2 leads to 16 different combinations. For the 16 sessions, all participants would be Thai-speaking Buddhists with no more than a secondary school education. In addition each session would include a mix of men and women as well as a mix of martial status for elderly participants. If one focus group were held for each combination there would be a total of 16 sessions, producing 8 sessions each for comparison on any one of the four break variables and 4 sessions each for comparison on any two of the four break variables taken in combination. Although it is unlikely that any researcher would want to make comparisons on the basis of three or more break variables taken in combination, there would still be 2 sessions each for comparisons of any combination of three of the four break variables.

Analysis

The most challenging step of virtually all research is the analysis of information collected. Unfortunately, far less has been written about how to go about analyzing focus group data, especially from a social science perspective, than about how to conduct discussion sessions. The approach described below has evolved in the course of several projects that made extensive use of focus groups. There is no intention to imply

Table 3.2 Use of Characteristics in Selecting Groups for a Study—
Exchange Systems Between Elderly and Adult Children in
Thailand

| | | Type of Characteristic | |
| | | Uniform | Composition |
Characteristic	*Break*	*Control*	*Control*
Life Stage			
Elderly Versus Adult Child	XX		
Region			
Northeast Versus Central	XX		
Residence			
Rural Versus Urban	XX		
Socioeconomic Status			
Poor Versus Better Off	XX		
Religion			
Buddhist		XX	
Language			
Thai Dialect		XX	
Education			
No Higher Than Secondary		XX	
Sex			
Male Versus Female			XX
Marital Status (of Elderly)			
Married Versus Widowed			XX

that it is the best or only way to go about the task. Undoubtedly, a
number of strategies can be usefully followed.

General Considerations

Given the qualitative nature of the data gathered by focus group
methodology, a considerable amount of subjective judgment is necessarily involved in their interpretation and analysis. Not all statements
can be taken at face value. Interpretation is facilitated by the fact that
statements can be examined within the context of the broader discussion
and in light of information available from other sources based on different
methodologies such as surveys, case studies, or in-depth interviews. Thus,
with proper scrutiny and interpretation, the information, perceptions,

opinions, and attitudes expressed by focus group participants can yield valuable insights not available from other sources.

The extent and nature of analysis to which focus group discussions are subjected can vary considerably and will ultimately depend on the goal of the study as well as to the skills and time commitment of the investigators. In the case of marketing research, for which the goal may be to arrive at some practical recommendations without carefully documenting their basis, analysis is often done within a very short time span and may be based simply on impressions gained and notes taken while listening to the actual session or to the tapes. In the following discussion it is assumed that a thorough analysis based on repeated examination of a full set of transcripts is to be undertaken with the goal of explicating and understanding the phenomenon under investigation from a social scientific perspective. Although a number of shortcuts may be tempting, they will likely compromise the quality of the analysis.

The topics for analysis are generally dictated by those included in the focus group guidelines. Sometimes other topics not explicitly incorporated in the guidelines will arise regularly enough that sufficient information was generated to include them in the analysis. On the other hand, some topics in the guidelines may have generated so little discussion or have required so much moderator intervention that they are little more than brief direct answers to specific questions and are better left out of the analysis. If a large number of full-length focus group discussions have been undertaken and a number of different topics or subtopics were covered, it may be best not to tackle all topics at once when proceeding with the analysis but instead to break up the analysis into more manageable subsets of topics.

Focus groups generate textual data for analysis in the form of transcripts. A typical 2-hour session yields an average of 40 to 50 transcript pages. Thus if 20 sessions are conducted, there will be close to 1000 pages of transcripts. Dealing with large amounts of textual data is common for social scientists who employ qualitative research approaches. Ethnologists typically have extensive field notes; qualitative sociologists often have long transcripts from in-depth interviews. Fortunately, the advent of personal computers together with word processing and special programs to help manage textual data have greatly facilitated the task of analysis.

In essence, there are two basic parts to the analysis of focus group data: a mechanical one and an interpretive one (Seidel & Clark, 1984). The mechanical part involves physically organizing and subdividing the data into meaningful segments. The interpretive part involves determining criteria for organizing the textual data into analytically useful subdivisions (in essence coding the data) and the subsequent search for patterns within and between these subdivisions to draw substantively meaningful conclusions. A major aspect of the mechanics of qualitative data analysis is equivalent in essence to cutting and pasting: cutting the material apart and pasting the pieces into categorical and conceptual collections. This unwieldy and time-consuming aspect of the mechanical part of the analysis is greatly facilitated by the use of computers programs: Word processing programs are used to put the texts into the computer, and other programs are used to organize and retrieve the textual data. An example of such a software package is *The Ethnograph,* which is quite suitable for use with focus group transcripts (Seidel, Kjolseth, & Seymour, 1988). *The Ethnograph* enables the analyst to code interactively textual data files into analytic categories. Segments of the text associated with a particular code or combination of codes can then be readily sorted and retrieved. In this way all statements relating to a particular topic covered by the focus group sessions or all of the views of a specific nature concerning that topic can be easily assembled for the analyst to study, once the transcripts are entered into the computer and coded.

Word processing and *The Ethnograph* are, of course, only tools to aid the analysts in exploring the data for developing and testing analytical ideas and questions. Interpreting the transcripts is the real challenge to the researchers. Several specific procedures can be followed, which should contribute to the quality and reliability of the analysis.

Code Mapping Transcripts

Central to an analysis of qualitative data such as focus group transcripts is the process of coding the material into analytically distinct segments that can then be examined together when drawing conclusions concerning one or more of the topics and related concepts under investigation. In addition, coding can identify segments for some practical purpose, such as use as quotations in the report or to alert the analyst of some special feature of the segment (e.g., responses elicited by a leading question posed by the moderator or comments said in jest).

The term *code mapping* is used here to describe the process of coding, because in effect the analyst goes through the manuscript marking in the margins where segments corresponding to different codes start and end. The term is borrowed from the manual of *The Ethnograph,* which is well suited for entering these codes onto a computerized focus group transcript (Seidel et al., 1988). Even if a computerized transcript is not being used, the basic process of marking codes on the transcript would still facilitate analysis considerably. It is generally useful to read through a sample of the manuscripts before coding is started. However, because material can be easily recoded and the coding can be expanded at any point in the analysis, it is recommended that coding begin quite soon in the analysis stage. When developing codes, the code words chosen should be short and summarize the contents.

It is unrealistic to think about coding a transcript in full detail the first time through, largely because many concepts and subjects that will be useful to code will only become apparent as the transcripts are read and as the actual writing up of the results takes place. The following steps are one way that the code mapping process might take place. They are suggested with the idea that the researcher will be using *The Ethnograph* or similar program eventually to enter the codes in a computerized version of the transcript.

Develop an Initial Set of Codes Corresponding to Each Item in the Focus Group Discussion Guidelines. Note that the guidelines will typically have both major topics and subtopics (or specific questions below them). In addition, the subtopics (or specific questions) may have probes below them. A separate code should be assigned to each item at every level. Thus some codes will be fairly inclusive and cover general topics under which the more specific codes are organized. The codes covering major topic headings will normally include very long segments of text. For example, if the guidelines are organized under three major topics, the code for one may cover a third or more of the entire transcript.

Note also that comments concerning any subtopic will usually be nested within longer segments covered by the major topic codes, as they will normally occur at the point in the discussion when the moderator has reached the subtopic in the guidelines. However, when comments concerning a subtopic arise spontaneously and are not within the text of the "correct" major topic, the segment of text given the subtopics's code should also be given the appropriate major topic's code, even though the specific segment appears within the text of a different major topic. In other words, any segment assigned a code of a subtopic should always be associated with the code of the major topic under which the subtopic falls in the guidelines. Likewise, any segment assigned a code associated with a probe under a subtopic should also be associated with the codes of the subtopic and the major topic under which the probe falls in the guidelines.

Create Additional Codes for Topics That Arise and Are of Special Interest. As you go through the transcript mapping codes according to the scheme developed in correspondence to the guidelines, invent additional codes for topics that arise and are of interest to you but that are not specifically mentioned in the guidelines. Different researchers may be struck by or interested in different topics so they will not necessarily chose codes for the same additional topics.

Develop Nonsubstantive Codes That Will Be of Particular Help in the Analysis and Write-Up Phases. In addition to codes relating to substantive topics, you may also want to use some nonsubstantive codes, which will facilitate interpretation and write up. Some examples of such codes are one that flags potential statements that could serve as illustrative quotations in the text of the report, a code that flags discussion in response to comments or questions by the moderator that appear to be leading and hence biasing the participants in their subsequent discussion, and a code that indicates a statement is made as a joke or that the participant is laughing while making the comment (perhaps based on comments by the note taker included in the transcript).

Develop Subsequent Detailed Codes to Use for Analyses of Specific Topics. After the initial code mapping is completed and the researcher is analyzing specific topics covered by the transcripts, it may be useful to develop a considerably more detailed set of codes for the topics on which the analysis is concentrating. The relevant details to be coded will generally become apparent as the analysis proceeds and will usually refer to considerably shorter text segments than those identified in the course of the previous code mappings.

Constructing an Overview Grid

An effective way to proceed with the interpretive part of the analysis of focus group transcripts is to construct a large chart or table that can be referred to as an *overview grid* and that provides a descriptive summary of the content of the focus group discussions. Such a grid would typically have topic headings as one axis and focus group session identifiers as the other. The cells would contain brief summaries of the content of the discussion for each group concerning each topic, indicating, for example, the extent of consensus regarding the topic and the direction of this consensus. Other brief relevant aspects about the discussion can also be noted within the cell, including your impression of the quality of the information. In reaching conclusions on quality, consider such factors as moderator influence, the number of people actually giving that opinion, and so on. The topic headings are largely determined by the issues addressed in the discussion guidelines. However, topics that persistently arise even though not explicit in the guidelines would also be added.

Although it is not imperative to have code mapped the transcript before constructing an overview grid, having done so can facilitate the task. This is especially so if the code mapping has been computerized through a software package such as *The Ethnograph*. Computerized coding of the transcripts makes organizing their contents by topic and session quite convenient. Construction of the overview grid serves as an effective way to familiarize the analyst with the content of the transcripts. Often the process leads to insights and suggests hypotheses that contribute to the later stages of the interpretive analysis.

Relationships between some of the variables of interest can be assessed directly during the stage at which the overview grid is being constructed, especially if direct questions addressing such relationships were included in the discussion guidelines. Table 3.2 contains examples of questions that directly address relationships, including the probe about whether the life cycle stage or sex of the adult child relates to various expectations for actual behavior affecting the elderly, the probe about whether place of residence affects the support that adult children provide parents, and the probe about whether the amount of property that an elderly couple retains affects the care they receive. Other analysis, however, may examine patterns existing between the analytical subdivisions used in forming the overview grid and require returning to the transcripts to develop appropriate interpretation. A program like *The Ethnograph* can be very useful at this stage, because it provides an efficient means to retrieve statements relating to any combination of analytical categories that the analyst specifies.

Clearly a considerable amount of subjective judgment is involved at this stage in detecting patterns as well as in the earlier stage when determining what views appear to be more pervasive among the many opinions expressed. Not all statements can be taken at face value but rather require interpretation based on the context in which they are made and sometimes in the light of information available to the researchers from external sources. It is advisable that several people read through all the transcripts and collaborate on the analysis to reduce the chances that the subjective portion of the analysis process leads to unwarranted emphasis or invalid conclusions.

Making Intergroup Comparisons

If the study design involved a set of break characteristics used to differentiate subsets of the target population, an important part of the analysis will be a discussion of the similarities and differences between the groups involving these various subsets. Note comparisons are not necessarily made between every unique combination of break variables but instead between clusters of combinations. For example, in a study that incorporates region (central versus northeast), rural-urban residence, socioeconomic status (high versus low) and religion (Buddhist versus Muslim) as break characteristics, there are 16 unique combinations of the characteristics. Nevertheless, interest is unlikely to focus on comparisons between all 16 detailed combinations. Rather comparisons are more likely to be made on the basis of only one or two characteristics at a time (e.g., Buddhist versus Muslim or possibly rural Buddhist versus rural Muslim versus urban Buddhist versus urban Muslim). It is unrealistic to think of exercising controls in the analysis of focus group data in the more rigorous sense of a quantitative multivariate analysis.

Incorporating break characteristics believed to be of substantive importance into a study design enables contrasts to be made between focus groups held with the differently defined subsets of participants. However, comparisons among groups differentiated by break characteristics may be even more useful for giving the analyst confidence that the views common across the groups are relatively general than in enabling the analyst confidently to contrast differences in views associated with the break characteristics. This is particularly true if only a small number of groups are available for each subset. The reason for this is that the analyst may have difficulty in distinguishing differences between any two groups that stem from more substantively based considerations from those differences that are a function of the circumstances under which the group took place (e.g., the particular way the moderator conducted the session or the particular group dynamics related to the personalities of the particular participants). However, when similar opinions are expressed by different subsets, despite the many differences that characterize the conduction of any two sessions, it is likely that views or experiences are being tapped that are common to a shared underlying culture within the broader population.

Assessing Reliability

Using a team approach involving several researchers when analyzing focus group data substantially facilitates reliability in the interpretation because various steps in the analysis can be done independently by each team member and later compared. Disagreements can then be discussed and generally resolved by reviewing the transcripts together and tracking down the source of the disagreement. By having each team member independently construct an overview grid, it is possible to establish considerable reliability early in the interpretive process. If both original language transcripts and translations are being used, a team approach is essential with at least one member being able to analyze the original language version.

Because the focus group approach inherently involves conducting a number of sessions, it is possible to assess the reliability of the data (in contrast to the analysis) by comparing statements within and, more important, across sessions. This advantage in assessing reliability is an important difference between the focus group approach and other qualitative research strategies. Assessing the internal reliability of the focus group is greatly facilitated by the construction of overview grids. Although some variation in views is to be expected from session to session, an important goal of a focus group study is often the determination of cultural expectations (e.g., about the role of the elderly and the support and exchange systems in which they are involved). The extent to which consensus is found within and between groups about their expectations, allowing for possible systematic differences by ethnicity or other cultural groupings of the sessions, can indicate the reliability of the information collected. The fact that a design often imposes some variation in key characteristics such as rural and urban residence and socioeconomic status permits confidence that views that are consistently found across groups represent cultural consensus.

The accuracy of the interpretive analysis is also enhanced if the analysts are intimately involved with the actual data collection (i.e., present at the focus group sessions and possibly even serving as moderators). This eliminates considerably the distance between the analyst and subject being studied that so often marks quantitative social science research in which only interviewers and not the eventual analysts have contact with respondents.

4

Understanding Communication Processes in Focus Groups

TERRANCE L. ALBRECHT
GERIANNE M. JOHNSON
JOSEPH B. WALTHER

Using focus groups as a setting for data collection can serve many important purposes for social scientists. The method of conducting group interviews to obtain data is increasingly useful as a way to generate qualitative and quantitative data about a wide range of social, cognitive, health, and behavior patterns. However, focus groups are events that have a life of their own; indeed, they occur in settings where the processes of interpersonal communication and social influence are omnipresent. As Yovovich (1991) suggests, "interaction among respondents stimulates new ideas and thoughts . . . yet group pressure challenges participants to be more realistic" (p. 43). Simply, the communication that occurs in focus groups is a phenomenon sometimes overlooked by researchers seeking to gather data from these sessions.

Most of the other chapters in this volume are concerned with exploring focus group methodology and, principally, with describing the different kinds of research projects that benefit from focus group data. In contrast, this chapter is about the process of communication that occurs in the focus group and how this process impacts the validity of the data obtained from focus group sessions (the answers that researchers collect from the participants in these groups). This chapter is a review of some key aspects of the interaction dynamics that facilitate or hinder the quality of the focus group method and the data. As communication researchers contributing to this volume, our tasks are to explicate the nature of the process of communication, to review principal characteristics of group communication in the focus group context, and finally, to describe ways those interaction processes impact the opinions (data) generated by the focus group. We conclude with some pragmatic suggestions for increasing the success of focus group interactions.

Definitions

Understanding how communication phenomena occur in focus groups begins with an expansion of certain key terms: communication, small group communication, and focus group communication. *Communication* is a transactional, symbolic process of mutual influence occurring between two or more individuals that alters their affective, cognitive, or behavioral states (see Burgoon & Ruffner, 1978; Cappella, 1981; Miller & Steinberg, 1975; Wilson, 1975). Transactional influence means that a change in any one aspect of the process may modify all others (Burgoon & Ruffner, 1978). When one person communicates a message to others, the process is not linear. Rather, verbal and nonverbal behavior can affect all persons' feelings and cognitions about themselves and the state of the relationship, future message sequences, and so on. These effects may or may not be "predictable" in a linear, if-then fashion. As messages are exchanged, all parties are caught in a web that is ongoing and dynamic in character (Burgoon & Ruffner, 1978).

Communication is also symbolic in nature. Meaning does not reside in the specific messages that are expressed but in the perceptual processes of each participant. Individuals attach referents or meanings to the symbols they exchange (the words they hear and use, the nonverbal behaviors they process and use) to create meaning. To the extent interactants have similar referents for the symbols they exchange, meanings are shared between individuals and understanding is achieved. In short, communication, both verbal and nonverbal, is a mutual influence process; the linguistic and nonlinguistic symbols transacted reflect and reinforce cognitive patterns for all participants involved.

Examining the *small group* as a context-based communication experience is best framed in the definition by Shaw (1981): "A group is defined as two or more persons who are interacting with one another in such a manner that each person influences and is influenced by each other person" (p. 10). In short, communication is "the essential characteristic of [a small] group]" (Littlejohn, 1989, p. 202). Discussions derived from *focus group communication* usually occur among six to eight participants as a way to gather in-depth information on a specific topic or related set of topics selected by the researcher (Hooper, 1989). The basis of the participants' interaction may include identification of key problems and/or solutions and enacting or informing outsiders (researchers) about cultural patterns or community (e.g., McHenry, 1992). For example, Grunig (1990) reported the use of focus group communication to generate strategies for educating a community about the stigmas of mental illness. The purpose for which a focus group is organized and conducted will naturally influence the way in which the discussion unfolds and the way the messages exchanged are tracked by the participants and by the researcher. The purpose of the group also impacts the interpretations that accrue as meanings are co-constructed and enacted by participants. To illustrate, members of a focus group who are evaluating potential new products that they themselves might purchase will likely interact with one another in ways that differ markedly from members communicating in a group involved in corporate planning; at a simple level, the former group is very egocentric whereas the latter group is very object oriented. One group is consumption and immediacy oriented, and the other group features more complex, long-term decision criteria and ambiguous goals.

Generating Group Opinions
in Focus Groups

It is common in many focus groups for members to discuss an issue and offer a unified voice in presenting their opinions to the researcher. This is the heart of the persuasion and mutual influence process in the small group experience, but therein also lies the challenge for the researcher. There are obviously many advantages and disadvantages to obtaining consensual focus group opinions (as opposed to collecting individual opinions). However, given that the focus group session is a *communication* event, the concern is to understand how the communication process determines the nature and quality of the data generated and how the opinion generation process may be thwarted during the focus group experience.

One of the advantages of the opinions generated through focus group interaction (over the opinions elicited from individual respondents) has to do with the isomorphism of group opinions to those of individuals in the population at large. This observation does not pertain to the qualitative nature of the comments made by focus group members, but refers to the process of opinion formation and propagation in normal life. From a communication perspective, focus group methodology has a degree of external validity based on the fact that focus groups are grounded in the "human tendency to discuss issues and ideas in groups" (Sink, 1991, p. 197). In this sense, personal opinions might be more appropriately described as derived from social, rather than personal processes. Opinions about a variety of issues are generally determined not by individual information gathering and deliberation but through communication with others.

This process is well documented in research on the two-step flow theory of media consumption (Lazersfeld, Berelson, & Gaudet, 1948). The theory has been supported and extended over several decades (see Katz, 1957, 1967) and is based on the notion that opinions about current events tend not to be drawn directly from media sources but from interactions with social partners. These partners, termed *opinion leaders,* tend to be well informed, cosmopolitan, and high media consumers (Rogers & Shoemaker, 1971). This and other research supports the notion that opinions frequently arise through group interaction, as opposed to situations of social isolation.

Other research has shown that decisions individuals make about various actions are affected by the reactions that such individuals predict that their significant others will have to their actions (e.g., Fishbein & Azjen, 1981; Triandis, 1980). Even in the case of deciding whether or not one might seek medical attention, the anticipation of favorable or unfavorable social reaction may be just as potent a predictor of medical attention as the severity of illness or one's belief that such attention will remedy the problem (see Becker, 1979; Montano, 1986; Seibold & Roper, 1979). Obviously, compared with the latter two criteria, anticipated social evaluations seem a far less rational basis on which to determine potentially life-threatening medical decisions. However, this factor represents the power of the social influence process in shaping people's opinions.

Given that focus groups are social events involving the interaction of participants and the interplay and modification of ideas, such a forum for opinion gathering may render data that are more ecologically valid than methods that assess individuals' opinions in relatively asocial settings. A focus group responding to a new product, concept, or idea might generate opinions more like those of the public than would even a large number of isolated respondents.

Although the above benefits of social interaction for opinion formation are compelling, the communication process in group settings is also subject to problems that pose serious potential threats to the validity of the data gathered in the focus group sessions. To outline some of these problems, a look at opinion articulation processes follows.

Of particular consequence is the fact that social interaction affects not only opinion *formation* but opinion *articulation* as well. A now-classic model of the process of opinion giving is Kelman's (1961) typology. Kelman suggested that opinions are produced through one of three processes: compliance, identification, and internalization. Each type of communication pattern may be seen in focus group interaction and may be deemed a potential threat to the internal validity of the focus group data.

Compliance is the act of responding in ways one believes are expected by a questioner, in anticipation of some immediate reward. These types of responses are superficial opinions at best or demand characteristics at worst. Yet, if focus groups are conducted such that short, conforming, flattering, or socially desirable responses are intangibly rewarded by a facilitator, just such compliant responses should be expected to prevail. For example, if conforming or flattering responses are not questioned or probed, they may be rewarded by an earlier adjournment of the focus group session. Although the sponsor of a focus group meeting may be fascinated by the process, respondents may be less committed (especially those being paid per session), and the opportunity to end the session sooner may lead to less valid, more compliant, responses.

A second process of opinion generation, *identification,* is related to the situation in which a respondent's position on an issue is similar to the position held by someone the respondent admires or with whom he or she seeks solidarity. Interpersonal attraction between group members may lead to such responses. One example is that respondents frequently assume that a focus group facilitator is professionally associated with a particular organization, product, or idea. The facilitator's own biases and preferences may be intentionally or unintentionally signaled. Given that respondents may wish to please (or at least not offend) the facilitator, their responses may reflect what it is they think the facilitator wants to hear. Finally, whether embodied by the moderator or another participant, some participants may naturally desire to affiliate with a skilled communicator and socially attractive other, and one way to signal affiliation is through the expression of similar attitudes (see

Byrne, 1971; Cappella & Palmer, 1992; Sunnafrank & Miller, 1981). In any of these cases, a respondent's stated opinions may grow to resemble those of the affiliative target. Thus identification may drive the formation of a "group" opinion.

One extreme case of opinion by identification is almost guaranteed to take place in a focus group involving participants from various hierarchical levels within a single organization or reporting structure. Regardless of whether the facilitator emphasizes that all responses and disagreements are legitimate, it simply may be too professionally and personally risky for a subordinate to disagree publicly with an opinion offered by a superior who holds fate control. Experiments using computer-based electronic meeting systems, in which all comments are displayed anonymously, show significantly greater substantive conflict within these groups than in face-to-face or nonanonymous electronic meetings (see Connolly, Jessup, & Valacich, 1990; Gallupe, DeSanctis, & Dickson, 1988). These results show that identification processes, when they appear, present very powerful inhibiting effects on opinion advocacy.

An additional condition based on Kelman's (1961) identification process leading to insincere or premature agreement is the notorious "groupthink" condition, in which participants' desire for cohesion preempts their critical examination of decision implications (Janis, 1972). The groupthink process is probably less frequent in ad hoc focus groups than in ongoing problem-solving groups in which group solidarity forces have had time to congeal. However, if the moderator's behavior suggests that quick decisions will be rewarded (e.g., move the group toward a faster exit) such premature consensus development is possible.

The third form of opinion disclosure, that based on *internalization,* is related to the report of opinions that are deeply ingrained and personal. Such opinions are less susceptible to transient effects of material rewards or social relationships (i.e., potential artifacts of the focus group setting). Thus these opinions are potentially the most valuable yet the most difficult data to obtain by researchers using a focus group methodology. Efforts to prompt participants to articulate such opinions not only are subject to the psychological and communication barriers noted above but are also affected by a sequencing effect common to the group setting. The classic conformity research by Asch (1952) demonstrated what experienced focus group facilitators have seen many times: When respondents are asked one at a time for their judgments, those responding last tend to echo the sentiments of those responding first. While Asch's experiments examined a minority of one as the last respondent (the majority was all but the one), similar effects inhibit responses in focus groups. In the focus setting it is common to ask the group to think about a concept, a message strategy, or a product, then ask them to express their evaluations. After a gregarious first speaker voices his or her opinion, others are frequently heard to say "pretty much the same as the first person who spoke," or otherwise indicate either that some type of social pressure is occurring or that the cognitive wheels have simply stopped.

Thus the key issue is how to facilitate the disclosure of internalized opinions. Several suggestions are offered below, based on the notions that not all communication is good communication and that there is a time and place in focus groups for *not* talking.

Research on group discussion has found that the group idea-generation process benefits when it begins as a parallel, individual process. In the public context of the group, this is most easily achieved by beginning with participants writing, rather than saying, their ideas. Such techniques have been examined formally as part of structured approaches in decision-making groups. One such approach, the nominal group technique (NGT; see Van de Ven & Delbecq, 1971) has received much attention by both researchers and practitioners (e.g., Gustafson, Shukla, Delbecq, & Walster, 1973; VanGundy, 1988). In NGT, the participants each write down his or her own initial ideas about a topic. The moderator then asks each participant, in turn, to announce his or her answers, after which group discussion commences. Another technique, the Delphi method, further restricts the amount of group interaction. Using the Delphi method, participants are asked to write their responses to a proposal. These responses are collected by the facilitator, and then posted for public reading. Although there are other differences between Delphi and NGT, the most important aspect to consider is the anonymity offered by Delphi.

Interest in these group discussion procedures generally focuses on the groups' decision quality, and some communication principles are readily applicable to the focus group setting. First, by using writing rather than speaking (as in the NGT approach) and then asking each participant what he or she has written, the group is likely to produce a greater number of unique responses (see Steiner, 1972). Even if many responses are similar, the researcher can rule out the effects of compliance or identification, because no one knows what anyone else in the group will be expressing. In this way, each person participates, no one can defer to someone else's idea, and no one can attempt an other-specific, socially desirable response (especially if each individual cannot see other people writing long versus short responses). After hearing each idea, the greatest advantages of brainstorming can be realized, as others' ideas stimulate further thinking by participants.

Second, masking authorship and posting or reading the group's responses while maintaining anonymity of idea creation (as in the Delphi approach) may change group dynamics dramatically. Knowing that one will not be associated with a suggestion may mitigate the potentially inhibiting influences of evaluation apprehension (see Gallupe, Dennis, Cooper, Valacich, Bastianutti, & Nunamaker, 1992). Hence, more risky or creative responses may be offered by individual members. In addition, ideas are discussed more critically when their authorship is hidden. More critical treatment of issues by focus groups is facilitated by anonymity, because (1) the author of an idea is protected and may be less likely to feel a personal affront because disagreements are directed more at a substantive, rather than an interpersonal level, and (2) given this relatively nondefensive climate, speakers may feel freer to criticize a group idea because the risk of interpersonal or professional retribution is somewhat curbed.

In general, such strategies for structuring the communication process alleviate those conditions that cause problematic interaction and that threaten the validity of focus group data. With these interpersonal barriers controlled, the group is primed for more creative types of interaction. One such pattern that results in the group connecting and mutually developing a kind of substantive "story" (as their response) is fantasy spinning (Bormann, 1972).

Fantasy Themes and Focus Group Communication

When the purpose of the focus group discussion is to solve a problem, some knowledge of communication theory and research on small group decision making is instructive for both the group moderator and the investigator who must interpret the discussion data. Hirokawa's (1983a, 1983b) studies of functional decision making have shown that members' discourse must fulfill certain key purposes, rather than follow specified linear steps, to result in an effective decision.

Alternatively, a more frequent use of focus groups and group interviews for social scientific purposes is to stimulate a discussion that functions to simulate a microcosm of the larger community or (as noted in the discussion about consensual group opinions) agreement on a significant social issue (e.g., plans for a major political campaign, a crucial verdict for trial simulation research, community attitudes on abortion or racism, or a description of unsafe working conditions in an organization). In these types of exchanges, the members of the group may unintentionally, although naturally, weave a story, constructing a fantasy as they build on one another's statements to describe collectively an ideal campaign, justify their verdicts and social attitudes, or describe the lack of safety in their workplace. When a fantasy pattern unfolds in a focus group session, Bormann's (1972) method of *fantasy theme analysis* is a more useful guide for the interpretation of these data than is a rational group decision-making model.

Fantasy themes include a recollection of something that occurred in the past or a dream about something yet to happen. For example, Putnam, Van Hoeven, and Bullis (1991) demonstrated that convergence in teachers' and school district representatives' discourse about common enemies and past negotiations became the basis for later negotiations about teacher salaries and benefits. Bormann (1972, p. 397) noted the drama that unfolds in a fantasy theme may often be a simulation of a here-and-now situation in the group. Smith (1988) extended this observation by stating that a good-versus-evil or the-powerful-versus-the-powerless fantasy theme commonly underlies narrative discourse about extant conflict.

Bloom (1989) and others have stated that the artificial or laboratory setting of the focus group threatens the validity of the meanings created and the messages produced, because of the subtle and overt restrictions on naturally occurring communication among members. Much has been written about creating a conducive environment for focus group discussion (cf., McDonald & Topper, 1988; Roller, 1992; Schwartz, 1991) and about adapting the setting to the focus group participants (cf., Fedder, 1990; Simon, 1987). The nature of the communication relationships between group members clearly has implications for the level of trust and patterns of self-disclosure that occur between members; both are crucial factors in determining the validity of discursive data. Some focus discussions are conducted within naturally occurring or nominal groups such as families (Pagnucco & Quinn, 1988), to capitalize on the realism and spontaneity provided by existing communication relationships. Accordingly, one way in which participants with no commonly shared history may create a type of trusting, disclosive group culture is by using references to fantasy characters (i.e., "common heroes, villains, saints, and enemies," Smith, 1988, p. 271). Group members can develop attachments to one another based on culturally shared symbolic realities. This creates common ground, bridging differences and relational uncertainties present between participants. They then have redundant, shared referents to use in their discourse about rational, logical topics. For example, members of the U.S. Democratic party may be unable to agree on the "best" way to salvage a flagging U.S. economy, but they can converge on a story that reflects their collective identification of George Herbert Walker Bush as the man responsible for the country's current economic woes. By participating in dramatized communication about a fantasy character (setting, situation, etc.) group members demonstrate or make public their shared commitments and attitudes about the topic under discussion.

Fantasy theme analysis brings communication theories about small group interaction together with rhetorical theories about language, meaning, and the effects of messages on audiences, groups, and speakers (Bormann, 1972). This is a method for critically analyzing topics in narrative discourse (the stories) to which group members refer as they ground their logical points in their discussion or debate. Bormann (1972; 1982) based the method on Burke's (1946) work about dramatistic criticism and on Bales's (1950) treatment of fantasizing processes in small interacting groups. The fantasy critic interprets discussion in terms of "how dramatizing communication creates social realities for [a group] of people and with a way to examine messages for insights into the group's culture, motivation, emotional style, and cohesion" (Bormann, 1972, p. 396). Fantasies begin to chain out (Bormann, 1972) through a group of persons as references to the central fantasy types serve to ground particular logical arguments about characters, their motivations, the context, and so on. Bormann (1972) argued that the fantasy theme has explanatory power as a mechanism to account for the development and dissolution of dramas that engulf groups of people and consequently change their behavior. He depicted what he termed systemic layering, or chaining, of fantasized elements in group discourse, beginning with individual references to fantasy characters, settings, or situations.

Such shared fantasies establish the nature of shared reality on which discursive logic, or reasoning, is based (Bormann, 1982). As part of the analysis, fantasy themes are referred to as the "proof" for logical arguments in discourse between group members. For example, the fantasy of a God persona allows biblical quotes to stand as proof in religious arguments, just as a fantasy about science entails proof in the form of empirical evidence for logical arguments about these topics. Smith's (1988) observation about the pervasiveness of the good-versus-evil fantasy theme suggests that shared attitudes about "the good" often stand as proof in logical discussions aimed at problem solving. ("The good" may be a low-cost solution or an environmentally safe solution or a decreased stigma, etc.) References to this "good" ground logical arguments about the best way to solve the problem in question. In addition, given that people sometimes have more cognitive information than they can articulate (Miller, 1991), projective discussion techniques (e.g., drama, pictures, stories) can be used to elicit emotional bases for opinions and undeveloped thoughts.

In a review of the method after 10 years of programmatic research, Bormann (1982) reiterated the "fundamental concern for message content" (p. 291) and stated that the claims of fantasy theme analysis are empirically supported. Specifically, the claims of the method include (1) fantasies are shared in all communication contexts, (2) there is a connection between shared fantasies and community consciousness, (3) the process of sharing fantasies is closely connected with personal motivation, and (4) sharing fantasies is a means to construct mutually understood and shared social realities. Thus, for focus groups that are designed to simulate a microcosm of community consciousness (versus those designed to solve a problem, per se), fantasy theme analysis provides a superior interpretive lens for the researcher. Fantasy themes are shared in focus group interaction; these themes help direct the formation of group opinion and the process of sharing these fantasies helps group members create their social reality.

Summary Implications for Conducting Focus Group Research

The communication issues described in this chapter are important concerns for preserving the internal validity of focus group data. The human communication behaviors occurring in focus groups are imbued with patterns that cannot be divorced from the specific content of the message responses given by participants. We caution researchers to consider the entire episode of the group interview when interpreting focus group data and to recognize that group responses are subject to social influence (e.g., compliance, identification, and internalization) and fantasy spinning as a means of developing shared meaning and rendering the experience sensible and accessible to all participants.

The following recommendations are offered for researchers and readers of this volume to consider as they plan studies employing a focus group methodology.

1. The focus group method necessitates that the role of the moderator be given critical consideration; many of the important considerations for moderator selection and participation focus on the communication implications of the moderator's experience, communication competence, and style.

The moderator's experience, competence, and style at facilitating group interaction and stake, or involvement, in the group's discussion will likely affect the quality of the data collected (Rigler, 1987). Moderators should use such skills as active listening (Woolridge, 1991) and projective techniques (e.g., pictures, drawings, and role-playing; Miller, 1991), particularly when managing emotionally charged topics. Focus groups are interactive events, meaning that the form of the discussion and substantive messages revealed may be unknowable in advance. The moderator must be rhetorically sensitive, that is, able to gauge accurately the perspectives or reactions of others in the group, to speak using language and terms common to the focus group members (see Eadie & Powell, 1991; Hart & Burks, 1972). In addition, the moderator must be able to respond neutrally to the discussion as it unfolds.

Reliability is also enhanced when the same moderator is used across focus group sessions (Klein, 1989). This provides greater shared relational history among group members, which is more likely to enhance trust, predictability, and honesty in responses (see Roller, 1992).

2. Communication patterns in focus groups may be useful for obtaining quantitative as well as qualitative information.

Most focus group sessions are designed as communication events that surface qualitative data, such as individual and shared assumptions, feelings, and themes. Yet the focus group can also be a useful forum in which to raise tentative hypotheses and test them on the spot. An example will help to clarify this argument.

One of these authors conducted focus group sessions for a newspaper publisher considering a change in the layout and features in its daily comic strip section. Two series of mock-ups were created for the groups, with each series containing several contiguous days of the old and potentially new comics. After examining each series, the group discussion raised several plausible hypotheses about what makes a comics sheet popular. Some participants suggested that day-to-day continuity was important; others were attracted to the better known, widely read comics seen in a variety of other news markets; some suggested they preferred series that contained feminist themes; and others liked plenty of soap-opera-type strips. These attributes could then be counted in the different layouts, and ranking tests administered easily, even on an impromptu basis. Small sample and nominal- and ordinal-level statistics allow for hypothesis tests. For example, the sign test (see Moses, 1952) is a useful measure of preference between two paired stimuli (e.g., two versions of a newspaper). Statistically, it is as likely as a *t*-test to detect differences 95 out of 100 times but is much more powerful with small samples (even $N = 6$) than with large ones (Siegel & Castellan, 1988).

Other two-sample tests also allow for stratification analyses by gender, income, or some other variable of interest. Using the newspaper example, a group of subscribers may indicate significantly different appreciation for various ratios of old-to-new comics, compared with infrequent readers. The Komolgorov-Smirnov test can detect such differences when they exist. Although these kinds of designs and statistics do not substitute for large-scale surveys or controlled experiments, they do serve as opportunities for pilot testing to begin confirming or disconfirming conclusions arising from qualitative methods in focus groups.

3. Several threats to the validity of focus group data exist related to communication phenomena. These include social desirability, low levels of trust, face-politeness needs, researcher bias, and deception.

Socially desirable information may be communicated at the expense of socially undesirable information (see Mariampolski, 1989, for question strategies to manage sensitive topics and techniques for question probes). It is also the case that sensitive and potentially embarrassing topics may incur participants' politeness and face needs (see Brown & Levinson, 1978). These should be anticipated and accounted for in the data obtained (e.g., Potts, 1990). Deception becomes a threat to validity, particularly when respondents are overly experienced with focus groups. The problem of a professional respondent (Hayward & Rose, 1990) arises when participants are solely motivated to join a group because of the compensation they will receive for their involvement. Such individuals may initially appear sincere, but their motivation to contribute fully and constructively may be negatively affected, thus skewing the sincerity and spontaneity of their participation in the group interaction. This attitude on the part of one or some can have a contagion effect on other focus group members.

4. Communication implications also extend to the issue of appropriate samples for focus group research. *Differences, especially in group size and demographic composition, have implications for language choices, cultural ways of speaking (Hymes, 1972), and disclosure levels.* Without moderator skill in managing focus groups, group size and group participation have long been inversely correlated (see the discussion on opinion generation). Status, ethnicity, and gender composition of the group can also impact communication reticence or assertiveness (Bortree, 1986; Simon, 1987). Furthermore, the developmental communication abilities of group members (e.g., children; see McDonald & Topper, 1988; Spethman, 1992; Winski, 1992) require moderators to adapt to participants' culturally native ways of speaking.

Final Note

Focus groups are clearly communication events that should not be taken for granted. Like other tools of opinion research, handling the interview may be part art and part skill (see Fowler, 1988). However, the artistic aspects of managing group interaction with facility, as well as the stimulation and interpretation of group opinion data, may be enhanced by consideration and implementation of lessons learned from communication theory and research.

5

Quality Control in
Focus Group Research

RICHARD A. KRUEGER

Years ago I heard a veterinarian talk about breeds of dogs. He was offering suggestions about which breed of dog to select. One tip was particularly interesting. The vet said that when a breed suddenly becomes popular, the quality of that breed begins to suffer because some dog breeders will attempt to meet the demand by breeding dogs without regard to quality standards. Popularity and quality are at odds. Perhaps this applies to research methodology as well as to breeds of dogs.

A decade ago few would have anticipated the widespread current interest in focus group interviewing. This interest has lead to a variety of applications and misapplications, to discoveries and opportunities missed, to enlightenment and confusion. Some of the resources invested in focus groups were well spent, others were spent foolishly. Differences in the quality of focus groups are more apparent now than they were a decade ago, owing in large part to the growing use of such groups. Unfortunately, there is a plethora of inadequate studies, involving poor design and shoddy reporting.

This chapter addresses specifically the problem of quality control in focus group interviewing; however, similar problems exist in all research methodologies. In our free-enterprise, entrepreneurial society no procedure is immune. In the past, telephone interviews and mail-out surveys were the methods most abused. Focus groups have now joined them.

Quality control problems occur for several reasons. Those who practice research (consultants, researchers, evaluators, experts, etc.) are free to experiment, practice without certification or even training, and only sometimes do they bear the consequences of their actions. In close-knit communities word-of-mouth recommendation is rather effective in maintaining quality or, at least, in satisfying clients. However, in larger communities these informal networks are less effective. No methodology escapes the erosion of quality that results from widespread adoption. In some respects, qualitative methodologies are particularly susceptible to abuse largely because they involve people, who must make judgments about the nature of questions to be asked, subjects to be studied, and analysis to be done. Moreover, in qualitative methodology it is easier for the researcher to overlook, ignore, or misinterpret a defect in the research procedure. Consequently, these problems are less apparent to the client.

The Two Dimensions of Quality

Quality consists of two interdependent dimensions: what the researcher does and what the client perceives. First, what steps or procedures does the researcher undertake? Over time, acceptable procedures for conducting focus groups have been developed. Some of this advice is situation specific, other suggestions are generally applicable. For example, open-ended or nondirective questions are recommended for use across focus groups, whereas the appropriateness of recruiting strangers to participate depends on the purpose of a given study. This chapter attempts to highlight these traditional and preferred procedures within the public and nonprofit sector.

Second, quality lies in the perception of the client or user of the focus group study. Quality in focus groups is not the absence of defects or the reduction of errors. It is the degree to which client expectations are met by the researcher. These expectations may be based on the client's past experiences, professional standards, or even whims. Whatever the source, they must be considered by the researcher. When the client's expectations are at odds with accepted traditions or standards, the researcher should work with the client to seek resolution. In this situation the researcher serves as a teacher or adviser, helping the client see the importance of certain actions.

10 Quality Factors in Focus Group Research

I offer as worthy of consideration and discussion the following 10 factors that can influence the quality of focus group interviews:

1. Clarity of purpose
2. Appropriate environment
3. Sufficient resources
4. Appropriate participants
5. Skillful moderator
6. Effective questions
7. Careful data handling
8. Systematic and verifiable analysis
9. Appropriate presentation
10. Honoring the participant, client, and method

Let's examine these factors along with the specific threats to quality that have emerged from focus groups, particularly in the public and nonprofit arena.

Clarity of Purpose

Quality is affected when the purpose is not clear or when focus groups are stretched beyond their limits. At times clients and even researchers forget that focus groups are primarily information-gathering processes and not means to facilitate group decision making, team building, or to create a public image of listening. Focus groups are not a substitute for the nominal group process that seeks to arrive at consensus or brainstorming when creative ideas are sought.

Focus group interviews provide a specialized tool for researchers. It is the methodology of choice in some situations, in others it may be acceptable or appropriate, in still others it is inappropriate.

Threats to Quality

Quality can suffer when focus groups are used to accomplish conflicting objectives. For example, an organization wants feedback from employees or clients but also wants to convey the impression of listening. Quality suffers when the perception of listening is overemphasized and attention to careful listening is subordinated in the focus group. Focus groups should not be used to make statistical projections to a given population. The fact that 80% of the focus group respondents hold a particular opinion does not mean that the same percentage of a given population does. Other research procedures are needed if the user wishes to make inferences to a population.

Quality suffers when those involved have differing notions of the purpose of the study. Misunderstanding among key partners can result in compromises that may jeopardize quality or the client's satisfaction with the outcome.

Appropriate Environment

The appropriate environment includes the physical location where participants meet as well as the sociopolitical ambience of the research project. A proper physical environment must be provided. The location should be neutral and easy to find, a place where participants feel comfortable and relaxed. The group should be arranged so that each participant can see others in the group, often around a table. The focus group is recorded on audiotape. Other features such as one-way mirrors, special focus group rooms, or video cameras usually do not add substantially to the quality of the focus group and may even distract. The guiding principle is to find an environment that participants find nonthreatening, convenient, and comfortable.

An emerging concern has been the sociopolitical environment. Focus groups have increasingly been used within organizations as a means for providing feedback to decision makers and for gaining insights about compensation or benefits or as strategies for fostering team building or total quality management. Perhaps the greatest challenge to these internal focus groups is creating the nonthreatening and informal organizational environment necessary for focus groups to be effective. Employee focus groups in the work environment routinely present special problems in achieving the relaxed, permissive environment where people feel they can openly share thoughts and opinions. Intimidation, conformity, and group traditions can profoundly influence sharing. Sometimes an organization dictates what is acceptable, what values are to be held, or what actions are considered appropriate.

Threats to Quality

Quality is threatened when confidentiality is not ensured. Organizations typically desire feedback when problems arise, budgets are cut, or reorganization is needed. These factors prompting the need to listen also tend to erode trust within an organization. The moderator attempts to create a trusting and confidential environment, but the history of activities within the organization can make this task virtually impossible. Also, the perception of the internal moderator by focus group participants may be determined by previous experiences with the moderator. If participants are distrustful, they may be skeptical about participating and, may, therefore withhold or be guarded in their comments.

Quality can be influenced by the physical location. The physical location of the focus group can evoke negative attitudes thus limiting participation. Religious, social, educational, or regulatory agencies and organizations may need to consider holding focus group meetings outside their facilities. Sometimes insiders feel it is easier to talk if they are away from the building, and outsiders may be intimidated by what the physical structure connotes.

In some situations one-way mirrors and video recorders can jeopardize the quality of the conversation. One-way mirrors are obvious to participants and have the potential for creating an atmosphere of suspicion and doubt. This is not of major consequence when the topic is toothpaste, soap, or house paint, but if the topic is at all complex or sensitive a mirror or video recorder may limit or hinder sharing. Public programs, by their nature, are complex, and personal values shape the participants' opinions. Serious thought should be given to the benefits and limitations of one-way mirrors and video recording of public-sector focus groups.

Visitors to the focus group can jeopardize quality. Normally, the focus group consists of a moderator, an assistant moderator, and the participants. Occasionally, another person can be included if there is a definite purpose for their presence, such as coordinating refreshments or registration.

Some groups need extra time and effort to establish trust. Participants may be particularly sensitive about the other people in the group, including the moderator. Focus groups with certain professionals (particularly medical and law enforcement personnel) are often affected when others in the group have backgrounds different from their own.

Duffy (1991) noted that FBI agents were not comfortable with the focus group process until they were convinced that everyone in the room had similar backgrounds. My experience with highly skilled and specialized groups indicates that these individuals are more open and willing to share when the focus group is strictly homogeneous.

Sufficient Resources

Research quality is related to cost. Nonprofit organizations typically have difficulty with the high costs of research. In private-sector marketing research, it is relatively common to spend $15,000 to $25,000 on a small focus group study or $30,000 to $50,000 on a mail-out survey. Yet, these same cost estimates shock nonprofit administrators. Too often the public sector shuts out quality at the beginning of the study because it is just too costly. An interesting myth about focus groups is that they are cheap. It may be that this misconception is a carryover from private-sector marketing research for which cheap means anything less than a $50,000 mail-out survey. Although they cost less than other market research procedures, focus groups are not cheap according to the standards used by academic and nonprofit organizations.

Cost is not the best predictor of quality, but too many studies have compromised quality because of an inadequate budget. Budget directly influences the range of choices available to the researcher. Focus groups take resources, and the quality of the results is often commensurate with the investment of resources. Individual focus group costs can range from $1,500 to $5,000. Furthermore, the low end can be even lower with in-loaded staff for recruiting, planning, moderating, transcribing, or analyzing. On paper, it may even appear that there are no costs except for postage, telephone, and refreshments. In fact, the in-loaded costs can be substantial.

Threats to Quality

Quality is threatened when resource estimates of time or money are not realistic. Underestimating costs and assuming that certain difficult tasks can be completed in the least amount of time cause difficulty. Three tasks in focus groups often require more time than anticipated: recruitment, question development, and analysis. Most other time demands can be reliably estimated.

Piggyback focus groups can erode quality. To minimize the use of resources focus groups are sometimes conducted during an already scheduled session. This process of piggybacking focus groups on existing meetings can be a viable alternative for limiting resources but it can also jeopardize quality. The climate of the conference or meeting can influence the nature of the comments made. In some situations, the speakers, themes, or workshops of the conference shape the perceptions and attitudes of focus group participants in such a way that they are responding primarily to the stimulus of the conference.

Appropriate Participants

Participants should be carefully recruited and should represent the individuals you intend to study. It is vital to have the right participants in a focus group. This may seem simple, but it is one of the more difficult aspects of a focus group study. When identifying focus group participants, give it a second or third thought. Too often the researcher or client makes this decision quickly without considering options. Issues that must be addressed are whom to select and how to do the selecting. Both issues go back to the purpose of the study. In some studies the decisions are straightforward—as when a known population is sampled.

Let's take an example from the religious community. It is appropriate to sample from the existing membership list when the problem or concern relates specifically to those members. However, if the intent is to reach new and previously unreached members, then sampling from the existing membership rolls would be a mistake. Indeed, a typical erroneous assumption is that current members have attitudes, values, and opinions similar to those of nonmembers.

Identification of the group is only the first step. Consideration must also be given to the specific means of selecting participants. A form of random sampling is often preferred to avoid bias that can subtly creep into the selection of participants.

Here's an example. The locally elected officials in my community were concerned about building a new fire station. For it to be built, they needed to pass a bond issue, a task that has been difficult for most municipalities in the past few years. To determine public sentiment on the issue, the officials commissioned a research firm to conduct a study. The market research firm conducted what they called "focus groups" around the community. The public was invited to attend any or all of the discussions held in various places in the community. The marketing firm indicated that the results suggested the vote would be favorable, and the city council decided to move ahead with the election. Advance publicity favoring the new fire station bonding election emphasized that local elected officials had listened to the residents and responded by asking for the election. The election results were a disappointment to the elected officials: The bonding bill was resoundingly defeated. The primary problem was the means by which participants were selected. What was called a focus group was more like a public forum or meeting where supporters of the fire station could promote their cause. Residents who were against the bill just ignored the meetings, but showed up for the election. In this situation, the lack of careful procedures for selecting respondents produced embarrassing and erroneous results. Furthermore, generalizations or projections to a population based on limited focus group interviews are risky.

Threats to Quality

Quality is threatened by using convenience samples. Identifying focus group participants can be complicated and time-consuming. It is tempting to take the easy route and recruit participants who are easy to obtain. However, convenience samples can be devastating to quality because of the potential for hidden bias.

Quality can be jeopardized in organizational focus groups when participants are selected by the line supervisor or manager. Focus groups in organizations must work within the chain of command. As a result, the immediate supervisor must be consulted or at least informed of the process. Typically this supervisor is also invited to participate in the selection of the focus group participants. There is a tendency for bias to occur in employee focus groups when supervisors unilaterally make the decision. A result of this bias is that the individuals selected may be outside the mainstream.

Quality is affected when recruitment overemphasizes compensation. A number of market research companies use public announcements, often newspaper ads, that offer money for participating in a focus group. This method of recruitment has the advantage of identifying hard-to-reach audiences but it may disproportionately attract people whose primary concern is to make $25 or $50. Participants enjoy the focus group experience, appreciate the financial incentive, and make special efforts to get into focus groups. Market researchers call them *focus groupies* and have become wary of these repeat participants.

Quality is threatened when insiders are assumed to be like outsiders. Assuming that insiders or past users are similar to outsiders or nonusers can lead to faulty focus group results. Educational, service, and religious organizations have established membership lists, and over the years those members have enjoyed and appreciated the opportunities offered. An interesting example is included in Martin (1977).

Quality is influenced by failure to segment or by using inappropriate segments. Segmenting in a focus group study requires resources because of the need to complete a wave of studies with each segment. Typically a *wave* consists of three or four focus groups. Two types of error emerge: failure to segment, thereby missing important data that would likely have surfaced if segments were added and developing too many segments that show no differences but increase the costs of the study.

Quality is threatened by using *dirty* lists for recruitment. Agencies and organizations have lists of varying quality. Some are checked regularly and updated to ensure accuracy whereas others are notorious for being out of date or inaccurate. For studies in which lists must be current or populations are changing it is critical to have highly accurate mailing and telephone lists.

Quality can be threatened when subordinates are required to participate in focus groups. The perception of the employees is the decisive factor. Most often, if employees sense that the focus group will be helpful or beneficial, that the request is sincere, and that past interactions with superiors have been satisfactory, then they willingly participate. Required attendance at focus groups is a mistake when employees are suspicious or even hostile owing to past experiences.

Skillful Moderator

The moderator must be skillful. Moderating a focus group might seem easy, but it requires mental discipline, careful preparation, and group interaction skills. The skillful focus group moderator must be able to project sincerity, have a sense of humor, be flexible, and have a keen memory. Perhaps most critical is the ability to listen. Over the past 5 years my colleagues and I have trained hundreds of moderators in the principles of focus group interviewing. For a considerable number of these aspiring moderators the most difficult skill to learn is that of listening. Novice moderators usually want to talk too much; offer their points of view; feel they must defend their product, idea, or organization; or simply are so interested in the topic that they want to share their own point of view. For some the discipline of listening comes easy, for others it takes constant effort.

The moderator influences quality. Some have a natural affinity for the moderator role: a ready smile; a sense of humor; the discipline to listen without interjecting their personal opinions; a warmth for and liking of people; and the ability to detach themselves from the issue at hand and recognize that the purpose is to obtain information and not to teach, preach, or correct the participants. For others, acquiring these skills requires effort, a desire to learn, and coaching from a master observer. Some individuals have profited from past experiences with groups. This is particularly true in the nonprofit sector, which has a considerable tradition with committee or group-process structure.

One of the first factors influencing quality lies in the words chosen in the introduction to the focus group. Problems emerge when the moderator inadvertently gives excessive attention to potential problem areas such as wanting both positive and negative comments, why the discussion is being tape recorded, or unnecessary details regarding the purpose of the focus group. Another problem occurs at the beginning of the focus group if the moderator inadvertently asks participants for their questions at the end of the introduction before proceeding to the first question in the questioning route. Asking for questions at the beginning of the focus group may result in the moderator losing control of the group.

Another factor influencing quality is the careful and deliberate use of moderator strategies. For example, moderators must know when to probe or follow up on questions, and how to maintain a balance of participation within the focus group by encouraging quieter participants and restraining dominate ones.

Focus groups conducted by nonprofit organizations often benefit from the use of an assistant moderator—as a means of enhancing quality control, improving subsequent analysis, and handling focus group logistics. By contrast, assistant moderators are usually not used in the profit sector because they add to the cost of the study. The nonprofit sector absorbs the cost of the assistant moderator and considers it a worthwhile investment.

Threats to Quality

Quality can be jeopardized when the moderator is too close to the topic. This has two dimensions. The first is that the moderator knows so much that he or she has already narrowed the relevant arguments into categories—categories that may be different from those of the focus group participants. The second dimension is that the moderator is perceived by participants to be holding a particular position or stand on the issue, which, in turn, provokes similar or different views from the focus group.

Quality is threatened when the moderator doesn't listen carefully. Some individuals lack the capacity or willingness to listen to other's views. Although this threat is rare, it seriously erodes quality. Unfortunately, when it occurs the moderator is usually unaware of his or her actions. By verbal and nonverbal communication the moderator signals the participants to say little and concentrate on certain aspects of the topic. Through the use of probes and follow-up questions the moderator concentrates the discussion on topics that elicit their personal point of view. The moderator is often highly committed to one point of view and seems to believe that if only the others knew as much about the topic as he or she does they would have the same opinion.

Quality is jeopardized when the moderator lacks warmth, energy, and diplomacy. Moderators can go through all the mechanics of leading the focus group but erode quality by not conveying sufficient warmth and enthusiasm or by failing to exercise necessary diplomacy. A comfortable, permissive environment is critical to successful focus groups. Abrasive comments and indifferent attitudes signal that the moderator may be less than sincere about the need for obtaining information. At times the moderator must diplomatically curtail dominate individuals or shift the focus of the discussion. The moderator should also project enthusiasm for and or interest in the topic and participants. If this is done with finesse and smoothness, the group proceeds effectively. Some moderators project an image of being so laid back that the participants doubt that their comments are needed or wanted.

Quality is threatened when the moderator telegraphs the wrong verbal and nonverbal cues to participants. For some moderators this is the most difficult task in focus groups. Verbal cues that present threats are those that might be interpreted as expressing approval or value. For example, "Great" and "Excellent" are typical verbal responses in normal conversation, but they present major threats in focus groups. Neutral verbal responses such as "Uh huh," "Okay," and "Thank you" do not imply approval or agreement. Participants may consciously or unconsciously respond to cues from the moderator and amplify or expand on areas that obtain approval from the moderator while ignoring other areas where positive cues were not provided.

Nonverbal cues can also threaten focus group quality. Of particular concern are moderator head nods (signaling approval), smiles, and eye contact that are offered to certain focus group participants expressing a certain position or point of view.

The underlying purpose of the study must guide the use of verbal and nonverbal cues. Quality erodes if these cues are used to amplify topics that are irrelevant or meaningless to the purpose of the study. Quality is enhanced when cues are tactfully used to elicit greater understanding on critical and central features of the study.

Quality is threatened when the moderator doesn't maintain effective control of the group. Dominant participants may influence what others are willing to say. These talkative individuals may inhibit some participants, speak on behalf of others, and for still others the comments may just not seem relevant. If the moderator does not seek out all opinions within the focus group, the subsequent analysis will be severely threatened. The moderator must provide an element of balance in the focus group by diplomatically shifting the conversation from the active talkers to those who have said less. It is a dangerous mistake to assume that silent participants are agreeing or not thinking. If the moderator does not successfully solicit the opinions of less talkative participants, some valuable insights may be lost.

Effective Questions

Without questions there is no focus group interview. In fact, the nature and sequence of questions may be the most distinctive feature of these interviews. Quality focus groups depend on quality questions. These quality questions typically follow a prescribed format (Krueger, 1988) that is intended to foster the permissive climate of the focus groups and also capture the nondirected nature of the interactions.

Threats to Quality

Quality is affected when the moderator plans for too many questions. About 10 to 12 well-developed questions are often adequate for a 2-hour focus group interview. In addition there may be follow-up questions to this core set of questions. The number of questions is also influenced by the topic, the specificity requested, and the nature of the participants. Reduce the number of questions if the topic is complex, if conditional responses are expected, if specificity of response is desired, or if the participants are experienced or knowledgeable.

Quality is threatened when the moderator fails to follow up. This follow-up is often accomplished in several ways. Immediate follow-up probes or requests for examples during the focus group can amplify the concept. Unfortunately, this is sometimes a difficult call for the moderator, because what seems like a perfectly logical and understandable answer at that moment in the focus group may not make sense to the analyst working with the transcript after the focus group. A second way this follow-up can be performed is in later focus groups. The moderator probes in more depth particular aspects that emerged from early analysis of results.

Quality is threatened when the questions are phrased in abstract, philosophical terms rather than in specific, concrete ones. Typically, the questions guide the discussion into broad-based comments about values that may or may not be personally espoused by the participants. It's easy for focus group participants to echo traditional and socially acceptable statements. Unless the questions are specific, the participants do not relate how they would actually respond. Sometimes in focus groups I have observed the phenomenon of inconsistent comments. This may be triggered by a number of factors, one of which is a discrepancy between community values and individual actions.

Quality is threatened by overreliance on expert logic. Often we assume that the focus group question posed by experts reflects how the participants see the situation or problem. Experts designing the questions may follow a logic that makes very good sense to them but that may be different from that of the participants, jeopardizing the results of the focus group process. This threat can be minimized in several ways. The first is to ask a final question at the conclusion of the focus group. For example, just before the participants are dismissed, the moderator might review the purposes of the study, amplifying the information given at the beginning of the meeting. This then is followed by the question, "Have we missed anything?" The second way to minimize the threat is to consider the first focus group as the pilot test of the questions and later adjust the questions as needed. Indeed, if in the first focus group the questions do not seem to flow logically or make sense to the participants, it may be wise to adjourn early and seek the participants' advice on rephrasing or repositioning the questions.

Quality is threatened if the participants respond prematurely. Participants must be ready to contribute. This is accomplished by following accepted guidelines for focus group questions in sequencing the discussion. Typically a focus group has several categories of questions that take participants deeper into the product, problem, or circumstance that is the topic of the discussion. The beginning questions help set the stage, allowing participants to reflect on their experiences and collect their memories and thoughts on past similar situations. Later the discussion moves into more specific and critical areas that are central to the purpose of the study.

Quality suffers when participants are asked for solutions instead of identifying problems. There is a tendency in focus groups to jump to solution strategies before the problems are adequately identified. A dictum that comes from marketing research is that the participant should not be put into the position of being the expert and asked to design, construct, or develop a solution. The participants are assembled because they have certain factors in common, such as the use of a product or the manner in which they encounter a policy or employment. Designing solution strategies—whether it be in architectural plans for buildings, designs for educational programs, marketing campaigns, or workplace communications—is a complex process, and experts are aware of the trade-offs and consequences of various alternatives. However, lay participants can provide valuable insights into how they respond to differing solutions that were created by experts.

Careful Data Handling

Quality is influenced by handling of data. This includes the use of background information, recording equipment, field notes, and transcriptions. Memories fade, blend together, and blur our perceptions of the focus group interview. Quality analysis depends on quality of data handling.

Threats to Quality

Quality is threatened by the lack of field notes. Focus group field notes are primarily the role of the assistant moderator, because the moderator is so involved in guiding the discussion and concentrating on the flow of the discussion that note taking is virtually impossible. The assistant moderator, often at the opposite side of the room from the moderator, is in a position to observe the discussion and note both verbal and nonverbal communication. Quality field notes are those that can be accurately interpreted several months later by someone who wasn't at the meeting. Word-for-word quotations are cited and are set off from the thoughts, ideas, or questions originating from the assistant moderator. Seating diagrams are included as are the most notable quotations on the questions of greatest importance.

The quality of electronic recording affects the quality of the focus group. Tape recordings of focus groups directly influence quality. When playing back the tape or reviewing the transcript of the focus group, the analyst may detect ideas or comments that have been overlooked during the discussion. Unfortunately, it is always difficult to obtain very clear sound when tape recording focus groups. Background ventilation, tapping on tables, multiple voices, difference in voice volume all affect the quality of the audio tape.

Quality of transcripts affect the quality of the study. A number of decisions are often left to the typist. Quality transcripts are those that identify the speakers—or at a minimum identify the moderator and then leave space between the different speakers. Some transcriptionists can provide the names of the participants by hearing their voices. Transcript quality is often affected by the number of distractions or interruptions encountered by the typist or by the kind of playback equipment. To foster quality, avoid distractions for the typist, get adequate playback equipment with ear phones and foot-operated stop and play-back buttons, and use a word processor. The word processor allows the analyst to edit the transcript easily, such as adding names of speakers or technical terms that were unfamiliar to the typist.

Perhaps the most subtle and frequent threat to quality of data handling is the human factor. This includes failure to have or follow procedures, lapses in memory, inattention to detail and a host of other preventable tasks. Several deserve mention because of the frequency with which they occur in focus group interviews. All field notes, transcripts, tapes, and other materials generated at the focus group must be carefully labeled and filed for later retrieval. Electronic equipment requires human operators to ensure adequate power because electric cords can be accidentally pulled out and batteries run down.

Systematic and Verifiable Analysis

Analysis often is the single biggest problem in focus group interviews. It is time-consuming, unstructured, and complex. The analysis must be systematic and verifiable. It is systematic in that it follows a prescribed, sequential process. The analysis must also be verifiable—a process that would permit another researcher to arrive at similar conclusions using available documents and raw data. There is a tendency for some to see selectively only those comments that confirm a particular point of view. Furthermore, the degree of intensity in the analysis and the nature of the reporting should be appropriate to the purpose of the study. At times the situation may demand that reports be quickly produced, and the analyst must be able to adjust to these constraints while maintaining appropriate quality control.

Several systematic procedures have proven to be particularly beneficial in the analysis process. One of these is to seek final statements from participants to clarify where they've ended up. It is not unusual for participants to offer several differing points of view during the course of the focus groups. This may be due to one of several factors: the participant didn't perceive the contradictions in the points of view espoused, the participant really believes that both points of view are valid, or the participant in fact shifted his or her opinion. If the participant does not have the opportunity to explain the differences, it is nearly impossible to determine what to do with the comments. A strategy used at the end of the focus group is to encourage each participant to summarize his or her point of view on the critical topics of interest: "If you were invited to offer 1 minute of advice to the top decision maker on this topic, what would you say?" or "After considering all of the topics (needs, concerns, etc.) expressed tonight, which one is of greatest concern?"

Another systematic procedure that improves the analysis is to seek verification from the participants of the key points of the study. One way of doing this is to ask the assistant moderator to offer a 1- or 2-minute summary at the end of the focus group interview. Instead of summarizing all points of discussion the assistant moderator directs attention to those topics that are of critical concern to the study. Following the summary, the participants are asked if the summary was complete. If they hesitate or appear doubtful, the moderator might ask if one of them would like to amend the summary. Following the amendment the participants are again asked if it was complete, and the process continues until the summary is satisfactory to the participants.

Still another systematic procedure is for the moderator team (the moderator and assistant moderator) to meet as soon as possible after the participants have left the focus group site. In addition, it is often helpful to turn the tape recorder back on and record this 20 to 30 minute conversation. The moderator and assistant moderator review what they consider to be the high points of the interview, the most notable quotes, and compare and contrast the interview with previous focus groups in the series. The debriefing serves two purposes: it enables the team to capture their first impressions at the conclusion of the focus group and, if the team is going into another focus group within the following several hours, it tends to help clear their minds for the next focus group.

Threats to Quality

Quality is threatened when too much or too little time is spent on analysis. The effort expended in the analysis should reflect the importance of the study. It is difficult to estimate the amount of time needed for analyzing focus group results. Two dangers exist: spending too much time analyzing content of trivial importance to the study and spending insufficient time analyzing topics of major importance, with little opportunity to correct mistakes or serious negative consequences.

Quality is threatened by ignoring the positive or negative potential of computer assistance. The challenge is for the researcher to find an appropriate role for computers. This will vary by individuals and by purposes of the studies. Some see the use of computers as the great hope for analysis. However, although it may prove beneficial, it may not be worth the added costs. Critical factors might be missed and a false sense of security provided. Recently, several excellent books have been written on computer textual analysis (Tesch, 1990; Fielding & Lee, 1991).

Quality is threatened by moderator fatigue. Novice moderators should plan to conduct only one group per day, and veterans should seriously consider limiting themselves to two per day. Conducting three focus groups per day is mentally and physically taxing and jeopardizes the ability of the moderator to follow up, owing to memory interference. The moderator remembers that a comment was made, but cannot recall if it was in this group, the one before, or the first one. As a result, the moderator begins to make small mistakes on follow-up comments or becomes tense and irritable, which, in turn, affects the participants' willingness to share their insights.

Another type of moderator fatigue also affects focus group quality. After about three or four focus groups, the moderator senses that he or she has heard all of this before and the newness of the focus group has worn off. The moderator may prematurely draw the discussion to a close, missing additional avenues of thought, conditions, or modifications provided by the participants.

Appropriate Presentation

The final presentation of focus group findings often has a major influence on the decision maker's ability to use the results. Therefore, oral reports highlighting important findings, conclusions, and recommendations and then allowing for questions and clarifications are most beneficial. In other situations, expectations call for a written report suitable for later examination and action. These written reports typically fall into a continuum ranging from the mere listing of raw data, to bulleted reports, to a descriptive report, to a descriptive report with recommendations.

Threats to Quality

Quality suffers when the results are confusing. The goal is data reduction, not confusion. Some reports are a collection of statements in a question-by-question format. This is hardly an analysis, and unless it is explicitly requested by the client, it is an inadequate focus group report. The task of the analyst is to draw the data together and present it in the report. The goal is enlightenment, not confusion.

Quality is threatened when the client receives a report in an unexpected format. Surprises may be beneficial in battle but are foolish in reporting. The client-decision maker and the researcher should have early on reached an agreement about what constitutes an acceptable report. Unfortunately, clients are sometimes surprised by the nature, length, or style of the final focus group report.

Quality is affected when the report is late. Sometimes focus groups need to be postponed, recruitment strategies get bogged down, or the analysis process unexpectedly takes additional time, resulting in the report being delayed. This can be of minor consequence in some situations and a disaster in others. The worst strategy is not to communicate anticipated delays to the client. Without question, the researchers and client should attempt to negotiate a revised deadline as soon as delays are anticipated.

Honoring the Participant,
Client, and Method

Honor the participants. Be respectful of those participating. The quality of the focus groups is affected when participants are not treated in a respectful manner. Be cautious of assumptions you make about their experiences and views.

Honor the client—those who are commissioning the study. Be sensitive to their needs. Some clients are uncertain of the problem, and focus groups represent a means of getting in touch with reality. The moderator-analyst-reporter is the link between the client and the focus group participant.

Honor the method. All research disciplines have advantages and disadvantages that depend on the personnel, location, and purpose. Focus group interviews fit into a niche—in some situations they are beneficial for obtaining information; in others they are worthless.

Threats to Quality

Quality is threatened by bad attitudes. Focus group participants react negatively when the moderator exhibits a condescending attitude. Respectful empathy and eagerness to listen do much to convey the positive impression that is the foundation of open communication.

Quality is threatened by deception. There is a distinct difference between avoiding a recital of the details of the study and deception. Standard practice in focus group interviews is to limit the details regarding the purpose, scope, and nature of the study—particularly at the beginning of the focus group. Too much information too early in the interview has proven to be distracting and tends to cause participants to focus prematurely on solutions as opposed to problem identification. Deception occurs when the participants are purposely told, or the moderator strongly implies, inaccurate information about the nature of the study.

Quality can suffer from focus group gimmicks. In recent years a number of companies have offered special tools that assist focus groups. These tools can inadvertently change the dynamics of the group and may run counter to some of the fundamental principles of focus group inquiry. One that has gained popularity is the rheostat knob or key pad with number that the participant turns or presses to indicate a level of preference, approval, satisfaction, etc. These devices are linked to a portable computer that displays an immediate average score that can be used for follow-up questions or can even be shown to the participants. Although these devices have some potential for immediate tabulation of results, they tend to lend a gimmicky atmosphere to the discussion and participants are more impressed with the knobs than with the issue being discussed. Often these devices are promoted as offering fast or immediate focus group results. These gimmicks may be beneficial in some situations, but it is questionable whether these experiences should even be called focus groups.

Strategies to Foster Quality

Although the researcher needs to be cognizant of threats to focus group quality, there are several proactive steps that also deserve mention. Collegial advice on design and procedures improves quality. Many tasks and decisions are improved when a team of people are involved. Research colleagues and people from within the organization under study can offer valuable formative advice on critical features of the focus group study such as recruitment, question development, incentives, and analysis.

Collegial feedback on results improves quality. Sharing focus group procedures and results with professional colleagues has been one of the most effective means of ensuring quality. This summative assessment could occur at a variety of levels, from the local sharing within the organization to the national professional meeting. Collegial feedback is a major advantage of the academic and public sector over the private marketing research environment, for which much of the results are proprietary and cannot be shared. Unfortunately, in the private sector many mistakes are buried or ignored.

Quality and confidence increases when focus group reports are audited. The focus group audit involves having an outside individual or group determine if the recommendations, summary, and major features of the report are borne out by the raw data. This is done by reversing the analysis process, beginning with the final report and tracing back each theme or concept to its source.

The skills and expertise of focus group researchers vary considerably and advice that is beneficial to some is not fitting for others. Here are some suggestions for novice moderators: Be sincere, agonize over questions, and actively listen to responses. Allow sufficient time for analysis, don't work alone—seek feedback from colleagues. No matter how much you know, how many degrees you have, or how much experience is under your belt, you are there to learn from others. You are the sponge, soaking up and absorbing information from the participants.

Of particular concern to experts is this advice: Don't trust your ability to hear it the first time, review the transcripts or tape. Be careful of your assumptions for they can lead to dangerous mistakes. Experts automate, but be careful that you haven't missed critical factors in your speed to accomplish the task.

Summary

The 10 factors that directly influence quality in focus group interviews are (1) clarity of purpose, (2) appropriate environment, (3) sufficient resources, (4) appropriate participants, (5) skillful moderator, (6) effective questions, (7) careful data handling, (8) systematic and verifiable analysis, (9) appropriate presentation, (10) honor the participant, client, and method. Quality in each of these areas may be jeopardized. Not all threats to quality are equivalent. Some are minor, some are major, and others are situational. These situational factors depend on the experience level of the researcher, the environment, and the problem.

PART II

Combining With Other Methods

6

Using Focus Groups to Adapt Survey Instruments to New Populations

Experience From a Developing Country

THEODORE D. FULLER
JOHN N. EDWARDS
SAIRUDEE VORAKITPHOKATORN
SANTHAT SERMSRI

A problem frequently confronted by researchers investigating phenomena in unfamiliar populations concerns the issue of obtaining valid information. At the core of this issue are questions about the portability of concepts, appropriate methodologies and measurement, and matters of interpretation. Stone and Campbell (1984), for example, warn us that using survey data alone can produce misleading results when researchers work outside of situations with which they are knowledgeable. Brislin (1986) provides some very useful suggestions for writing questionnaire items for use in such research, but other than the chapters of this volume, relatively little has been written on integrating focus group

AUTHORS' NOTE: A previous version of this chapter was presented at the conference on Focus Groups and Group Interviews: Advancing the State of the Art, Menucha, Oregon, October 4-6, 1990. The research reported in this paper was supported by grant SES-8618157 from the National Science Foundation. We are grateful to the Institute for Population and Social Research, Mahidol University, Bangkok, for additional support for this project.

interviews and survey research to help ensure the validity of one's data and interpretations. Knodel and his colleagues (Knodel, Sittitrai, & Brown, 1987) very effectively used focus groups to provide insight into questions remaining after exhaustive analysis of survey data and by their example suggest the value of combining these methodologies. A recent paper by Ward, Bertrand, and Brown (1991) reports that sets of focus group interviews and surveys have produced comparable results in family planning studies. Desvousges and Frey (1989) show that focus group interviews can be extremely helpful in developing questionnaires for use in environmental risk studies. But none of these papers discusses the use of focus group interviews as an aid in questionnaire design in the context of cross-cultural research.

We used focus group interviews as the initial stage of research in a study of the effects of household crowding in Bangkok, Thailand. As social researchers, we started with a set of ideas concerning the impact of high levels of household crowding on psychological well-being and family relations, ideas that had emerged primarily from crowding research in the United States, which had documented selective, and essentially modest, effects of household crowding (Booth, 1976; Gove & Hughes, 1983). Our basic research question was whether household crowding has more severe social and/or psychological effects when the levels of household crowding are substantially higher than those typically found in the United States and other developed countries (the average number of persons per room is about 0.5 in the United States but more than 2 persons per room in Bangkok).

With this in the way of background, we address three issues in this chapter. First is the question of the portability of research instruments from familiar to unfamiliar situations. We were attempting to take a set of ideas developed primarily in one cultural setting and test the applicability of these ideas in another setting. Focus group interviews, it seemed to us, might be a particularly useful starting point for such an endeavor. Rather than simply translating existing questionnaires, with their scale items, and carrying out a survey in Bangkok, we felt that we needed more information about several topics, including Thai perceptions of and reactions to crowding as well as sources and manifestations of conflict in Thai families.

Second, we discuss the focus group procedures themselves. Principally, this concerns the size and composition of the groups, the location of the group interviews, the use of a moderator, the design of the discussion guide, and the coding scheme for the transcripts.

Finally, we focus on the articulation between the focus group interviews and the household survey we subsequently designed. The key question discussed in this section is, "What would we have missed if we had not begun with focus group interviews?" This involves (1) the role of the focus group interviews in determining the concepts to measure, (2) hypotheses derived from the group interviews, (3) how lessons learned from the focus group interviews were applied to the actual writing of questionnaire items, and (4) how the groups helped generate new survey items. Although our research is cross-cultural in nature, our experience suggests lessons that, in our opinion, will be useful to any researcher working in an unfamiliar context.

Background of the Project and the Issue of Portability

Our research, as we have indicated, focused on the potential social and psychological effects of household crowding. In basic outline, the crowding model we were testing suggests that the more crowded households are, the more stressful the situation. The greater the stress experienced, the more likely disturbances in family relations and mental health are to occur. While prior studies have shown crowding to have some relationship with these phenomena (Booth & Edwards, 1976; Gove & Hughes, 1983), research has been conducted largely in Europe and North America where there is a limited range of crowded conditions. The effects of crowding have not always been easily detectable and where they have been found, the effects are often mild, leading some researchers to speculate that there may be some *tipping point* or threshold beyond which crowding effects become more pronounced (Booth, Johnson, & Edwards, 1980). To provide a rigorous test of the model and to isolate more adequately possible crowding effects, theoretically it was necessary to conduct such research in a site where a higher level and, perhaps more important, a greater range of household crowding is to be found. It was for this reason that we chose an Asian city, Bangkok, as the research site.

The plan, ultimately, was to conduct a large-scale household survey, using a representative sample and appropriate statistical controls. The survey instrument was to include items tapping the subjective dimension of crowding, lack of privacy, felt demands, psychological well-being, and a variety of aspects concerning marital and family relations.

In conducting this research, we quite obviously had to confront the issue of cultural differences. Asians and Westerners do not necessarily respond to crowding in an identical manner. Indeed, some have suggested that Asians are indifferent to, or actually prefer, crowded living conditions and that humans are highly adaptable to such conditions (Loo & Ong, 1984; Baldasarre, 1979). Given this, it was plainly necessary to learn more about the cultural context of Thailand and, more specifically, about that of Bangkok. We needed to gain a greater appreciation for relevant concepts and behavioral patterns in the Thai context. Several key questions were foremost in our minds. The first had to do with the Thai concepts of crowding and privacy. Do Thais consider high levels of crowding to be undesirable and, if so, why? What aspects of privacy are most salient to Thais, and in what ways do crowded living conditions violate this concept of privacy? What interaction sequences surround episodes of family conflict in Thai households? That is, what sorts of behavior on the part of family members do Thais find to be irritating or to violate some family norms, and how do these irritations manifest themselves in family relations? And which household members feel the effects of crowding most acutely? Who, in short, have the greatest demands and constraints placed on them?

At a minimum, a creative application of our theoretical concepts to a new cultural context would be needed. But as an alternative, we had to consider that household crowding is not necessarily perceived as a problem in Bangkok. Although the level of household crowding in Bangkok is high by North American standards, suggesting we might find strong effects, there are several cultural factors that could, contrary to this hypothesis, result in finding crowding effects more modest in nature.

First, the typical household structure found in Bangkok suggests that there may be normative tolerance for household crowding. Very few Bangkokians live alone, extended families are not uncommon, and the average household size is more than five persons. Whether these living arrangements are a matter of necessity or choice, social norms may facilitate harmonious relations among crowded family members. Second, even in rural areas, where land is relatively abundant, similar levels of persons per room (2.1) are found. This history of crowding may make it easier for Thais to accommodate to high levels of crowding. Third, the tropical climate allows household members to be outdoors many hours every day, during all seasons of the year. Living space is not confined to the housing unit itself but expands to adjacent communal areas. Moreover, in Bangkok, those who work outside the home often work long hours and may have a time-consuming commute to work. This means that some household members are absent during most of their waking hours. Hence, the effective level of crowding might be lower than indicated by a simple head count. Fourth, Thai normative structure stresses the avoidance of interpersonal conflict and encourages the maintenance of harmonious relations (Klausner, 1972, 1981). The emphasis placed on self-control might moderate any potential effects of crowding. Finally, Thais appear to value social interaction more than Americans do, while placing less value on privacy. Whereas an American may wonder whether it is appropriate to disturb someone who is alone, Thais are more likely to think that a person who is alone may need companionship. For many Thais, high levels of household crowding may simply provide protection from loneliness and offer many opportunities for social interaction. Consequently, it was quite unclear at the outset whether higher objective levels of crowding necessarily would lead to more deleterious consequences, or whether Thais would even perceive household crowding to be a stressful or otherwise detrimental circumstance.

One strategy we used to evaluate the adequacy of the concepts and to operationalize them in the Thai context was to assemble a research team integrated both in terms of nationality and disciplinary training. Fuller is U.S. trained and based but has worked extensively in Thailand; Edwards has published research on crowding and is an expert on family relations. Sermsri and Vorakitphokatorn are Thai nationals holding academic appointments at a leading university in Bangkok; they received their Ph.D.s in the United States. Thus on both sides there is an appreciation of the culture of the other. The combination of Americans familiar with Thailand as well as Thais familiar with the United States has proven to be a useful mix to address the theoretical and methodological issues raised in the research.

Focus group interviews made up, though, a crucial strategy to obtain a better understanding of how typical Thais conceptualize and react to household crowding. Our focus group interviews thus preceded, and contributed to, the formulation of a survey instrument.

The Design of the Focus Group Interviews

Like most focus groups (Morgan, 1988; Krueger, 1988), ours had moderators and were fairly small, usually having eight participants. In most focus groups, the members are fairly homogeneous with respect to characteristics that are of importance to the research problem. A somewhat unusual feature of our design was that whereas the groups were homogeneous, we selected several different types of groups, following a factorial design.

The topics of interest, as0 already mentioned, included concepts such as subjective crowding, lack of privacy, norms about family interaction, family conflict, and felt demands. We anticipated that men and women might have different needs for privacy, different reactions to crowding, different levels of felt demands, and different abilities to cope with crowding; that perceptions of crowding and problems associated with crowding would vary by level of household crowding; and that issues of crowding and privacy might weigh more heavily on members of extended families than on individuals living in the context of a nuclear family. Thus gender, level of household crowding (high or low), and household type (nuclear or extended) became the defining, or *break*, characteristics for the groups (Knodel, Sittitrai, & Brown, 1990, p. 7). These three dichotomies defined eight types of focus groups. One focus group interview was conducted for each type of group.

Of course, dividing the population of Bangkok into these eight types does not produce completely homogeneous categories. Several other dimensions were of interest. Some crowding research in the United States points to subcultural variations in reactivity to crowding (Gove & Hughes, 1983). In Bangkok, Chinese comprise a substantial minority of the population. The question arose as to whether ethnic Chinese react to crowding in the same way that ethnic Thais do. To keep the groups relatively homogeneous, the people recruited to participate in the eight focus groups were all ethnically Thai. Two additional groups were made up of ethnic Chinese—a male and a female group. The Chinese focus group members were all recruited from households with high levels of crowding but without regard to household structure.

In conducting focus groups, it is desirable continuously to create a situation that stimulates genuine discussion among members of the group, with all members participating. In Thai society, there tends to be considerable deference to older people. We were concerned that if the groups included a broad age range, the younger members would be reticent in participating openly in the discussion and, especially, that they would be reluctant to contradict their elders. Hence, we limited the age range in each group to a 10-year range. Not wanting to limit our research to a single 10-year age range, different age ranges were used in different groups.

With respect to group composition, we believed that it would be most informative to concentrate on more crowded households. As a consequence, while we distinguished between more crowded and less crowded households, we selected all participants from low income areas. All of the participants resided in either slums or low-income flats (i.e., four- or five-story apartment buildings).

Focus groups are rarely, if ever, composed of random samples of a target population. Our groups were no exception. We can make no claim that our focus group participants are representative of a broader population in any statistical sense. Because we did conduct group interviews in 10 widely dispersed neighborhoods in Bangkok, however, we do feel that the interviews provide a broad cross-section of Bangkok, particularly of lower-income groups.

The members of each focus group were recruited from one neighborhood. This was done as a concession to logistics. Very few, if any, focus group members had automobiles or telephones. In effect, it would have been very difficult to arrange for focus group members from different neighborhoods to meet at a single interview site.

At most, two focus groups were conducted each week. Members of the research team canvassed a specific neighborhood to locate potential focus group members who met the desired characteristics. Volunteers were then asked to meet at a designated time and place, e.g., a school or meeting hall in the community. In selecting the interview site, we thought it was important to meet at a neutral site where all group members would be on an equal footing, rather than, say, at the home or workplace of one of the group members.

Most methodological discussions of focus group interviews suggest that it is desirable for group members to be strangers before the discussion (Morgan, 1988, p. 48) so that they are not reluctant to share information and opinions that they might wish to conceal from friends and relatives. Our practice of recruiting all members for a given focus group from the same neighborhood violates this principle. However, it should be noted that the discussion topics for our interviews did not involve illegal, immoral, or taboo topics, and that it is difficult, at any rate, to keep secrets in Bangkok's slums and low-income flats. Neighbors live in close proximity to each other and are subject to a great deal of mutual scrutiny. Furthermore, at least in the Thai context, there is a genuine concern that complete strangers might not be willing to speak frankly about family matters. Focus group members, we found, were quite willing to discuss intimate details of family life, including some aspects of their sexual lives.

We had a fairly lengthy agenda that we wanted to cover in the focus groups, and so we elected to have moderators who followed a discussion guide. After an introductory ice-breaker question (concerning the cost of living), the discussion guide contained several major categories: (1) family size and definition of crowding; (2) household control, that is, the extent to which one is a decision maker about the use of space in the household; (3) the need for privacy and coping mechanisms; (4) satisfaction/dissatisfaction with the personal habits and behavior of the spouse and other household members; and (5) discipline of the children. Under each heading, there were several questions and follow-up questions. The content and structure of the discussion guide evolved through a series of discussions among the four co-principal investigators and the person who was to be the moderator for the male groups, and it was modified somewhat after the first group interview. The moderators were free to vary the order and wording of the questions but were encouraged to introduce all of the topics on the guide. After the group interview, group members were asked to complete a short questionnaire.

There were two moderators, a male for the male focus groups and a female for the female focus groups. The female moderator, who was also the female co-principal investigator, had previously conducted scores of focus groups. The male moderator, who also supervised the task of recruiting focus group members, had also conducted numerous focus group interviews before our project.

The focus group interviews lasted approximately 1.5 hours each. They were tape recorded (with two recorders) and then transcribed. The transcripts were then translated from Thai to English. A translator was hired for the task, and the translator worked closely with one of the Thai co-principal investigators to discuss how best to translate difficult phrases. Differences between Thai and English colloquial expressions, slang, idioms, and language structure in addition to profound differences in the typical life experiences of North Americans and Bangkok slum dwellers made the process of translating hundreds of pages of transcripts particularly challenging and time-consuming.

After the focus group interviews were translated, the English transcripts were imported into *The Ethnograph* program, and segments were coded.[1] Even though we had a discussion guide, it was not immediately apparent how to code the transcripts (cf. Morgan, 1988, pp. 64-69). The coding scheme was devised through an iterative, bootstrap process. After reading all transcripts at least twice, we began to code one of the transcripts. "Interesting" passages were marked with an appropriate code. In the process, many discrete codes were created. At times, we realized that it would be better to make distinctions that were not originally incorporated in the codes. This necessitated rereading, and recoding, portions of the transcripts that had already been coded. When a passage was marked, enough of the transcript was included in the marked passage to make the context clear. Often, this required marking a half page, whole page, or more. *Ethnograph* permits the same line to have several different codes and to be part of several different passages. Most of the codes were devised on the basis of the first transcript, but a large number of additional codes were devised while reading the second transcript. After the coding was completed for the second transcript, very few additional codes were needed. In all, more than 100 codes were created.

Ethnograph thus aids in the mechanical aspects of qualitative data analysis (e.g., the process of accessing all instances of material that deals with a common theme or concept, as identified by the user). *Ethnograph* cannot, however, perform the creative work of interpreting the data, nor would qualitative researchers want to turn such a task over to their personal computers.

Lessons From the Focus Group Interviews

Conceptual Considerations

Did we learn anything from the focus group interviews that we could not have learned from the survey alone? One aspect of this question is, "Were there any theoretically important concepts of which we were ignorant at the outset of the research project whose importance was realized as a result of the focus group interviews?" Another question is, "Were there variables that we would not have included in the questionnaire if we had not first conducted the focus group interviews?" Regarding the former question, in contrast with some investigators who have used focus group interviews, we were already aware of the major theoretical concepts of relevance before conducting the focus groups.

From the outset, we had already identified, for example, objective crowding as the key independent variable. We already knew that we wanted to measure subjective aspects of crowding and perceptions of the demands placed on respondents by other household members. We had already decided that psychological stress was an important outcome that we wanted to investigate and that it was probably a significant intervening variable affecting marital and family relations. We already suspected that psychological withdrawal and physical withdrawal might be mechanisms to deal with the hypothesized stress associated with crowded living conditions. Moreover, we already had identified marital relations, parent-child relations, and sibling relations, especially disharmony in those relationships, as variables that might be affected by crowding.

What we did learn from the focus group interviews was both more general and more specific. One of the most important lessons emerging from the group interviews was that the theoretical concepts we brought with us were, by and large, meaningful in the Thai context. Before conducting the focus groups, we had some uncertainty, as some Thai academics had suggested to us that Thais were used to being crowded and did not mind. The focus group interviews convinced us that Thais do indeed find high levels of crowding to be undesirable. This is a conclusion, in fact, that would be very difficult to support from standardized interviews alone.

Are Thais motivated to protect their privacy or is this a singularly Western concept? Again, the focus group interviews convinced us that Thais are concerned about privacy, and take various concrete measures to preserve privacy in their homes (e.g., partitioning of rooms). Thai parents seem to be particularly sensitive to the privacy needs of teenage daughters.

In general, then, we found that the concepts of concern were quite relevant.[2] But what are the impacts of crowding? Does household crowding produce stress? Does crowding have detrimental impacts on family relations? These questions could not be answered with confidence from the focus group interviews. The interviews did convince us, however, that many of our group participants were under considerable stress—whatever the source. We had already planned to study psychological stress, but seeing the level of stress among the focus group participants further encouraged us to thoroughly examine psychological well-being. In the survey questionnaire, in consequence, we included more items pertaining to psychological well-being than originally planned, eventually constructing eight different scales measuring aspects of well-being.

We also noticed that there were a lot of overtly unhappy families represented in our groups. Just as the American family is not a peaceful oasis in which the only emotions of note are love and mutual respect, so too Thai families have their problems in various types, forms, and magnitudes. Learning this gave us more confidence to proceed as planned in examining what may be considered some of the more adverse manifestations of marital and family relations.

Hypothesis Formulation

The focus group interviews further produced hypotheses to be tested during the analysis of the survey data. It became evident, for example, that to be a son-in-law or a daughter-in-law in the household is a disadvantaged position. These are positions that seem to be very stressful, precisely because one has little control over what takes place in the household. We later found selective statistical support for this hypothesis. Among respondents living in three-generation households, the feeling of being crowding increased *manifest irritation* and reduced supportive behavior toward children even more for those living with their in-laws than for those living with their own parents.

The idea that household members in different positions respond differently to crowding is not entirely new (Baldasarre, 1979, 1981). But sons- and daughters-in-law had not been singled out before, perhaps because these groups are relatively rare in North American households. Moreover, the focus groups added weight to the notion that the degree of household control has an important impact on how individuals respond to crowding. This was a variable that had previously been only indirectly, and inadequately, measured. Based on the focus group interviews, we were prompted to devise a scale measuring household control directly, including specific examples of types of lack of control mentioned by focus group participants.

Another hypothesis emerging from the group interviews concerned how household members attempt to reestablish privacy when it is threatened. Focus group participants were asked, for instance, what they needed to do to have privacy for sexual relations. Several participants indicated that this is much less of a problem when the children are very young. Older children, they suggested, stay up later at night and are more aware of what is going on. Much later, after the survey data became available, we were able to confirm the hypothesis that the frequency of sexual relations is significantly lower when the oldest minor child is 4 or more years old.

Conducting the focus groups also forced us to become more familiar with the research site, and in the process of recruiting focus group members and talking to members of the community, we learned about the types of housing, the types of households, how space is used, and so forth. We already had some notion about these matters, of course, and we could have visited selected neighborhoods without conducting focus groups, but the interview process focused our attention on conditions in these neighborhoods more than otherwise would have been the case.

Definitions and Translation
Considerations

We learned that the definition of even such apparently straightforward terms as *room* and *bedroom* had to be clarified. In Bangkok, various kinds of rooms may be used as bedrooms and many households subdivide their space in various ways, for example, by hanging blankets or using furniture as room dividers. This led us to ask about room partitions and to keep a record both of the number of rooms as constructed and the number of rooms formed by partitions. This resulted in an objective measure of household crowding not previously used in crowding research. Noticing that rooms varied greatly in size also suggested the importance of obtaining a measure of the area of each housing unit.

The focus group interviews, in addition, proved to be invaluable in the actual writing of the questionnaire. A project of the sort described here requires a careful and sustained effort to translate creatively theoretical concepts from the language of one culture to the language of another. Although we did not want simply to take a questionnaire that had previously been used in crowding research, translate it, and go into the field, we did want to replicate, at least in a rough sense, previous studies of household crowding. The focus group interviews helped to bridge the gap between the language of the researchers and the language of Bangkok. Translation of specific questionnaire items required a great deal of clarification of the nuances of meaning in both the Thai and English versions of the questionnaire. Through a series of back-translations, not only the Thai version but also the English version of the questionnaire evolved, with the group interviews making an indispensable contribution to the precision of the questionnaire.

In translating specific existing items, the Thai members of the research team changed some words based simply on their general knowledge of the meaning and connotation of words in Thai. They believed, as one example, that the phrase *too tired to do anything* would not be meaningful and that the phrase *too tired to move* would more meaningfully communicate the idea that an extreme tiredness had gripped someone. Similarly, translating the question, "During the past few weeks, how often have you felt particularly excited or interested in something?" presented difficulty because, in the Thai context, *excitement* has the connotation of misfortune. Also, because Thais are supposed to remain calm and peaceful at all times, it would be socially undesirable to admit being excited.

In constructing the questionnaire, as noted earlier, we borrowed many items used in prior crowding studies. A major problem with this procedure was that many of the English-language items were too abstract. By listening to the way the focus group participants talked, we realized (that is, our Thai colleagues realized) that the focus group members used simpler local language. We thus tried to reformulate the questionnaire items into a language that would be readily understandable to the average Bangkokian. While the majority of people in Bangkok are literate, the modal level of formal education is 4 years for men and women alike. This educational level needed to be taken into account in wording questionnaire items, and the focus group interviews helped us to do so.

Sometimes the Thai word that would be the obvious choice as a translation of the English was deemed to have a different connotation in Thai than in English. Several items from the Rosenberg (1965) Self-Esteem Scale, for example, needed to be reworded because no direct Thai equivalent could be found. The difficulty stemmed from the fact that Thais reflect on the self in different ways than do North Americans. In an item on positive affect borrowed from Bradburn (1969), the obvious translation for *proud* (in the phrase "felt proud because someone complimented you on something you had done") was believed to be more appropriate for the feeling one gets from a major accomplishment (e.g., raising three healthy children). Because we wanted to include minor triumphs, a different Thai word was used, and the phrase was back translated into English as "felt good because someone complimented you on something you had done." Another item in the original scale—"feel happy all the time"—was changed to "in a good mood," because the word *happy* was deemed to be too abstract in the Thai context. A related example pertains to translation of the concept *self-respect*. The literal translation of *self-respect* (*kaow kop tua eng*) makes no sense to most Thais; it is seen as just a string of Thai words that have been placed one after the other. The term *dignity* (*sak sri*) could be translated in a more meaningful manner. There were, in sum, many such cases for which our Thai colleagues recalled a specific phrase from the focus groups that served as a more appropriate translation.

Besides sensitizing us to the issue of word choice, the focus groups also taught us to make the questions simple and concrete. A number of revisions were made to make the questions more specific and closer to the phrases used by our focus group participants. The proposed item "Even members of a family need to get away from each other now and then" was changed to "In this house, I have almost no time alone." Another proposed item "Home is a place where people get in each other's way" was changed to "In my home, people get in each other's way."

Other revisions used specific examples mentioned by participants. For instance, we changed: "At home, do you have a place which you consider to be your own?" to "At home, do you have a place where you can get away from the children?" The reason for the change stemmed, first of all, from learning that no one has his or her "own place" in most households and that, in addition, when asked if other household members ever moved their possessions, several focus group participants indicated that only the children, not other adults, disturbed their things.

Conceivably, a good translator would have made the same choices, but we believe the Thai co-principal investigators were sensitized to issues of word choice and more aware of the idiom of our prospective respondents as a result of having been intimately involved in the focus group interviews, and that they therefore made more appropriate decisions in the translation process. The focus group interviews thus helped us learn the *natural vocabulary,* or colloquial expressions, of Bangkokians (Morgan, 1988, pp. 18, 34). The standard recommendation concerning proper translation practice is that after a questionnaire has been translated it should be back translated into the original language by a new (blind) translator. Unfortunately, the resulting back translation can correspond exactly with the original questionnaire and still not be fully understood by the intended target audience. Bilinguals who work with research teams are almost certainly from an educational elite and may not, in fact, speak the "same language" as the target population. We suggest that a questionnaire will be more appropriate for the target population if the translation is accomplished by individuals who are thoroughly familiar with the focus group discussions, even if this does not involve blind back translation.

Generating New Questionnaire Items

In addition to guiding our revision of existing items, the focus group interviews provided the raw material to construct many new questionnaire items, particularly items dealing with family conflict. In the group interviews, we spent some time discussing what husbands and wives quarrel about. Knowledge of the kinds of things that spouses argue about aided us in constructing a series of items that comprise what we call a *marital arguments* scale. Many participants mentioned quarrels about irritating habits, spending too much money, talking to members of the opposite sex, drinking alcohol, gambling, household chores, and disciplining the children. These complaints provided very concrete issues to include in the questionnaire, ones that we were fairly confident would be relevant to the survey respondents. We would never have thought to include many of these items if not for what we learned from the focus groups. Their inclusion, we believe, enhanced the validity and reliability of the scales developed from the questionnaire items.

In a similar vein, in our question about physical conflict between spouses, we included probes for slapping, hitting, and kicking, because all of these actions were mentioned in the focus groups. Our item on the physical discipline of children included a probe to determine if the respondent disciplined his or her child(ren) with the hand, the foot, or a piece of wood, each of these having been mentioned in the focus groups. Another question ("Do you ever go into another room to get away from other members of the family?") was included because several focus group participants mentioned this in response to a question that asked, "Do you have a personal space?" (or words to that effect). This item is used in our scale measuring physical withdrawal. On a more positive note, the focus group interviews also provided examples of ways in which parents were supportive of children, examples that became part of a scale measuring supportive behavior toward children.

In some cases, the experiences relayed to us by the focus group interviews led us to keep items from previous studies of crowding, because these items were obviously relevant in Bangkok. In other cases, we omitted items that we might have included, because our experience with the focus groups suggested the items were not relevant. This allowed us to shorten the questionnaire with minimal loss of information, while avoiding rapport-damaging irrelevant questions.

Conclusions

In our view, focus group interviews clearly are not a substitute for surveys (or, for that matter, for more intensive types of qualitative research). Nor are focus groups a substitute for pretests. We would highly recommend conducting at least one pretest before collecting the main survey data, for our experience suggests that even after carefully following the above procedures, problems with particular questionnaire items can still exist.

However, as Desvousges and Frey (1989) write, focus group interviews "are an excellent tool for making an unfamiliar topic familiar to the research team that must write questionnaires and interpret results" (p. 359). We would echo their assessment, noting that in our case what was unfamiliar was not the topic but the cultural context. A limitation of quantitative research is that the researcher is somewhat removed from the data. Focus groups help the researcher get closer to the data.

Focus group interviews were an enormously valuable element of our particular research project. The focus group interviews (1) provided a rich source of information about family interaction, family conflict, manifestations of stress, and perceptions of crowding in the context of Bangkok; (2) furnished insights into the effects of crowding on family relations; and (3) contributed vitally to the development of our survey instrument. The focus group interviews, we believe, enabled us to measure the theoretically important variables with greater validity and reliability.

More generally, when focus group interviews are used as an aid to questionnaire design, they can (1) contribute to the identification of the relevant theoretical concepts (and weed out irrelevant concepts), (2) assist in the formulation of relevant hypotheses, and (3) suggest how best to communicate with the target population. Our experience leads us to believe that focus group interviews can profitably be used whenever researchers attempt to conduct empirical research in an unfamiliar cultural context. Without such preliminary work, important explanatory concepts may be overlooked and measurement may be invalid, unreliable, irrelevant, or misleading.

Notes

1. *The Ethnograph* is a computer program developed by Siedel that provides the capability to index textual material (e.g., transcripts, field notes, and documents), using categories designed by the user (Siedel, Kjolseth, & Seymour, 1988).

2. One focus group participant mentioned that he would sometimes go out and ride the bus simply to relax. It should be noted that buses in Bangkok are often extremely crowded, with standing room only. This would suggest the importance of physical withdrawal and anonymity in reducing crowding effects.

7

Improving Survey Questionnaires Through Focus Groups

KERTH O'BRIEN

Focus groups hold many advantages as a method of gathering qualitative data. As Basch (1987) has noted, group interviews provide a valuable tool for gaining insights into how people think and learn about their personal life situations. Group interviews are an effective and relatively inexpensive means of interviewing several persons at once. They produce useful data on new research topics while requiring relatively little structure on the interviewer's part, and they allow an investigator to hear the richly contrasting viewpoints that become evident when group members react to each other's comments (Morgan, 1988).

Quantitative researchers have often conducted focus groups to acquaint themselves with new research areas before constructing their

AUTHOR'S NOTE: This work was supported by grants from the National Institute of Mental Health (1R03MH45640-01A1), from the Medical Research Foundation of Oregon, and from Portland State University. An earlier version of these findings were presented at the conference Focus Groups and Group Interviews: Advancing the State of the Art, sponsored by the American Sociological Association, October 1990, Portland, Oregon. The Cascade AIDS Project (CAP) of Portland, Oregon, provided its collaborative commitment to this research. Staff and volunteers of CAP and members of many lesbian, gay and bisexual community organizations and businesses provided their assistance. Julie Reynolds-Kwee assisted in conducting the focus groups. Thoughtful comments on this chapter were provided by Berit Ingersoll-Dayton, Leslie McBride, David L. Morgan, Susan Wladaver-Morgan, and anonymous reviewers. This chapter is based on a similar work by Kerth O'Brien now in press at *Health Education Quarterly,* published by John Wiley & Sons. Copyright © 1993. Reprinted by permission of John Wiley & Sons, Inc.

questionnaire measures (Converse & Presser, 1986). These practices are receiving increased attention and a few published accounts of such procedures now exist, mostly on topics in the health arena (Bauman & Adair, 1992; Desvousges & Frey, 1989; deVries, Weijts, Dijkstra, & Kok, 1992; Joseph et al., 1984; Steckler, McLeroy, Goodman, Bird, & McCormick, 1992). Even so, there is almost no published information on how a survey researcher would conduct focus groups for this specific purpose or implement focus group findings to construct a questionnaire.

To address this gap, the present chapter describes the use of focus groups as a resource for the design of a quantitatively oriented survey of social relationships and health behavior. The examples given pertain to groups conducted as part of the Portland Men's Study (PMS), a psychosocial study of gay and bisexual men at risk for acquired immunodeficiency syndrome (AIDS). Although the illustrations here are specific to AIDS and human immunodeficiency virus (HIV) infection, they are provided so that quantitative researchers in a variety of areas may see the benefits of focus groups to their own work.

Focus groups contribute to the development of a quantitative investigation in two major ways. First, focus group data can inform the actual content of the survey questionnaire—its wording, item development, and even the research questions that affect its design. Second, and quite different, focus groups can provide an understanding of what the given research project means to members of the study population. Below, both of these benefits are discussed using the PMS as an example.

Background: The Portland Men's Study

A series of focus groups took place as part of a long-term program of research examining the features of social relationships among gay and bisexual men at risk for AIDS. Goals of this program are to identify which features of social ties enhance the psychological health of men in this population as well as the ability to adhere to widely publicized behavioral guidelines for preventing transmission of HIV. The author and her research assistants conducted these groups to (1) learn the language the men used to discuss their private emotional and sexual experiences, (2) gather information about participants' experiences that would illustrate the concepts under study, (3) consult members of this community about recruitment procedures for the eventual survey, and (4) build support for the survey among members of the local community. Although the group discussions were not expected to provide new research hypotheses, the examples presented show that the groups did, indeed, yield this additional benefit.

Men in the study population differed from others at risk for HIV infection, such as hemophiliacs or injection drug users, because gay and bisexual men have personal networks that are largely structured around same-sex interaction and they are more likely personally to have known individuals who died of AIDS. In addition, gay community members have provided leadership in educating themselves and the larger society about HIV infection since early days of the epidemic (Gonsiorek & Shernoff, 1991).

Developing, Conducting, and Analyzing the Focus Groups

Planning for the focus groups began in fall 1988, through conversations with key informants in the gay male community of Portland, Oregon. We discussed the fact with these informants that focus groups sometimes yield more useful information if participants hold important background characteristics in common such as race or economic status. Participants feel freer to express their views and share personal experiences with similar, rather than dissimilar, others (Morgan, 1991).

Based on prior literature, we expected it would be especially instructive to hear the perspectives of men who were in primary relationships. Our key informants confirmed this idea, also directing us to other segments of the population that might have differing contributions to make toward the ultimate survey content, such as younger men and older men. Informants pointed out that ethnic minority men not only might have differing perspectives but also might feel more comfortable discussing their experiences with other minority men. Furthermore, informants indicated that at least some of the men who were HIV seropositive would feel more open about sharing their perspectives in groups with other seropositive men. Thus we planned to recruit participants for several groups that would be homogenous along some dimension in addition to sexual orientation. All participants in the homogenous groups were to be aware of these special group characteristics.

The discussions with informants yielded suggestions of 13 organizations and five individuals whom we approached for help in recruiting focus group members. Typically, for one of these groups, we contacted the group's leader to ask permission to visit one of their meetings. Upon visiting, we described our study and solicited the first names and telephone numbers of interested people; later, we telephoned these individuals to arrange times for the discussions. Men were invited to join the homogenous groups at this point. In addition, if a participant belonged to more than one of these special categories—as some respondents did; for example, some were seropositive men in relationships—he had the opportunity to join whichever group he wanted to.

Some participants were recruited in a slightly different way. For example, a discussion with older men met after the monthly scheduled meeting of an older gay men's social organization. This plan was announced in advance on the meeting schedule, and it was made clear that men who did not wish to participate would not be expected to do so (as, indeed, some opted to participate in a barbecue instead).

A total of 86 men signed up for group discussions; of these, 78 actually participated in 1 of 10 focus groups. A typical focus group had 5 to 8 participants. Groups were held in locations familiar to Portland's gay male community.

Before conducting the groups, we prepared a group discussion outline that addressed procedural issues and listed four basic questions (Taylor & Bogdan, 1984). All groups had these questions in common so that we could be sure they would be addressed during the 90-minute format. The structure of the discussion guide was influenced by our attendance at community events before the start of the study. For example, based on these interactions we determined that a discussion of private sexual activities should not take place at the beginning of the group. Therefore, our discussion guide included a first question to break the ice and get the men talking about their experiences—"How is your life different because of the AIDS epidemic?" This part of the discussion also served our purpose of becoming acquainted with participants' language for their experiences, so that we could employ this language in later, more personally oriented, phases of the discussion.

We began each meeting by reading a statement of voluntary informed consent, describing procedures, and answering questions. We told participants that our purpose was to learn more about their experiences and perspectives regarding the AIDS epidemic to develop a study questionnaire, adding that we also wanted their ideas about how to recruit a large, diverse sample of gay men in Portland to respond to such a questionnaire.

We structured each group to maximize participants' responses to each other's contributions, stating, for example, "There are no right or wrong answers to the questions I'm going to ask you—only your own experiences and perspectives." We assured them that if the topic of discussion wandered, they themselves would probably refocus discussion to the topic at hand. This suggestion proved a self-fulfilling prophecy that kept us from dominating the discussion (Morgan, 1988).

Diversity of commentary was encouraged. For example, we said, "Often you will find that if some of you talk about having a certain kind of experience, soon another person might say that his experience is different." We added, "Our discussion might remind you of another gay man you know who had a different experience. It would be okay if you tell us about his experience so long as you don't let us know who he is." This underlined the importance of each man's experience and offered a shield for participants who might want to contribute their own experiences without having to identify them as such.

In each focus group, three questions were asked in a *funneling* sequence (Kahn & Cannell, 1957) that led from a general topic to the specific interest area—the influence of social relationships on psychological health and on safer sex practices. The structure made these transitions easy. First we asked participants, "How is your life different because of the HIV/AIDS epidemic?" As noted earlier, we asked this to break the ice and to learn what language participants used for talking about their experiences. Second, we asked, "When people get involved sexually, why is it that sometimes they have safer sex and sometimes they don't?" This question was designed to focus the discussion on experiences of safer sex and eventually to allow the conversation to move toward a discussion of social interactions. Third, we asked the central question, "What are some things other people have done that you have found supportive in dealing with the HIV/AIDS epidemic?" We asked this question so that specific interactions, such as expressions of support for safer sex activities, could be identified. As each group drew to a close, we asked a fourth, methodologic question, "How can we best recruit men for the large-scale, questionnaire phase of this study?"

Coding the Content of the Group Discussions

The focus group audiotapes were replayed to note discussion climate and to consider areas of apparent awkwardness, emphasis, or conversational pause. The tapes were also transcribed. Based on these transcripts, particular words or phrases used to describe experiences were listed and grouped together on the basis of similarity. The concepts expressed were summarized in the transcript margins and listed together. These concepts were then grouped into categories, based on their similarity in content or emotive tone; categories were examined for the possible formation of subcategories. The categories were evaluated across focus groups to determine the range of experiences as well as the dominant experiences that participants had offered (Cartwright, 1953; Folch-Lyon & Trost, 1981) (for other approaches to the analysis of focus group data, see, e.g., Richards & Richards, 1991; Tesch, 1990).

***Using Findings From the Focus Groups
to Construct the Questionnaire:
Survey Content—
The Wording of Survey Items***

Focus groups inherently allow an investigator to learn the phraseology that participants use to describe their own experiences. With this information, the investigator can design a questionnaire using words and phrases to enhance respondents' understanding and, hence, to enhance data quality (Lown, Winkler, Fullilove, & Fullilove, 1991). For example, when we began conducting our groups, we referred to the human immunodeficiency virus as *HIV*—the name used by most health researchers working in this area. The focus group participants were more likely to refer to HIV as *the AIDS virus* and to the epidemic as *the AIDS epidemic*. Had the questionnaire used *HIV,* some respondents might have been confused. But through use of the population's own wording, the questionnaire presumably obtained more valid information.

Focus groups also informed us of participants' own phraseology on the topic of primary sexual relationships. Comments from participants indicated that some men considered themselves to be involved in a primary relationship with someone even if they were no longer involved sexually with that person. Others considered themselves to be primary partners while also participating in sexual activities outside the relationship. If the questionnaire had asked simply about a "primary sexual relationship," many participants would have found this vague. To incorporate this perspective, the questionnaire defined *primary partner* more carefully: "By 'primary,' we mean a relationship where you consider yourselves lovers or a couple, and where you have had sex together at least sometime in the relationship. This does not necessarily mean you are monogamous."

Construction of Survey Items
to Measure a Given Concept

Before designing their instruments, survey researchers typically know the research questions they will ask and the constructs they will measure. But specific indicators of their constructs—particular questions to address them—may be unknown, especially when the investigator is exploring a new research area. Focus group participants can provide qualitative examples of their own experiences and perspectives that, in turn, can shape the investigator's measurement decisions.

In the PMS, we wanted to ask questions about particular situations in which gay men engaged in sexual activities widely regarded to carry a risk of HIV transmission. The model we used held that both interpersonal and intrapersonal barriers (reference group attitudes and personal preferences) could interfere with adherence to the safer sex guidelines (Fisher, 1988; Kelly & St. Lawrence, 1988). The model lacked specific questions to address such dimensions as partners' attitudes or situational influences. In response to the question "Why is it that sometimes people have safer sex, and sometimes not?" participants described experiences that were readily translated into questionnaire items. For example, one man said, "I talked to a partner once about it afterwards . . . that I was disturbed by the fact that he was willing to engage in unprotected anal sex. . . . He didn't really say much." Such comments were rephrased into a questionnaire format in which respondents were asked whether they had experienced one particular risk activity within the past year. Those who had were then asked, in a checklist format, whether each of several interpersonal or intrapersonal conditions had existed when they experienced the activity, for example, "My partner would not have minded if we had used a condom."

Focus groups also provided examples of supportive social interactions that facilitated the development of social support measures. In response to the question "What are some things other people have done that you have found supportive in dealing with the HIV/AIDS epidemic?" one participant talked about how people close to him might remind him to follow the safer sex guidelines: "I can tell the difference between 'Be careful because I love you' and 'be careful because I don't want the neighbors asking me questions.' " The message this participant preferred—"Be careful because I love you"—was also a very good example of emotional support. His experience lent itself readily to the following survey item, with which respondents were asked to agree or disagree: "My friends want me to follow the safer sex guidelines because they care about me."

Development of New Hypotheses

Focus groups can generate hypotheses that merit further quantitative investigation, even if the groups have not been designed with this in mind. In the PMS, this fact became evident when participants talked about the different ways they communicated their interest in safer sex to a potential partner. Two participants had this to say:

> I think that one of the best approaches [to safer sex] is to make protecting yourself an important part of foreplay. It could be fun, just in doing it. Why waste time talking?

> Maybe when you're involved in sex you're going to have to deal with it . . . by ignoring it, or talking about it or just doing what you think is the right thing to do. But I don't think there is a lot of talking in the bar. . . . It would take all the spontaneity out of it, for most people.

In another group, a participant added,

> I went to a safer sex workshop and . . . the assumption there was . . . you would never end up in bed with someone before you had talked about safer sex, and that you would have negotiated this, and I thought that was out for a lot of men. . . . I thought it was sort of an upper-class thing.

Despite the verbal emphasis in AIDS-preventive education (Hochhauser, 1987), participants made it clear they did not consider it important to talk about safer sex in order to practice it. Their perspective raised an interesting research question: Are men who prefer not to talk about safer sex more or less likely to engage in safer sex practices than other men? Questionnaire items were written to pursue this question, with which respondents could agree or disagree: "Talking about safer sex gets in the way of enjoying sex" and "If I want to have safer sex, the way I tell my partner is I talk to him about it."

Focus groups led directly to the inclusion of these questions about communication style. They fit very easily within the framework of the study, because they pertained to social interactions, safer sex attitudes, and risk behavior.

Another unexpected contribution pertained to the conceptualization of AIDS-preventive behavior. In discussing how their lives are different because of the AIDS epidemic, participants talked about changes in sexual activity that went beyond most published studies of AIDS-preventive behavior. Most studies have focused on the frequencies of risk behavior, such as anal sex without the use of condoms; AIDS prevention is regarded as abstaining from activities that carry risk. Many studies have also asked about modifying activities to include condoms (Becker & Joseph, 1988; Stall, Coates, & Hoff, 1988). Few studies have asked about sexual activities that carry no risk, such as telephone sex or mutual masturbation, which were safe before the AIDS epidemic and remain safe today. These activities have great value as replacements for risk-related behaviors and are thus AIDS preventive. Participants in the focus groups were aware of this:

There's more mutual masturbation [than there used to be 10 years ago].

There are so many more people . . . saying, "You know, I would much rather live my life giving myself a hand job than risk any type of exposure." Video rentals have gone up, you know.

The idea that such behaviors could, perhaps even should, be regarded as AIDS preventive is consistent with the principle from learning psychology that the best way to be rid of an old habit is to replace it with a new habit (Guthrie, 1935). In the PMS, questions about masturbation were included to test the hypothesis that men who practiced masturbation were more likely than other men to avoid the sexual behaviors that carried risk of HIV transmission.

Development of Survey
Recruitment Procedures

The problem of sampling is critical for research with gay men. The population as a whole is difficult to define precisely, partly because many gay men prefer to remain private, or closeted, about their sexual preferences (Walter, 1985). Many psychosocial researchers try to approximate the benefits of a representative sample by recruiting a sample that is as diverse as possible (Kaplan, 1989).

Focus groups conducted for the PMS were unusual in that participants were aware these groups were the first phase of a long-range research program and knew their input would influence the questionnaire content. This enabled participants to help to recruit for the survey phase. They were asked, "How can we best recruit men for the large-scale, questionnaire phase of this study?" Participants suggested several new ideas, including posting a notice on electronic bulletin boards used mostly by lesbians and gay men, working with the staff of businesses owned by members of the gay community, and advertising in the performance program of the local gay men's chorus. Importantly, minority men who participated in the focus groups indicated that personal contacts would be the best way to recruit other minority men for the questionnaire phase: "We know that we can call each other and exchange information and stuff like that, and . . . we've got some informal networking that goes on . . . but there's not a formal network."

Several focus group participants offered to see whether the organizations to which they belonged would be willing to send out notices about the study to persons on their mailing lists. Most of these suggestions for reaching a diverse sample of men were pursued during the questionnaire phase of the project.

Participants also offered their opinions about research procedures for the current phase of the study—the focus group phase—particularly in regard to their own anonymity as participants. Before the focus groups were started, we received approval from the appropriate institutional review board for procedures that would require participants to sign consent forms as indications of their voluntary informed consent to participate in the study. But as the participants indicated, their signatures on the consent forms were the only aspect of the research that carried risk:

> I've got complete confidence in you, but if something comes up and there is just some problem with the study . . . I'm not sure that just one locked file drawer would provide the confidentiality that all of us here need.

We returned to the institutional review board with these concerns. The board approved a change in study plans, no longer requiring participant signatures. The board also asked us to thank respondents for their willingness to work together with the university on these issues.

Description of the Study Goals and of the Questionnaire Itself

Members of a population that has been understudied—or, in the case of gay and bisexual men, actively exploited (e.g., Socarides, 1970; Zucker, 1966)—may be reluctant to participate in subsequent research efforts. By inviting input from population members, research investigators can establish credibility with the community, build or rebuild a sense of community trust, and develop research procedures compatible with community values. This is a second way in which focus groups informed study operations. Focus group participants welcomed the opportunity to have input into the design of the questionnaire, but some participants remained suspicious of any research, especially funded research, that would ask gay and bisexual men for information about which they felt vulnerable. What would be the benefit, they wanted to know, of such information? Would these questions show respect for the value this community places on privacy? How would respondents' confidentiality or anonymity be maintained?

These concerns led to the development of research procedures characterized by accessibility and directness. The survey questionnaire included a removable cover sheet with our telephone number that respondents could keep. In addition, we recruited most of the survey respondents in person rather than through the use of graduate assistants, so that potential respondents could address their questions directly to the individual responsible for the entire project. Typical questions pertained to the nature of our collaboration with the local AIDS service organization, our educational background, current organizational memberships, commitment to confidentiality, and the source of our interest in the topics of HIV and AIDS. The directness, respect, and face-to-face interactions that characterized these focus groups provided an early positive step in establishing the investigator's local credibility.

We gave further evidence of our investment in open collaboration by sharing the focus group findings with community members. Several months after the groups were completed, copies of a brochure-length report were sent to the organizations and key social network members through which participants had been recruited. Enough copies were sent that all members of these more than dozen organizations received copies. As a result, members of these groups believed that their organizations—not just a collection of men who happened to belong to those organizations—had contributed to the research effort. Thus the survey was established as a community project (O'Brien, 1989). When we approached community groups again in the questionnaire phase of the project, we found that all organizations that helped during the focus group phase were willing to help again by distributing questionnaires. Indeed, a few organizations even contacted us rather than waiting for us to contact them, to ask whether there was some way they could be helpful in the questionnaire phase. The questionnaire phase itself suggested these collaborations were highly productive: although participation was sought from 500 survey respondents, in fact more than 750 individuals completed and returned questionnaires.

In sum, focus groups provided multiple benefits. They informed the survey procedures and the content of survey measures in terms of question wording, item development, hypothesis generation, and descriptions of the study's purposes. They also created a sense of involvement for members of a community previously alienated from research and established the local credibility of the investigator.

Evaluating the Benefits of the Method

What evidence do we have that the survey questionnaire was made better by our having used these procedures? The questionnaire might be evaluated through an examination of the internal reliability coefficients for scales that were developed from the focus groups. One scale was designed to test a new hypothesis regarding nonverbal behavior that emerged from focus group discussions. This showed the weakest level of Cronbach α (0.411), suggesting there may be an inherent contradiction in the use of a verbal self-report measure to tap nonverbal communication style. Other scales showed higher reliabilities: Three items designed to assess interpersonal skills for negotiating AIDS-preventive behavior attained an α coefficient of 0.625, two items measuring emotional support from friends had an α of 0.648, and four items assessing the influence of primary partners on AIDS-preventive behavior had an α of 0.715. Focus group discussions played a primary role in the development of these items.

Clearly, this is a standard criterion by which survey effectiveness may be evaluated. But the question remains whether our α coefficients would have been lower if focus groups had not been used. A proper test for this or any other study would compare survey instruments that have been developed with those developed without the use of focus groups. We know of no researchers who have such data at this time, but we propose this as a direction for further methodologic study.

Discussion

Focus groups are not a methodologic remedy for all of the problems involved in questionnaire design (Basch, 1987; Desvousges & Frey, 1989). Compared with individual interviews, focus groups offer a researcher less control over the data generated (Bauman & Adair, 1992; Morgan, 1988). Individual interviews might also be preferred for topics that are particularly complex, because the interviewer can use probes and follow-up questions to explore aspects of a participant's experience that may not come to light in a group setting. Even with these limitations, group interviews still bring certain advantages. Participants sometimes share very personal experiences in a group setting—especially one in which they feel comfortable with similar other participants—more readily than in a dyadic interaction. They sometimes respond to each other's experiences with reports of their own quite different experiences, allowing the investigator to discover information that might not come up in one-on-one settings. Focus group interviews also provide the practical advantage of collecting valuable data within a short timeframe. We hope that researchers who want to use qualitative data to inform their survey development will consider the possibility of a focus group methodology (Steckler et al., 1992).

In summary, focus groups are important to the survey research process. Not only can they help the investigator know the language that his or her populations use to describe their experiences but they can acquaint the investigator with the population members' values and styles of thinking and communicating about the research topics. In short, they can help a quantitative investigator to ask useful questions and to ask questions in a useful way. Finally, they can be helpful in any ongoing research effort with populations that are vulnerable or understudied, because they demonstrate to members of the population that the investigator is not just treating them as numbers but is truly interested in listening to them.

8

Focus Groups and Surveys as Complementary Research Methods

A Case Example

BRENT WOLFF
JOHN KNODEL
WERASIT SITTITRAI

Combining qualitative and quantitative techniques within a single research design represents a methodological union between two divergent research traditions within sociology. Survey research, the paragon of quantitative analysis with its emphasis on measurement standardization and representativeness owes much to the Durkheim tradition of broad, comparative analysis and the search for social facts. Research approaches that favor qualitative methods to analyze social phenomena may be seen as closer descendants of Weber, emphasizing the importance of finding the subjective meaning of actors in a social setting. Because conclusions about meaning are necessarily interpretive and usually contingent on the context in which the actions take place, such qualitative analysis is typically resistant to either quantification or standardized comparison. Implicit in the two approaches to social research are fundamentally different, some might say fundamentally incompatible, views about reality and the best way to explain it. It is not surprising, then, that the respective practitioners from quantitative and qualitative domains of sociological research have been known to react with as much skepticism as enthusiasm to this eclectic mix of methods.

Our major aim here is to concretely illustrate how incorporating a qualitative approach, represented by the focus group method, into an integrated research design with a major sample survey component can enhance the quality of the resulting analysis and the confidence that can be placed in it. As elaborated in several recent publications devoted to the method, focus groups typically bring together a small number of participants from a well-defined target population to discuss a set of preselected topics under the guidance of a trained moderator (Merton, Fiske, & Kendall, 1990; Morgan, 1988). Transcripts of the discussion serve as the source of data for qualitative analysis.

Although survey and focus group techniques are derived from divergent theoretical approaches, there is nothing inherent in the methods themselves that forbids their combination. In fact, the particular strengths and limitations inherent in different methods might suit them ideally to complement one another in a unified research design. Focus groups can never claim to be representative of a much larger inferential population that surveys obtain through random sampling methods. In the first place, the selection of group participants is typically purposive and based more on suitability or convenience rather than representativeness. Second, the absolute number of focus group discussions feasible in a single research design will always be small by survey standards.[1] The time-consuming nature of data collection and textual analysis in addition to the general qualitative nature of conclusions limit the utility of large numbers of group discussions, at least for the sake of replication alone. Finally, although the level of structure imposed on discussion can vary considerably, focus groups will never be able to attain the degree of standardization possible through adherence to a fixed questionnaire format.

By the same token, surveys lack the flexibility of qualitative approaches to pursue particular issues in any greater depth or to accommodate a wider range of explanatory categories than foreseen in the original questionnaire design. Surveys are also less adept at capturing the kind of in-depth contextual detail that focus groups can provide.

Most important from a qualitative research standpoint, survey research may be seen as hostage by its own design to conceptual research priorities of the investigators. Survey research is characterized at every step by the extraordinary unilateral control exercised over measurement and interpretation by the researchers, guided by their own theoretical concerns. The selection of items on the questionnaire certainly reflects research priorities established before data collection, even if new hypotheses can be generated and tested using the same data. Questionnaire pretests may provide critical feedback on the choice or wording of questions, but this process is inherently conservative, sensitive to design flaws arising from questions included and not from questions omitted. In the analysis phase, the relationship between measurement categories is either tested or presumed in the modeling process, whereas the relevant context for the relationships is determined through the choice of control variables. In focus group research, both the social context of the relationships under study and the subjective meaning attached to them by the social actors themselves are allowed to emerge more or less spontaneously within the framework of discussion guidelines. While qualitative analysis need not be accepted as the authoritative truth, it can provide independent verification of original theoretical conceptualization on which an isolated survey research design relies so completely.

In summary, survey and focus group approaches to social science research each offer a distinct set of strengths and limitations that are markedly different yet potentially complementary when combined in a mixed-method research design. Given their association with different approaches to social science, however, it is essential to be clear about what theoretical assumptions are guiding the use of these methods, what are the goals of the research project, and what are the limits of interpretation of the resulting data.

Combined Uses of Focus Groups and Sample Surveys

Focus groups can be used to complement sample surveys in several ways, depending on the sequential order with which the research components are combined. Conducted before the survey, focus groups can be used to facilitate questionnaire design, from the formulation of whole question categories to fine-tuning wording on particular questions (e.g., Knodel, Havanon, & Pramaulratana, 1984; Morgan, 1988). They have also been used before surveys to anticipate survey nonresponse or refusal problems in hard-to-reach populations and to explore ways to minimize these potential sources of sampling bias (e.g., Desvousges & Frey, 1989). A second approach is to conduct focus groups among actual survey respondents shortly after the survey has taken place to evaluate the survey process. Discussions might be used to assess reaction to the survey and to trace more carefully the cognitive and social processes that influenced respondents' comprehension of survey questions and their subsequent responses.[2] A third approach is to conduct focus groups after the survey results have already been analyzed with an aim to corroborate findings or explore in greater depth the relationships suggested by the quantitative analysis (e.g., Knodel, Chamratrithirong, & Debavalya, 1987). Yet a fourth approach is to conduct focus groups more or less concurrently with surveys as complementary components of a unified research design. Survey questionnaire and focus group discussion guidelines are designed in advance to yield independent quantitative and qualitative research perspectives on the topics under investigation. Focus groups might be held during the same time as the survey fieldwork, with participants drawn either from the survey respondents themselves or from others who are similar or complementary in their characteristics.[3] The results of the survey would not inform the contents of the focus group discussion guidelines, or vice versa, in the sequential manner that characterizes the previously described approaches. Instead, the survey questionnaire and the discussion guidelines would have been jointly designed before the results of either component were known. Survey data and transcribed texts from focus group discussions could then be analyzed together or independently according to the research objectives. The goal of such a complementary research design is the mutual enhancement of the analysis and understanding of each component by the other, sometimes called *triangulation* between qualitative and quantitative data (Denzin, 1970; Miles & Huberman, 1984; Webb et al., 1965).

This last approach is the focus of this chapter, drawing illustrations from a study of the consequences of family size for socioeconomic well-being in rural Thailand. Examples of three different ways in which the focus group findings complemented the survey results are discussed. More specifically, the examples chosen show how focus groups may be used to illustrate and confirm survey findings, how they may be used to clarify or elaborate survey results that might otherwise lead to unexpected or contradictory conclusions, and finally, how they may be used in a more exploratory fashion to suggest explanatory categories that were unanticipated at the time of project design. Before proceeding to these examples, however, a brief description of the project design is necessary.

Project Description

The concurrent use of focus groups with sample surveys was an integral part of the design of a study titled the Socioeconomic Consequences of Fertility Decline for the Thai Family, conducted in 1988 in Thailand. The project was carried out by the Institute for Population Studies at Chulalongkorn University to explore the impact of dramatic changes in the demographic regime in Thailand on several dimensions of family well-being. The average family size in Thailand declined from more than six children per couple in the early 1960s to just above two children by the mid-1980s (Chayovan, Kamnuansilpa, & Knodel, 1988). This represents a remarkably short period of time for the kind of fertility transition that required half a century or more in North American and Western European countries. The purpose of the study was to test assertions commonly made by advocates of family planning in Thailand and elsewhere that fertility declines resulting in smaller average family size should yield direct short- and long-term benefits for the well-being of individual families. The addition of a focus group component allowed the study to examine the consequences of changing family size through the perceptions as well as through more objective measures gathered by the survey.

The degree of success in combining different methods in a single study may ultimately depend on a research design that can accommodate the strengths and limitations of each measurement instrument. In the study under consideration, the use of survey and focus groups was coordinated to ensure that the resulting data would be reasonably comparable. The survey was limited to two small areas that were purposively selected to exploit regional differences in the timing of the onset and subsequent pace of fertility decline.[4] The first consisted of two adjacent districts in northern Thailand, where fertility decline began early, probably by the early 1960s, and proceeded rapidly to approach replacement level fertility by the end of the 1970s. The second site consisted of two adjacent districts in central Thailand. There fertility decline started later and proceeded at a more moderate pace than in the north.

The sample within each site was split evenly between couples with small families having a completed size of one or two children at the end of child bearing and large families defined as having four or more children. Roughly equal numbers of couples were selected in each study site and typically both husband and wife were interviewed jointly. Eligibility was limited to couples who started their child bearing between 1962 and 1974, thus controlling loosely for access to modern contraceptive methods, which started to be widely available sometime during the 1960s. A detailed description of the study design can be found in the first report of the project (Knodel, Podhisita, & Sittitrai, 1988).

The focus group component was also designed to enhance comparability between qualitative and quantitative analyses. Focus group participants were purposively selected from among survey respondents, based on considerations of convenience and suitability to contribute to a group discussion. The usual practice of choosing participants who do not know each other was not practical to enforce in a local rural setting.[5] To minimize primary group dynamics that may impede the flow of the discussion and threaten the validity of the results, eligibility to take part in a focus group was restricted to only one member of a couple, either the husband or wife but not both. The groups consisted of seven to nine participants, one moderator and a note taker and lasted approximately 2 hours. The composition of each group was homogeneous with respect to family size. A total of 12 focus group discussions were conducted altogether, evenly divided between northern and central study sites and, within each site, between large and small families. The symmetrical design produced 3 focus groups for each family-size category in each of the two regions, sufficient to discern differences in the qualitative analysis between any two cells in this two-by-two research design. Note that the consideration of region and family size was employed to introduce a simple level of analytic control that might be similarly accomplished in a quantitative analysis through the use of statistical methods.

A uniform set of focus group guidelines was used for all sessions. Research categories reflected in the discussion guidelines were decided in advance, based on theoretical considerations and on exploratory in-depth interviews conducted during the preparatory stages of the project. The moderator maintained a relatively high level of control over the discussion, introducing general issues from the guidelines for discussion and probing or interjecting to make sure the groups covered all the essential points and to keep the conversation focused. Although the main discussion topics were generally introduced in the same order, there was a good deal of variation between groups in how the moderator introduced questions and how much discussion was devoted to any one point in the guidelines. The transcript record leaves little doubt that considerable latitude was maintained to permit free discussion of issues, unsolicited opinions and unanticipated responses. Despite these variations, the relatively uniform structure of the focus group discussions achieves a minimum level of standardization in the language of survey research that permits comparison on particular guideline questions across groups.

Analysis

Although the strategy of triangulation has been advocated for quite some time, the specific combination of focus group discussions and surveys as an integrated multimethod approach appears to be relatively recent. A primary aim of this chapter is to provide a realistic assessment of the potential for the combined use of the methods with examples of how it works in practice. We have selected examples from the study described above to suggest a range of possible applications of triangulated analysis.[6]

The main aim of the study was to explore the relationship between completed family size and three socioeconomic outcomes: educational attainment of children, the ability to accumulate material wealth in the form of savings and assets, and the ability of women to participate in income-earning activities outside the household. Although the main conclusions of the study will not be discussed in any detail here, examples of the interplay between focus group and survey findings have been selected from each of the three outcome categories. As summarized previously, each example illustrates one of the three ways focus groups complemented survey analysis within the constraints of this research design.

**Example 1: Illustration
and Confirmation**

The use of focus groups to illustrate and confirm conclusions from the survey analysis represents the least ambitious if most reliable objective of this type of multimethod design. To the extent that survey questions are well conceived, well understood, and accurately measured and to the extent that focus group discussions yield unbiased information from participants roughly typical of the survey population, the two should point to similar conclusions. Of course, the qualitative method inevitably adds a degree of contextual nuance that is impossible to extract from the cold parsimony of a statistical analysis. Consequently, the argument could be made that combining methods enriches the analysis, even if the substantive conclusions are the same for both.

One example of this illustrative function of focus groups is the analysis of family size and educational attainment. Theory holds that families with fewer children are better able to concentrate resources and invest proportionally more in each child's education. Such a mechanism would be mitigated, however, if children work to pay for their own education or if costs could be defrayed by the public sector or among an extended kin network that might include the grandparents, aunts and uncles, or elder siblings. Information was gathered in the survey and focus groups to explore how Thai villagers finance the education of their children, particularly past the primary level, when the cost of tuition is no longer covered by the government. The conclusions from both survey and focus groups were unequivocal: regardless of family size it is the parents and the parents alone in these rural Thai settings who are expected to shoulder the main burden of education costs. Relatives or siblings may contribute some on an occasional basis, but such support is clearly limited.

The results from the survey question on education finance are presented in Table 8.1. Alternative means of educational support were assessed for each child in a respondent's family. Two main conclusions may be taken from these figures. The first is the low level of financial support parents receive to educate their children. With little child fosterage or direct support from outside the nuclear family, the largest category of nonparental support comes from siblings within the family; 8% to 14% of children reported having given such support. Net monetary contribution of children to their own education was usually quite small, under 500 Baht or $20 U.S. The second main conclusion that can be taken from Table 8.1 is the lack of meaningful differences with respect to how small and large families shoulder education costs. Note that with respect to sibling support, typically the direction would go from older to younger siblings. Thus the largest difference found, namely for support of another sibling, is probably an artifact of the greater chance that any particular child in a large family will have younger siblings. It may also reflect the fact that the wider age difference between siblings in larger families will make it more likely that an elder sibling could be old enough to work while a younger sibling is still in school.

Evidence from the focus groups strongly confirms the survey findings and reflects some of the human complexities that enter into the decision to help or not to help. The following excerpted quotes are typical of the dominant opinions expressed in the focus groups:

Participant 1:   One grandma has a lot of grandchildren. If she supports one, the others complain. The solution is to support none at all. [Large family group, central region]

Table 8.1   Percentage of Children in Small and Large Families Whose Education Was Partially Supported by Sources Other Than Parents

	Small Families	*Large Families*
Children who lived at least a year with someone other than parents before reaching age 12	5	2
Children who received educational support from someone other than parents or siblings	5	3
Children over age 12 who helped pay own educational expenses	8	12
Children over age 12 who paid more than 500 Baht ($20 U.S.) toward their educational expenses[a]	4	3
Children over age 12 who provided support for siblings' education[b]	8	14

SOURCE: Knodel, Havanon, and Sittitrai (1990).
NOTES: a. Includes those who covered all their expenses as well as those who covered their tuition fees.
b. Excluding children from one-child families.

Moderator: Have you heard that grandparents sometimes help support the children's education?

Participant 1:   Rarely.

Participant 2:   If the grandparents have some money they might help a little, but not continuously.

[Large family group, central region]

Moderator: Do any relatives help share the expenses?

Participants, together: No, no one does.

Moderator: Do uncles, aunts, grandmas, grandpas, or even great grandparents help?

Participant 1:   No one helps.

Participant 2:   No one helps. Parents have to support their own children.

[Small family group, north region]

Example 2: Clarification
and Elaboration

The second example is drawn from the analysis of the effect of family size on material wealth accumulation. It is hypothesized that smaller families who are spared the cost of raising many children should have a relative advantage over larger families in their ability to accumulate savings, invest in housing improvements, and acquire modern consumer goods. Of course, a number of mediating factors such as educational investment or wealth status before child bearing begins may affect this empirical relationship. The task of assessing current and retrospective wealth status was left to the survey component of this study for obvious reasons (see Havanon, Knodel, & Sittitrai, 1990).

The study was also interested in how family size affects the perceived ability to accumulate material wealth, a topic well suited for a combined approach. Focus group participants were asked if the number of children in a family affects its ability to save money or afford housing improvements and consumer goods. Survey respondents from large and small families were asked to speculate on the effect of having as many or as few children as the opposite group on their relative wealth status. For example, respondents from small families were asked whether they would be able to afford more, fewer, or the same number of consumer goods if they had decided to have four or more children. Respondents from large families were asked the same question, but supposing they had decided to have two or fewer children instead. Three variants on the same question were posed for overall material well-being and two specific aspects of material wealth, consumer goods and housing quality.

The survey results shown in Table 8.2 indicate that a strong majority of respondents from large and small families—81% and 84%—respectively, perceive that families with one or two children enjoy a relative advantage over families with four or more children when gauged by overall economic status. Only a small proportion of respondents, between 5% and 8%, reported they would be better off economically with many instead of few children. The same attitudinal measure for consumer goods yielded far more equivocal results, however, seemingly inconsistent with the previous finding. Although a majority of respondents in each family size category still support the general perception that small families experience a relative advantage over large families with respect to the ability to purchase modern consumer goods, 22% or roughly one in five of small family respondents thought they would own

Table 8.2 Percentage Distribution of Perceived Effects of Opposite Family Size on Current Economic Status and Number of Consumer Goods by Actual Family Size

| | Actual Family Size | |
	Small	Large
Economic status if family size were opposite		
Better	8	81
Worse	84	5
Same	7	11
Depends, don't know	1	3
Total	100	100
Number of consumer goods if family size were opposite		
Better	22	59
Worse	54	8
Same	23	29
Depends, don't know	1	3
Total	100	100

SOURCE: Havanon et al. (1990).
NOTE: Percentages do not necessarily sum to 100 due to rounding.

more if they had a larger family. Moreover, a relatively high proportion of respondents from both family size categories thought the number of children would not make a difference one way or the other. How can these attitudinal measures be reconciled?

The focus group discussions on this topic helped clarify the relationship of family size to material wealth accumulation. Two points emerge from the focus group analysis that suggest the hidden logic behind the somewhat inconsistent findings of the survey. First, the extent to which children detract from the ability to accumulate wealth is a function of where they stand in the life course. There was strong consensus that while children were still dependent, and especially when they were attending school, they represented a distinct economic burden on the family. In a poor rural setting where cash incomes are low, many children of school age or below can represent a real economic drain on the couple's finances. The length of time children can be net contributors to the family income is ultimately limited by marriage, after which little direct support to the parental family from either sons or daughters can be expected. Before marriage, however, children who are old enough to work for a wage or help with family farm work or home improvement may become real assets to the family's economic status. In addition, children themselves often provide the main incentives to buy modern consumer goods, even sometimes lobbying their parents to make purchases and offering to share the costs.

Moderator: And the children, when they get some money from their work, do they help you pay for these things, when they grow up?

Participant 1:   Have they separated their family from us [the parents]?

Moderator: Suppose they still live with you.

Participant 1:   Then they do help. Like when they get some money from cutting sugar cane, we'll contribute for a television.

Participant 2:   Yes, contribute.

Participant 3:   They'll spend more than us.

Participant 1:   They'll say, "Let's get a TV, Dad."

Participant 2:   [We respond,] "Let's help each other if you want one."
[Large family group, northern region]

Participants 1 and 2:   Children won't help us any more after they get married. They help themselves.

Participant 3:   They help their spouse and children.

Participant 4:   After they have left home, they belong to a different family. They will help only when it is necessary or an emergency.
[Large family group, northern region]

The discrepant results of the attitudinal measures on the survey can then be understood as the result of poorly conceived question wording that did not anticipate either life course dynamics underlying the link between family size and material wealth or the active role of children themselves in the accumulation of material wealth. This particular point may be trivial in itself, but it exposes a potentially important role of triangulation in the interpretation and explanation of study results. Two independent observations are better than one, and similar conclusions derived from different methodological approaches are stronger than those derived from one approach alone. In this case, triangulation revealed a conceptual flaw in the survey instrument that alone might lead to erroneous or contradictory interpretations.

Example 3: Determination of New Explanatory Categories

In its most ambitious form, triangulation involves the complementary use of methods to examine different dimensions of the same underlying concept, thereby arriving at a better understanding than would be possible using either approach alone. This last example, from the analysis of the effects of family size on women's employment, illustrates the use of focus groups to suggest a new explanatory category that was not fully anticipated at the time that the project was being designed and, moreover, would have been difficult to accommodate within the more rigid constraints of the survey questionnaire.

The study of this complex subject is simplified to some extent by the virtually universal precedent in rural Thailand for women to participate in agricultural and income-earning activities, often working together with their husbands. Consequently, women's work cannot be seen as a matter of individual tastes or preferences. Rather work appears to be more of a cultural and economic imperative for women, one that poses competing demands on time devoted to child care. The fertility-work relationship in this setting can be reduced to three dimensions: exclusion of women from income-earning activities while dependent children are present, temporary interruption of women's work for a variable period following each birth, and interference with women's work when child care and work responsibilities overlap.

Both the survey and focus groups were used to explore the first two dimensions, and both provided mutually confirmatory information. The exclusion of women from income-earning activities to assume full-time child-rearing responsibilities can be quickly ruled out as a viable alternative for rural Thai women. Detailed retrospective birth and work histories collected by the survey reveal that more than 90% of women worked between marriage and their first birth, between every pair of consecutive births and following the birth of their last child (Podhisita, Havanon, Knodel, & Sittitrai, 1990). The inescapable conclusion is that regardless of completed family size or birth order, virtually all women contribute directly to household economic productive activities. Qualitative analysis yields similar conclusions. The contribution to the household income by women was frequently described as a matter of necessity, making full-time child care a fanciful notion at best.

> If we don't go out to work, we won't have anything to eat. No food to take in if we spend all of our time bringing up children only.
>
> [Small family group, northern region]

The extent to which child rearing and ultimately family size relates to the temporary interruption of economic activity for women was also explored in the survey and focus group discussions. Quantitative analyses of survey data seen in Table 8.3 show very slight differences between small and large families in the median length of time that women spent away from work outside the home after each birth, on the order of 2 weeks. For both family sizes, the time of work interruption was short, between 2 and 4 months on average. Consequently, the survey suggests that the only real effect of family size on women's work would appear in the cumulative sum of time spent not working after every birth. A woman with six children by this calculation would spend up to 1 year longer away from work than a woman having two children—a relatively insignificant difference when measured out over a full lifetime (Podhisita et al., 1990).

Focus groups similarly found little difference between small and large family groups with respect to the timing of work resumption following birth. Most participants emphasized the economic pressure placed on the household and the husband when the wife is not working, and the strong incentives to return to work as soon as the child is old enough to accompany the mother out to the fields.

An additional dimension of the relationship between family size and women's work emerged from the focus group discussions, namely the tendency of child care to interfere with the productivity of the mother once she resumes economic activity following the child's birth and initial withdrawal from the labor force. The focus group discussions also make clear that, as in the case of education finance, rural parents must assume almost all of the responsibilities for early child care themselves. Until children reach school age, little support outside the family is available. Thus although rural Thai mothers manage to accommodate both work and child care at the same time, it often comes at some cost to their economic productivity. Even if we had been fully cognizant of this effect at the time of the study design, we doubt there would have been any easy way to obtain survey data to quantify work interference. As the following quotes make clear, the focus group transcripts suggest that work interference represents an extremely salient factor in the view of villagers and an important if poorly measured cost of high fertility.

[We are] very busy! While the mother works, the child asks for this and that. Now food, now drink. The mother has to frequently leave her work to take care of the child. She can't work fully.

[Small family group, northern region]

Moderator: When they are still breast feeding, do you still go out to work?

Participant 1:   We do. If there's nobody to take care of him, we take him with us.

Moderator: Is it hard?

Participant 2:   Quite hard. We can work only when the child is asleep. When they're awake, we can't.

Participant 3:   [She] has to feed him.

Participant 4:   If the child is easy, that helps because he'll sleep quite long. He'll get up to be fed before noon. But if it's a difficult child, he'll be crying when we haven't finished transplanting two bunches of sprouts, then we'll have to tend to them. Then they sleep, we resume work.

[Large family group, northern region]

The analysis of the relationship between family size and women's work demonstrates the truly independent yet complementary use of survey and focus group methods to measure one underlying concept. Focus groups are clearly limited in their ability to produce detailed individual-level information that allow the kind of retrospective birth and work histories seen in Table 8.3. Surveys suffer from their selectivity in measuring only that which can be easily quantified. Ardent advocates for either method might argue that this study might be done using only one methodological approach, but it seems clear that the combined approach in the project under discussion has extended the limits of the analysis and contributed to a better understanding of the phenomenon under study.

Table 8.3 Median Number of Months the Mother Is not Economically Active in Her Main Occupation Following the Birth of a Child, by Order of Birth and Family Size

Order of Birth	Small Family Median	N	Large Family Median	N
After 1st birth	3.5	302	2.9	306
After 2nd birth	3.4	281	2.9	302
After 3rd birth	2.1	45	3.0	303
After 4th birth	—	10	2.8	306
After 5th birth	—	2	3.7	162
After 6th birth	—	2	2.0	73

SOURCE: Podhista, Havanon, Knodel, & Sittitrai (1990).

Conclusion

The preceding examples demonstrate the ability of focus groups and surveys to complement each other in a social science study. When they are concurrently designed and implemented, focus groups and surveys provide asymmetrical but independent observations of the study population that strengthen the ability to draw conclusions as well as confidence in the nature of the conclusions themselves. When surveys and focus groups point to the same conclusions, the results of independent analyses tend to confirm each other. When analysis of either one appears to be internally inconsistent or contradictory, the other source of data may help to elaborate or clarify the underlying mechanisms that produce these inconsistencies. On those occasions in which surveys and focus groups examine different dimensions of the same underlying concepts, such as the relationship between women's work and fertility examined above, the results may lead to deeper insights into the nature of those concepts than would be possible using either methodological approach alone.

Before the implementation of the study, in the design phase of focus group guidelines and survey questionnaire, it is impossible to plan or predict how analyses will be distributed among these three possible outcomes. Unpredictability means that investment in a complementary design is a risk with no guaranteed gains, but on the other hand the gains possible usually justify the extra effort involved, and in some respect, it is precisely the unpredictability of outcomes that adds to the interest and excitement of doing this kind of research.

From a broad social science perspective, the justification for integrating survey and focus group methods might best be summarized as the potential gains to the validity of conclusions from any one study and to the generation of new hypotheses that advance research agendas. Mutual enhancement of validity provides the underlying theme for the illustrative examples of triangulation selected above. The survey research component strengthens external validity or representativeness that are the inherent weakness of small-scale, in-depth qualitative studies (Campbell & Stanley, 1966; Cook & Campbell, 1979). The focus group component in this integrated design reinforces internal validity, or the extent to which conclusions from the analysis can be said to be true of the original study population. In the alternate design language employed by Kish (1987), such a combination of qualitative and quantitative methods would mutually enhance the respective qualities of realism and representation that can be used to judge quasi-experimental and observational studies.

From the standpoint of advancing research agendas, two independent measures of the same phenomena, particularly if they involve separate methodologies, should yield not only greater analytic leverage than one approach alone but very likely conflicting, inconsistent, or unexpected results that naturally prompt the development of new explanatory hypotheses. The more conventional path to advancing theory is through repeated measurement over time, incorporating the findings from one study into the design of those that follow. Mixed method approaches simply concentrate and accelerate the process by combining the testing of hypotheses with the generation of new ones in the same step. In this respect, the combination of surveys and focus groups also synthesizes elements of grounded theory with a more conservative hypothesis-testing approach (Glazer & Strauss, 1967).

The most problematic aspect of combining different methodologies is the comparability of results. A basic ability to generalize the findings of both surveys and focus groups to some common inferential population is implicit in the notion of triangulation. Yet the same properties that make these two methods mutually complementary from a substantive analytic point of view—the breadth and abstracted individual-level detail possible in surveys and the narrow focus and depth of contextual detail possible in focus groups—tend to restrict the ability to reach common conclusions about a study population, at least not without bold simplifying assumptions. This is the juncture where instincts learned through the different training received by qualitative and quantitative researchers begin to make them feel uncomfortable. Proponents favoring quantitative approaches caution skepticism of anything labeled *typical* without careful definition and positivistic verification of the fact. Qualitative researchers may be equally skeptical of the need to generalize at all. Generalization and interpretation will continue to be a point of issue when combining methods. In the study reviewed above at least, we believe we have shown that appropriate research design can address potential incompatibilities in the analysis of these two different but complementary methods.

Notes

1. The number of focus groups in the type of research design described in this chapter is determined by the structure of the analysis. Focus groups were organized according to break and control characteristics to provide analytic contrasts between groups (see Knodel, Sittitrai, & Brown, 1990). Within any comparison category, three focus groups were conducted to reduce the possibility that the analysis would be based on an unusual set of participants or an aberrant discussion dynamic. In principle, a study design calling for numerous contrast categories and multiple groups within each category might require very large numbers of discussion sessions, although the potential cost in time and money would be considerable.

2. This use of focus groups would yield at best qualitative, approximate indicators of response error or bias. The literature reviewed by Groves (1989) on cognitive and social processes that give rise to survey error or bias relies primarily on measures embedded in the survey instrument itself. This type of interpenetrated design allows more precise estimation of error or bias for particular response items. It assumes, however, that questionnaire designers anticipate measurement error in advance.

3. It is not necessary, however, that the focus group sessions and the survey be strictly concurrent. Under some circumstances it might be more convenient for logistical reasons to conduct the fieldwork of each component separately, although typically there would not be a long gap between them.

4. The decision to limit the study frame to two sites rather than conducting a nationally representative sample was based as much on budget constraints as on compatibility between surveys and focus groups.

5. For a thorough exposition of the guiding principles and practice of this application of focus group research, see Knodel, Sittitrai, and Brown (1990).

6. All tables and focus group quotations presented below are taken from previously published reports issued in connection with the project. Each of the tables indicates the specific reference from which it is taken. In the case of the focus group quotations, those dealing with education are taken from Knodel, Havanon, and Sittitrai (1990). All other focus group quotations come from Sittitrai, Wolff, Knodel, Havanon, and Podhisita (1991).

9

Selecting Individual or Group Interviews

BENJAMIN F. CRABTREE
M. KIM YANOSHIK
WILLIAM L. MILLER
PATRICK J. O'CONNOR

Reverend Alex Trevor has devoted his life to helping people with their problems, but he has not had much success with his own problem of living with diabetes. Trevor was diagnosed with diabetes 17 years ago at the age of 52 and for 16 years has been on insulin. When he talks about having diabetes, his stories center around his struggle with weight, issues surrounding food, and the technical aspects of daily glucose monitoring and insulin injections. He describes his doctor throwing up his hands and proclaiming, "I don't know what to do with you." This, Trevor believes, is the worst thing a doctor can do for him. Overall, Trevor wishes that technology and science had more to offer. Nevertheless, Trevor is now guardedly optimistic since changing to a specialist in endocrinology whom he hopes will be more knowledgeable about the day-to-day reality of living with diabetes and more familiar with recent advances in diabetes care.

Herbert Oliver is a family physician who has cared for many people with diabetes during 20 years of private practice. During the early years of his practice, he thinks he tried to "medical school them to death," resulting in his losing patients. He now tries to "soft-pedal the whole thing," thinking it is sufficient to "see their random blood sugar under 200." He prefers that his patients not be on insulin and thinks the vast majority of his diabetic patients are under good control. Oliver feels these patients go through stages and that if they accept their identity as a diabetic and listen to their physician, they can enjoy a longer, healthier life. The key for them is to cooperate with the rules and understandings presented by the physician. He does not yet know that Trevor, one of his well-controlled diabetics, has left his practice for a specialist.

The frustration that both patients and physicians often have with respect to diabetes appears to transcend the physiology of the disorder. Clinical experiences such as the above indicate a need for a better knowledge base about the social, cultural, psychological, and physiological issues that surround the daily reality of having diabetes and the daily reality of being a health-care provider for people with diabetes. These types of complex concerns are well suited for qualitative research. Focus groups and individual in-depth interviews are two qualitative collection methods recommended and used to generate the necessary rich stories for analysis. But when to use which?

In this chapter, the decision-making process for selecting focus groups and/or individual in-depth interviews will be explored. A multimethod approach to research will provide the context for the discussion. The characteristics of focus groups and individual in-depth interviews will be compared and contrasted from this multimethod perspective. The decision-making process will then be illustrated by exploring studies that focus on the perceptions of both individuals with diabetes and the physicians involved in the care of these people.

An Introduction to Multimethod Research

Recently, qualitative research methods have made a dramatic resurgence in many disciplines that were long dominated by quantitative methods. These include such diverse disciplines as education (Lincoln & Guba, 1985), psychology (Packer & Addison, 1989), evaluation research (Patton, 1990), nursing (Morse, 1989), family studies (Gilgun, Daly, & Handel, 1992), and medicine (Crabtree & Miller, 1992; Mishler, 1986). This greater openness to qualitative methods is associated with a call for a paradigm shift, which has often led to pleas for the out-and-out rejection of the dominant positivist paradigm. Many researchers, however, are suggesting that research should be multimethod, such that data collection and analysis approaches are selected for their suitability for answering the immediate research question (e.g., see Brewer & Hunter, 1989; Miller

& Crabtree, in press). This approach is less concerned about shifting paradigms and more interested in identifying the relevant paradigm.

An essential criterion for conducting multimethod research is understanding the distinctions among paradigms, research styles, research traditions, and research methods. Three paradigms currently guide social research. *Materialistic inquiry*—also called positivism, postpositivism, and the objectivist pattern of knowing—seeks objective truth and the scientific method is the final arbiter of whether the revealed truth is objective. *Constructivist inquiry*—also known as naturalistic inquiry and the subjectivist paradigm—seeks to understand the constructions of reality created by the people being studied and by the researcher through a circle of inquiry. *Critical ecological inquiry*—also called critical science and critical theory—seeks to understand the systemic and structural issues at large and is primarily concerned with the distribution of power and elements of domination. Each of these paradigms serves as a different filter or template through which the empirical world is screened.

Different research styles and associated research methods are commonly linked with one paradigm or another. For instance, a field style of research using qualitative observational and interview methods is often used by constructivist inquirers. Materialistic or positivist researchers tend to do survey style research and use questionnaires and structured interviews. It is important, however, not to equate commonality with necessity. While research styles and methods are commonly associated with a particular paradigm, the three are independent.

This is particularly true when some people confuse constructivist inquiry and qualitative methods and use the concepts interchangeably. Although constructivist inquiry often uses qualitative methods, the two are not synonymous; furthermore, both quantitative and qualitative methods may be used in any of the three paradigms. For example, researchers operating from within a materialistic paradigm can use a qualitative method such as focus groups to help design research instruments and enhance survey style of research (see O'Brien, in this volume). Conversely, those operating under the constructivist paradigm can use the results of a survey to assist in sample selection and in better defining the topical areas for focus groups.

From a multimethod perspective, "the choice of research style for a particular project depends on the overarching aim of the research, the specific analysis objective and its associated research question, the preferred paradigm, the degree of desired research control, the level of investigator intervention, the available resources, the time frame, and aesthetics" (Miller & Crabtree, 1992b, p. 6). Thus the actual research methods employed are not a driving force and become subservient to the research goals, the immediate research questions, and the research context.

Focus Groups and In-Depth Interviews in a Multimethod Context

Multimethod research starts with goals and questions and identifies the design and methods best suited for achieving these. At one level, as noted above, this requires some thought about the fundamental ways of knowing, or paradigms, that the researcher brings to the research. At another level, the actual methods need to be delineated, including the full range of observational techniques (e.g., unstructured, direct, or participant), various types of recordings (e.g., audio, visual, or audiovisual), and documents, and many styles of unstructured, semistructured, and structured interviews and questionnaires. For many social and behavioral scientists this often becomes a decision on which interviewing strategy to use.

Focus groups and individual in-depth interviews are two forms of interviews from among a wide range of possible interviewing techniques, including key-informant interviews, life-history interviews, ethnoscience interviews, pile sorts, surveys, and questionnaires. There are also a diversity of group interview techniques (see Frey & Fontana, in this volume). In many ways, focus groups and in-depth interviews are very similar and can be equally effective in answering certain research questions. In fact, Merton and colleagues (Merton, Fiske, & Kendall, 1990), who are often cited as developing focus group research, present the focused interview as an interviewing technique that can be used with either individuals or groups. However, most researchers distinguish between focus group interviews and individual in-depth interviews, as is apparent from available sources on how to conduct each. Focus groups are covered extensively elsewhere in this book; descriptions of individual in-depth interviews include Merton et al. (1990); Douglas (1985); Gordon (1975); Lofland (1971); McCracken (1988); and Brown and Sime (1981). The approach to depth interviewing used in this chapter was influenced by the long interview, first described by McCracken (1988) and later by Crabtree and Miller (1991) and Miller and Crabtree (1992a).

Advantages and disadvantages of group versus individual interviews are briefly discussed by Merton et al. (1990), Morgan (1988), Stewart and Shamdasani (1990), and Krueger (1988) among others. With the exception of Merton et al. (1990), who cover both methods, very little on this topic is mentioned by authors who describe individual in-depth interviewing. Much of the discussion in the focus group literature centers on highlighting the advantages of using groups, particularly in the areas of dynamics (e.g., release of inhibitions, widening the range of responses, and activating forgotten details) and efficiency in time and money, and are generally limited to a few pages. Thus, the concentration is on why to select a focus group and not on the decision-making process. In fact, with the exception of Fern (1983), there appears to be very little in the way of systematic comparison from which to base any of these discussions. Empirical studies are needed to clarify some of these arguments such as systematically comparing and contrasting results from focus groups and individual in-depth interviews, perhaps by comparing some of the same participants or as a case-control type design.

The following discussion is not based on the type of empiric data just advocated but, instead, is based on the authors' experiences using both focus groups and individual in-depth interviews, including their combined use. Comparisons between focus groups and individual in-depth interviews are made in terms of economy (both time and money), depth versus breadth, interview dynamics, communication context, analysis and sampling issues, method as intervention, and logistic considerations. Within each section, the debate will focus on how design decisions relate to goals and questions.

Economy: Time and Money

Savings in terms of both time and money are cited as particular strengths of focus groups (Krueger, 1988; Stewart & Shamdasani, 1990); however, systematic studies documenting differences appear scarce. Nevertheless, our experiences working with both methods have left a number of impressions about the economy of each method.

Not unexpectedly, issues of time and money are not all that clear cut if systematically examined—there is considerable give and take in the costs of each method. The up-front planning and organizing time for focus groups is clearly greater than that of individual interviews. Many people need to be gathered together in a mutually acceptable location and time. This cost is often offset by the ability of group interviews to gather broader data more quickly, that is, there are more ideas per transcript. Payment, larger space, and refreshments are often required when conducting focus groups and the use of financial incentives for participation is more often necessary. Individual interviews are often conducted at the homes or offices of participants and financial incentives are required less often.

The number of interviews needed varies considerably with the research context for either method. The rule of thumb for conducting in-depth interviews is that it usually requires 8 to 10 interviews, although some applications might require 20 or more. Morgan (1992) cites 4 to 6 groups as typical, although he describes a study in which 30 were conducted! Thus in-depth interviews require more interviewer time, and there are often more tapes to be transcribed. The argument that using focus groups increases the sample size, however, is not valid—a focus group is not analyzed as individuals but as a group, a point we discuss further (see "Interview Dynamic").

Depth Versus Breadth

Both focus group interviews and individual in-depth interviews are touted for their ability to get at individual's perceptions of a topic of interest. Both also tend to use open-ended interview guides that allow respondents to address issues in their own terms. These similarities aside, it should be apparent that the results are going to be considerably different if 6 to 10 people are discussing a topic over the course of 1 or 2 hours than if only one person is doing so. Not only is there a different dynamic (discussed below) but there is a broader range of ideas expressed.

The difference in depth is highlighted when looking at the interview guides for each. The conversation in both focus groups and individual in-depth interviews is generally stimulated by a series of "grand tour" questions and some probes and prompts. Although it is possible to use a detailed interview guide in focus group interviews, placing too much structure may dramatically impinge the group dynamic that is found so valuable. Conversely, in depth interviewing, a detailed interview guide is generally created that includes a fairly lengthy biographical introduction and multiple, often fairly specific, probes and prompts for each grand tour question (see McCracken, 1988; Miller & Crabtree, 1992a). The goal is to probe deeply into the topic and to get an individual to tell lengthy stories with opportunity to clarify meanings and intentions.

Making decisions based on differences in depth versus breadth relates directly back to understanding the goals and questions. Many marketing applications need a broad scope—individual details are not all that relevant and certainly not worth the added effort. Focus groups, and a relatively unstructured analysis, are a natural fit. Similarly, anthropology, especially applied anthropology, is often concerned with the shared cultural understanding of a group of people and could probably make much wider use of focus groups.

Many clinical research questions, however, require a detailed understanding of what makes individuals different. The goal is to describe the unique individual and his or her perceptions. The shared understanding that comes from a group interaction may sometimes be important, but may miss the subtle individual variation that can be vital to understanding a particular health concern.

A common research goal is to quantify concepts using survey methods. It is widely recognized that both focus groups and in-depth interviews are particularly useful in the design of survey instruments (e.g., see Fuller, Edwards, Vorakitphokatorn, & Sermsri, in this volume); the goal is to identify topical areas and appropriate language. For this endeavor, focus groups may be much more economical, because the depth of information gleaned from individual in-depth interviews may be overwhelming and more than is needed.

Finally, another role of both in-depth interviews and focus groups is as a follow-up to a quantitative study. If the goal is to provide understanding of results, the greater depth of in-depth interviews might prove useful. On the other hand, if the goal is to generate working hypotheses, the breadth of focus groups might be more useful.

Interview Dynamic

There is an interpersonal dynamic in both focus group interviews and in individual in-depth interviews; however, this dynamic is very different. In the individual in-depth interview format, the dynamic is between an interviewer, who tries to set an agenda, and an individual selected to tell stories that provide insights into that agenda. The interviewer seeks rapport, creating empathy, privacy, and intimacy, as a way to gather data. The focus group uses a moderator to facilitate and manage the course of the group discussion by setting topical areas. In the focus group, the moderator often plays the part of being a guide, but within the group, a multitude of interpersonal dynamics occur and through this group interaction data are generated.

Focus group interviews use group interaction to generate data and gather insights into a research topic that would be less available without the interaction found in the group. Morgan (1988) notes "that focus groups offer a stronger mechanism for placing the control over this interaction in the hands of the participants rather than the researcher" (p. 18), and Stewart and Shamdasani (1990) present a series of "respondent interaction advantages" (relative to individual interviews) that include synergism, snowballing, stimulation, security, and spontaneity (p. 19). Stewart and Shamdasani even begin to delve into the group dynamic literature, although they fall short of discussing the many group-based intervention programs that exist (see Basch, 1987).

Setting up this group dynamic is not without costs, especially if viewed in light of the group dynamic literature—people change during the process. The unit of analysis becomes the group; the results are a shared understanding of the participants (perhaps with some minority opinions attached). Respondent's perceptions may change as they relate to others in the group and may not be consistent throughout the focus group. It may become difficult to distinguish the individual's beliefs from those expressed as a result of group pressures. Although it is possible to pick out the individuals from transcripts, the unit of analysis remains the group—focus groups are not a convenient way to bolster the sample size. The group dynamic can be particularly attractive for certain research goals and questions. The obvious examples are in marketing, where the targets of marketing strategies are consumer groups, but this also extends to educational and medical research. Understanding how people learn from each other and share strategies for coping can help highlight unintended consequences and the group dynamic can serve as an intervention strategy as participants realize they are not alone (see below, "Method as Intervention").

Communication Context

Research interviews are communicative events. Researchers selecting any interviewing technique should consider the communication style of potential respondents, including an understanding of the contexts in which the research topic is typically discussed (Briggs, 1986). There are situations in which the group is not an appropriate forum for communication or where social pressures prevent a topic from being discussed in groups. For example, the sensitivity of the topic makes it very difficult to study incest among fundamentalist Baptists in focus groups. Sometimes it is impossible to ensure that topics can be honestly discussed, because group members are necessarily known to each other. For example, in a study seeking to understand why physicians treating inner-city adolescents with sickle cell disease tend to underuse pain medications, the number of potential respondents is small and they generally know each other. The physicians would need to discuss their perceptions of African-American youth and drug use and might feel judged by people they know if interviewed in a group setting.

Analysis and Sampling Issues

Within the qualitative research literature there are a large number of possible analysis options for text data, ranging from very structured content analysis techniques to very open "immersion-crystallization" styles (for a discussion of analysis options see Miller & Crabtree, 1992b; Tesch, 1990). As Stewart and Shamdasani (1990) note, "the nature of the analyses of focus group interview data should be determined by the research questions and the purposes for which the data are collected" (p. 102). This is true not only for focus groups but for qualitative research in general, making it imperative that researchers be familiar with different methods of analysis. Researchers should not be making design decisions based on analysis considerations, but should be aware that certain analysis types may be less optimal with certain types of data. For example, the group dynamic of focus groups may make certain topics appear more important than they really are if quasi-statistical basic content analysis strategies (e.g., see Weber, 1985) are used. More methodological research is needed in this area. The unit of analysis in focus group interviews is the group and should be sampled and analyzed accordingly. Thus it might be argued that 6 to 8 focus groups are necessary for meaningful comparisons. The use of inferential statistics with focus group and individual in-depth interviews requires both an adequate sample size and a probability sample for the significance value (p) to be meaningful. The purposeful sampling generally used in qualitative interviewing makes the use of such inferential statistics very hazardous.

Method as Intervention

Small group process has long been used in health education as an intervention tool. As Basch (1987) notes,

> Focus group interviews have been employed primarily by marketing research organizations as a research tool to collect strategies for influencing consumer buying behavior. In contrast, small groups as used by health educators have been used for bringing about increased knowledge or skills or promoting planned change. (p. 414)

Clearly, it is possible to use focus groups as both a data-collection tool and an intervention simultaneously. Careful study of the group process could prove invaluable at understanding how people's perceptions change. People can recognize previously hidden parts of themselves in others. They can also reconstruct their own life narrative from others' stories.

Logistic Considerations

A final consideration that might influence the selection of focus groups and/or individual in-depth interviews involves the logistics of setting up the interviews. Individual interviews are easy to set up and are often conducted by having the interviewer travel to the residence, place of work, or some mutually acceptable location. Focus groups require a larger space and getting respondents at the same place at the same time. Some potential participants may not be mobile (e.g., home-bound elderly) or may have difficulty finding mutually agreeable times to get together; care must be given that systematic sampling bias is not introduced.

Two Illustrations

Diabetes is a chronic disorder that is frequently frustrating for both those with the disease and for those providing care for them. Many people with diabetes attend outpatient educational programs in which a multidisciplinary diabetes team articulates clear treatment goals and designs a plan to achieve these goals. A prospective epidemiological study of one such program identified four fairly distinct groups that had attended the program: (1) newly diagnosed individuals (< 2 years since diagnosis) who improved, (2) newly diagnosed individuals who did not improve (3) individuals of longer duration since diagnosis (>2 years since diagnosis) who improved, and (4) indviduals with longer duration since diagnosis who did not improve (O'Connor, Crabtree, & Abourizk, 1992). Statistically, those who had been diagnosed as diabetic for less than 2 years were nearly 2 times more likely to respond than those who had been diagnosed 2 or more years before the program. One of the goals of the research was to help improve the educational program; however, the statistical association did not provide an understanding of why there were differences. The finding prompted the question, "Who are these people and what factors lead the groups to differ in response to the program?"

**Understanding the Response
to a Diabetes Educational Program**

One approach to answering this question is to investigate the meaning that diabetes has for these individuals and to focus on understanding their perception of diabetes and the everyday impact diabetes has on them. This was conceptualized as four case studies (see Yin, 1989), with the goal of exploring and discovering the social, cultural, psychological, and physiological complexity of the issues. The researchers sought working hypotheses, breadth, and overall group differences. Focus groups could elicit detailed stories from each group and generate stories for this exploratory research whose overarching goal was to discover shared perceptions and lived understanding about diabetes. In addition, people like to share diabetes stories, making this a communication context in which focus group interviews would be ideally suited. However, in our planning we failed to account for some logistic considerations (although, in the end this contributed greatly to the findings).

In the actual study, participants for focus groups were drawn from the 163 people participating in the epidemiological phase of the project. Each group was divided into two homogenous groups based on gender. The decision to use focus groups as the primary data-collection strategy was hampered by the reality of living with diabetes. The first focus group was drawn from the largest group of patients—women with long duration of disease who had not improved more than 20%. A total of 15 women were contacted before 6 assented to participate. The reality of having diabetes for many of these women included living with some very severe health problems, which made it very difficult to travel. Many of these women, however, were willing to be interviewed at home in a face-to-face individual interview. The final study included six focus groups and 16 in-depth interviews.

One of the key distinguishing features that separated the successful and unsuccessful groups in this study was related to whether the individuals had undergone a conversion experience that changed the way they saw diabetes. Interestingly, these epiphanies had nothing directly to do with the health-care system. There were nevertheless some important implications for health-care providers. Just as Trevor at the beginning of this chapter changed physicians, many of these individuals reported that they took their diabetes more seriously and they wanted their physicians to change with them—when the physicians didn't, the respondents changed physicians. This leads to a subsequent question, "How do physicians understand diabetes and why is there so much variation in diabetes management?"

Physician Understanding of Diabetes

The second research question seeks to discover how physicians understand diabetes and select management strategies. The goal is to know the individual and not to get a shared understanding. As with the patient perception study, this research question is clearly best addressed with qualitative interviewing methods; however, the goal is to get a detailed understanding of how each individual physician makes decisions. Individual in-depth interviews are better suited to provide the personal stories that make up the individual. Although primary care physicians tend to share these types of stories in either groups or face-to-face conversations, making both focus groups and individual interviews appropriate for the communication context, past research experience has found that convening physician groups is particularly time-consuming and expensive as well as being a logistical nightmare.

In the study, 10 internists and 10 family practitioners were contacted and all agreed to be interviewed in their offices. They all also agreed to be interviewed without reimbursement. Each interview lasted approximately 1 hour and was tape recorded and transcribed. The individual face-to-face approach worked well; the physicians were very willing to discuss their strategies and the influences that led to those strategies.

Discussion and Conclusions

The illustrations in this chapter use a multimethod approach that focuses on specific goals and questions deemed important at a given point in time of a continuous research spiral. As goals and questions change, it is necessary to reassess research designs and methods to address emerging concerns. In addition to the strategies outlined, many other combinations of quantitative and qualitative methods are possible, ranging from qualitative data collection methods that include life history interviews and participant observation fieldwork to quantitative surveys and randomized controlled trial. Within this multimethod framework, if a subsequent goal of the research is to understand the culture of the care center providing the intervention better, participant observation and key-informant interviews may be useful. If, on the other hand, it was discovered that the group process in the focus group resulted in participants changing their perceptions and behavior with respect to diabetes, a randomized control trial using this group process as an intervention might be a logical next step.

Focused interviews are particularly powerful research tools that have many applications, both with individuals and in groups. The special characteristics unique to each makes it necessary to decide whether a particular project is better addressed using one method, the other, or perhaps both. Unfortunately, there are few empirical data on which to base these decisions. There is a critical need for more studies comparing focus groups and individual in-depth interviews to better understand the differences the group process has on the data and to assist in the decision-making process. Until that time, in deciding between focus groups and individual in-depth interviews, or a combination, researchers need to be cognizant of the research goals and questions and identify interviewing strategies based on the degree to which depth and/or breadth is desirable, the role interview dynamic should play, and the communication context as well as issues related to economy, analysis strategies, sampling, and logistics.

PART III

Conducting Self-Contained Research

10

Using Dialogical Research Methods in Group Interviews

RAYMOND V. PADILLA

Dialogical research uses group discussion as a means to reveal the ways in which individuals experience and act on problematic aspects of everyday life. Based largely on the work of Brazilian educator Freire (1970), dialogical research also redefines the purposes and outcomes of inquiry and recasts the roles of researchers and subjects in ways that lead to greater empowerment for the subjects. In contrast to traditional research approaches that focus on satisfying the curiosity of the investigator or the information needs of a client, the results of dialogical research are intended primarily to benefit those who agree to collaborate with the investigator in the research process. In a sense, the real investigators and clients of the research are the subjects themselves for whom the researcher becomes a facilitator of the group discussions.

As the name implies, dialogical research relies on specially structured dialogue in small groups as the chief method for revealing to the investigator and to the subjects themselves the overt and hidden aspects of problematic experiences in everyday life. Through group discussion, it is possible for individuals to make connections between personal troubles and social structures and conditions. In this respect, dialogue can be revelatory not only about the social connections to life's difficulties but also about alternative social arrangements that could improve the subjects' lives. The power of dialogue to increase awareness and to help individuals to change their circumstances derives from the potency of language itself. Language is an effective instrument both for basic communication and for critically examining the structures of meaning that individual's regularly use to articulate their understanding of things and events around them (Denzin, 1989; Gubrium, 1988). This chapter provides a summary of dialogical research methods as proposed by Freire and as implemented by me in several research projects focusing on U.S. Hispanic students. The emphasis will be on the methods rather than in the substantive results, which will only be summarized. Two examples from actual research are given. The first example follows closely the procedures described by Freire, whereas the second demonstrates how the dialogical approach can be combined with other qualitative techniques to carry out applied research in the field.

Elements of Dialogical Research

At the most general level, Freire's dialogical method involves the following items or conditions: (1) a team of investigators who are committed to improving the lives of the people that they study, (2) a group of individuals—the subjects—who are situated in a specific social, cultural, and historical context, usually under oppressive conditions with respect to economics and political power, and (3) a commitment by both the investigators and the subjects to collaborate in the investigation as a means to achieve greater empowerment for the subjects. The goal of the dialogical method is overtly political in the sense that its aim is to help the subjects achieve a higher level of awareness about the sociopolitical structures and cultural practices that have shaped their lives. By critically examining through dialogue the problematic aspects of their own lives, the subjects are able to gain the critical understanding that is necessary to identify viable alternatives to existing social arrangements and to take appropriate actions to change and improve their lives. Dialogical research, therefore, has its roots in a larger project of political freedom, cultural autonomy, and liberation from oppressive economic and social conditions.

This larger project of political emancipation and rational autonomy provides a rich intellectual and sociopolitical context within which dialogical research has evolved. Indeed, much of the discussion regarding Freire's method often focuses on this larger intellectual and political framework at the expense of methodological specificity. For those whose chief interest is ideological or political, too much attention to method and procedure seems to be a distraction. But for those who are research oriented, it is crucial to determine the specific methods and procedures used to carry out any activity labeled an investigation. At the risk of offending the sensibilities of those who might believe that Freire's thinking is too rich and complex to be reduced to a set of procedures, the following items represent one possible rendition of dialogical research as described and practiced by Freire.

1. Assemble a multidisciplinary research team. A team approach is used to bring a multidisciplinary perspective to the project. The idea is to gain a deep and comprehensive understanding of the field site to effectively fuel the dialogue that will take place among the subjects. The more that different perspectives can be brought to bear on this task, the better.
2. Select a field site that is appropriate for the research interests of the investigators and that is compatible with the underlying philosophy of the method.
3. The research team studies any available secondary sources relevant to the field site (e.g., previous studies, media accounts, documents, etc.) to develop a specific context for the fieldwork that is to follow.
4. The research team analyzes the research site using data from secondary sources and from site visits. In effect, an ethnography is produced by the research team that aims to achieve the following:

   a. Objectify the totality of the culture under investigation, i.e., the research site is seen as an object for analysis, one that is constituted as a complex social system.
   b. Break down the cultural totality of the research site through analysis. This involves finding out what is going on in the site through fine-grained analyses of events, life experiences, social structures, cultural patterns, etc.
   c. Through discussion within the research team of the various analyses made by its members, retotalize the culture under investigation. The object here is for the research team to reach a synthesis, a critically informed and integrated view, of the social system under investigation.
   d. Items b and c are performed iteratively until the research team reaches its best understanding of the situation under investigation.

e. Through the process of analysis-synthesis as described in b and c, the research team identifies the fundamental social contradictions that characterize the problematic aspects of life in the research site. These contradictions form the basis for subsequent fieldwork.

5. The research team returns to the field site to convene discussion groups among the collaborating subjects. The researchers become facilitators for the group discussions and focus dialogue on the key contradictions that were identified by the research team earlier in the investigation. However, the contradictions are not presented raw, but in codified form. Codification of a contradiction means that the essential elements of the contradiction are captured through a sketch, a picture, a song, a film, a minidrama, etc. These stimulus objects are presented to the subjects as a means to focus the group discussion. As the participants dialogue about the contradictions coded in stimulus objects, they express explicitly and implicitly their perceptions of things and events, their sense-making structures, and their fundamental orientation to the world around them.

6. The discussions of the participants are tape recorded and transcribed. These transcriptions constitute the raw data that the research team now uses for the second phase of analysis. In this phase the object is to decode the transcriptions of the group discussions. The purpose of decoding is to identify the generative themes that express the subjects' understanding about their situation. Generative themes are synthesized by the research team based on the dialogical data and reflect the basic cognitive orientations of the subjects to their daily life, how they give shape and meaning to the problematic aspects of their life experiences.

7. Like the contradictions in the first phase of the research, the generative themes also are encoded by the research team. The codified generative themes become the stimuli for further discussion by the subjects while the investigators continue to play a facilitating role. Viewed from a pedagogical perspective, the encoded generative themes form a curriculum that systematically fosters the development of critical awareness by the subjects about themselves and about the conditions that surround them. Through the development of critical awareness, or conscientization, the subjects have greater power to identify and enact viable alternatives to existing social arrangements that may not be serving them well.

Although there are many similarities between Freire's dialogical research and other qualitative methods, there are some interesting contrasts. For example, in dialogical research the subjects of the investigation also are the recipients of the knowledge gained through the investigation. Furthermore, the subjects are allies and collaborators in the research project along with the investigating team. Thus dialogical research is centripetal in that it tends to fuse the roles of subject, researcher, and client. Under such conditions, the results of the research are not necessarily evidenced by the typical ethnographic report or publication but by the actions that the subjects may take to change their world. The investigation results not in isolated knowledge but in knowledge in action. Thus the research act is aimed directly at changing social structures first by changing participant perspectives about existing social relations, conditions, and arrangements and then by allowing the participants the opportunity to envision viable alternatives. These alternatives then can be implemented by the subjects through appropriate cultural and political actions.

Another contrast is the role of the investigator. Because the object of dialogical research is action by the subjects themselves, the role of the investigator becomes one of facilitating the research of the subjects as they critically examine their world. This facilitating role requires a great deal of research in its own right because the investigator must carefully select the stimuli that will guide the subjects' dialogue along productive channels. Success would be highly unlikely if the investigator simply put forth his or her own preconceived ideas about what the subjects need to make their lives better. The contradictions that are used as stimuli for dialogue must be genuinely grounded in the life situation of the subjects. It is up to the investigators to do the necessary work to capture effectively the internal contradictions of the situation in question. It is in this phase of the investigation that the work of the investigators appears more like conventional fieldwork. Indeed, many of the standard field methods could be used effectively in this phase of dialogical research. However, once the contradictions are identified, the investigators shift the locus of knowledge from themselves to the subjects. The shift is carried out in two ways—in terms of knowledge production and knowledge consumption. Thus the essential role of the investigators in dialogical research is to facilitate the production of knowledge by and for the subjects.

Hispanics, Schools, and Universities

The first example is a pilot study that was conducted by me and several graduate students to test the feasibility of using dialogical research methods in a non-third world country, namely the United States. Although a developed country, the United States still can be viewed in some respects as containing within its population some sectors that display social, cultural, economic, and political characteristics quite similar to those found in third world populations. Some scholars have gone so far as to argue that the United States manifests internal colonialism with respect to certain segments of its population, for example, U.S. Hispanics, blacks, and native Americans (Acuña, 1972; Bailey & Flores, 1973; Flores, 1973). Others (Ogbu, 1978) argue that American society can be seen as incorporating castelike groups as exemplified by African-Americans and other minorities. These arguments provide a basis for testing Freire's dialogical methods with minority groups in the United States. Because he explicitly developed the methods as a way to change social, political, and economic relationships between those who hold power and those who do not, it seems plausible that the methods could be used with minority groups in the United States who also are significantly disenfranchised and powerless in comparison with the larger society.

The specific aim of the pilot project was to implement Freire's dialogical method as outlined above, paying particular attention to the research team's analysis of the research site and the identification of key contradictions, to be followed by the encoding of those contradictions, presenting them to small groups of Hispanic students, and then decoding the resulting dialogical data to identify generative themes. At this point the pilot project came to a conclusion; no attempt was made to use the generative themes for further discussion by the subjects or to implement an action agenda.

The research site was a large southwestern university that enrolls a substantial number of minority students in the context of a predominantly white institution. The minority students—largely Hispanics, blacks, and native Americans—constitute significant ethnic enclaves on campus even though these minority groups are considerably underrepresented compared with their numbers in the state's population. These enclaves are active in the area of student affairs (including student recruitment and tutoring) and in promoting cultural diversity activities such *Cinco de Mayo* week and Martin Luther King Day. The corresponding ethnic communities in the surrounding area also are quite active politically and continuously pressure the university to increase the enrollment levels of minority students as well as their degree attainment rates.

The subjects for the pilot project were Hispanic undergraduate students, mostly juniors and seniors. Three dialogical group sessions were organized in which six to eight subjects participated. Membership in the three groups was fluid and overlapping. Both males and females participated in the groups. The students were recruited on an opportunity basis, largely from the local Movimiento Estudiantil Chicano de Aztlán (MECHA) organization. Discussions were informal; the graduate students and I acted as moderators.

Before organizing the discussion groups, the research team spent considerable time identifying the salient contradictions that were experienced by the subjects both at the university and during their prior schooling. This analysis was driven mostly by reading various reports that had been produced by the university dealing with minority issues and by interviewing Hispanic students to determine how they were experiencing the campus and, more generally, how they had experienced schools. On the basis of these discussions, the research team identified the three following contradictions.

1. *The isolated individual.* The isolation contradiction reflects the subjects' contention that while they were going to school their parents' advice was seen as inconsistent with reality. This may have something to do with the low levels of educational attainment of Hispanics generally and the consequent unfamilarity with educational institutions, particularly high schools and colleges. Another element of this contradiction is that on occasion students found themselves to be "acting Anglo." They also believed that they had been subjected to ridicule and to deferential behavior in their social relationships. In addition, they sometimes felt singled out in class in the sense of having to represent their group or being obligated to assume an ethnic role regardless of whether they felt like doing so or not. Finally, they reported receiving double messages from Anglos concerning schooling. For example, high school counselors would not encourage the students to go to college, whereas the virtues of higher education were generally extolled.

2. *Achievement at a cost.* The second contradiction has to do with a sense of social disconnectedness as the price for academic achievement. Students thought that they were forced to choose between achievement in a socially disconnected Anglo environment and a socially connected

ethnic environment but with little achievement. Also, achievement was only possible for the *super-Mex,* that is, a Hispanic who was a super performer. One could not simply be average and blend with the rest of the crowd. Another aspect of this contradiction is that students sometimes kept their academic plans secret because of fear of failing. Similarly, they sometimes doubted good grades because they were unsure as to whether the good grades represented their ability or simply the instructor's concession to ethnicity. On the whole, the university was seen as impersonal and as posing many difficulties. Academic failure was attributed to the lack of adequate role models.

3. *Ethnic identity as problematic.* The third contradiction reflects the sense of ambiguity, indeterminacy, and transition that Hispanic students reported with respect to their ethnic identity. Students felt that they belonged yet that they were distant from the Hispanic groups on campus. They wondered if on occasion they were passing for Anglos. Some concealed the financial aid that they were receiving, because the Anglo students might feel offended by it. They also were concerned about interethnic dating. Finally, some had noticed that others who were not Hispanics desired to be so.

After these contradictions were identified, the research team proceeded to encode them to produce stimulus objects that would guide the subjects in group discussions. The procedure chosen was to prepare short narrative vignettes that captured the essential elements of each contradiction. These vignettes would then be distributed at the group meetings and read aloud by the moderator while the subjects read them silently. One group session was devoted to each contradiction. A following sample vignette encodes the first contradiction.

Josefina Goes to College

Josefina Amésquita is a freshman at Large State University (LSU). She lives at home with her parents in the south part of town.

While in high school, Josefina's mother encouraged higher education; her father said nothing. They felt very proud of Josefina when she graduated, because they did not have the opportunity to even complete the sixth grade.

During Josefina's high school years there was little motivation or encouragement from her counselor to attend college. Josefina also had a boyfriend who dropped out of high school and joined the army. He kept in touch with Josefina and wanted to marry her. Josefina received a scholarship to attend LSU.

As a freshman at LSU, Josefina enrolled in English 101, and on the first day of class she was amazed at the number of students in her class. She also noticed that there were no Hispanic students besides herself. As the professor went through roll call he came to Josefina's name and could not pronounce it correctly. One of the professor's assignments was discussion of various topics. Josefina was assigned to chair the group investigating "Hispanic issues."

Josefina found LSU to be very large and at times uncomfortable. During lunchtime, she usually ate by herself. She also did not have time to make new friends because she commuted to LSU.

Recently, Josefina received a letter from her boyfriend. The letter stated that he would be coming home for Christmas.

This narrative vignette, along with the others that encoded the other two contradictions, formed the stimuli that guided the discussion groups. The discussions were tape recorded and analyzed by the research team. On the basis of this analysis two generative themes were identified: Education as a struggle and the problematic nature of maintaining an ethnic identity.

The struggle to obtain a good education is fueled by social barriers originating in the larger society or in the ethnic group itself. These can be labeled external and internal barriers, respectively. Examples of the external barriers include racist or insensitive school counselors and teachers, lack of economic opportunity, prejudice among majority students, and tracking in schools. Examples of internal barriers include a tendency by peers to mock school achievement, pressures to stick to one's own, and family obligations.

The second generative theme is a complex of social and cultural pressures that can be summarized as community-family-identity. This theme reflects the changing roles that Hispanics in college experience as they become an educated elite. It also reflects the ongoing transformation of the group itself as it interacts more intensely with mainstream institutions and across a broader spectrum of social structures. College-educated Hispanics have multiple options in terms of languages, cultures, and social relations. As they assume professional roles, Hispanics feel the need to define the relationship between professional status and membership in an ethnic community, particularly the obligation that they may feel to advance the economic status of people still in the barrios. At the same time, traditional roles within the ethnic culture seem to be shifting quite rapidly. Children's relationship to parents, gender-based relationships, and the status of the family itself may be changing as a result of influences from American mainstream culture and economic necessity. These family-centered roles can become problematic as the ethnic culture itself shifts and as individuals adopt new rolls within the larger culture. All of these cross-pressures are further intensified by the tension that exists between ethnic loyalty and assimilation or acculturation into the mainstream culture. This is a historic process that forces Hispanics to reassess their preferred ways of relating to, and identifying with, both the ethnic and the majority cultures. Hispanic students are subjected to strong pressures by peers and significant others to maintain their ethnic allegiance and heritage while equally strong pressures are exerted by the majority culture and institutions for assimilation.

These two generative themes, identified through dialogical research, could be used as a foundation for making positive changes in the ways that Hispanics deal with the problems, opportunities, and choices that they face in a rapidly changing society. More specifically, the generative themes can become the focus of further dialogical research to improve college performance and degree attainment. As a starting point, the themes could be codified and presented to small groups of Hispanic students as part of an orientation program when they get to college and as a way of providing support as they progress through the curriculum. Through such dialogical groups, the students themselves could fashion viable solutions to the problems of ethnic affiliation, changing social roles, and their obligations to the Hispanic community.

Dialogical Research Combined With Other Field Strategies

The first example shows how dialogical research can be applied in a developed country in much the same way that it was applied in the underdeveloped countries for which it was developed. In this application, the method is literally transplanted and applied to a special segment of U.S. society in which the social conditions seem to parallel those in the third world, namely a set of colonial relationships that in the context of the United States are expressed as internal colonialism. The method is applied in both instances as a means to help colonized people to achieve greater autonomy and freedom from oppressive social conditions. But the dialogical method can be made more general if it is combined with more traditional field methods such as ethnography and focus group research. The second example illustrates this hybrid version of dialogical research.

The research problem was to find ways to improve the success of Hispanic students in a large, multicampus community college system in the Southwest. The project was initiated by high level administrators of the community college district who felt the need to improve the recruitment and retention of Hispanic students. In this respect, the research project had a recognizable sponsor or client who was interested in the results of the research. However, the goal of the research was to help the Hispanic students become more successful in college; in this sense, they were the ultimate clients of the research.

Often a research project of this type might focus on the causes or dynamics of students dropping out of college. There is a large body of literature, particularly influenced by Tinto's (1987) model of institutional departure, that can be brought to bear on this issue. However, the researchers working on the project decided to frame the issue differently: What do successful students know and do to make them successful in the target college system? The idea was to understand better the experiences of successful students to shape accordingly the experiences of new students so that they also could be successful.

The research was approached from the perspective that successful students must overcome a number of barriers as they enter college and finally exit with their diplomas in hand. The problem then was to find out what specific barriers the successful students had to overcome, determine what they had to know to overcome them, and identify what specific actions they took to overcome each barrier. In terms of dialogical research, the college setting was problematized with the successful, rather than the unsuccessful, students as the focus of attention. The implicit contradiction that the subjects were to address dialogically was that students had to overcome barriers if they wanted to be successful. By focusing the subjects' attention on successful students, the relevant barriers could be identified along with the knowledge base and action repertoire needed to overcome them in the specific setting that was studied.

Procedurally, several sets of discussion groups were organized in two campuses of the target community college district. In each campus, discussion groups were organized among students, faculty, and administrators, including counselors. The three types of discussion groups made it possible to contrast the views of students, faculty, and staff on the key question of how successful students overcome barriers to success. The stimulus used to guide the discussion was an empty matrix (Miles & Huberman, 1984) that began with a single word—*barriers*—as a cover term (Spradley, 1979) that was to be expanded exhaustively by the subjects. The matrix was taped to a wall and filled in by the moderator as the subjects dialogued about the various barriers that successful students had to overcome. Tandem group interviews were used to complete each matrix by the various types of respondents (students, faculty, and staff). In tandem group interviews, one small discussion group contributes as much information as possible within the allotted time then a second group continues the discussion adding data to the various vectors of the matrix until collectively several groups fill the matrix entirely. The matrix itself had a number of columns, including the lead column headed by the *barriers* cover term and two other columns to capture the knowledge and the actions needed to overcome each barrier. Thus *knowledge* and *actions* were the cover terms for their respective data vectors. The rows of the matrix were used to capture the essential points made by the subjects regarding the topics that were identified by the cover terms. Such a matrix can be expanded dynamically both in terms of the relevant concepts that are to be explored (cover terms) and the elaboration of those concepts by the subjects (rows of data). In theory, the matrix allows the investigators to expand the group discussion to any practical degree of information saturation without losing the open-ended quality of the discussion.

Analysis of the completed matrices revealed that the identified barriers could be categorized into five classes. There were institutional barriers such as the admissions process, lack of mentors, and lack of student input into academic affairs. Another class of barriers was directly related to the classroom and instruction. Exemplars of this class included the student's lack of academic preparation, lack of study skills, the delivery of instruction, and the instructor's sensitivity (or lack thereof) to the students. A third class of barriers focused on the student's environment outside of campus. Examples of this class included cultural differences, lack of family support, and lack of social acceptance within the community. The fourth class of barriers had to do with financial matters. Some students failed to qualify for financial aid, they needed part-time work, and they lacked money management skills. Finally, the fifth class of barriers focused on the individual in the sense of personal characteristics. Examples of this class included unclear educational goals, lack of self-esteem, "unfair world" attitude, and culture shock from lack of ethnic students in classes. Thus through dialogical research an exhaustive listing of barriers to student success was made and reduced to a handful of classes by the analysts.

In a similar manner, the knowledge and action vectors were submitted to analysis and each reduced to a small number of classes. For example, the knowledge vector was condensed into four classes. The first class, general knowledge, restricts in meaningful ways the search space for a solution to a given barrier. This type of knowledge also can be likened to awareness of the general nature of a solution. The second class is specific knowledge. This type of knowledge points to a specific solution to a given barrier. Thus each barrier is mapped to at least one viable solution. The third class is incremental knowledge. Such knowledge is typically an extension of existing knowledge to improve a particular skill or to enlarge a specific knowledge base. This type of knowledge usually is acquired by special instruction, such as tutoring or by accessing sources of knowledge such as textbooks and libraries. Finally, the fourth class of knowledge is procedural knowledge. This type of knowledge provides specific directions or the steps to be taken to overcome a barrier. Thus procedural knowledge is prescriptive or formulaic.

The richness of the dialogical data provided an opportunity for more than cataloging and categorizing the items contributed by the subjects. By taking the matrix as a whole, one can begin to see connections and relationships between the discrete items in the cells, the concepts implied by the cover terms, and the extended discussion of the subjects among themselves and with the moderator. In this particular study, it became clear that the dialogical data could make an important contribution to theory. The knowledge and actions of successful students implied that successful students are in fact experts at being students. The knowledge that makes them experts is not the formal knowledge that they are seeking and acquiring as they attend classes. Rather it is the locally and experientially acquired knowledge, the heuristic knowledge (Harmon & King, 1985), of the campus that enables them to survive the college environment and then to master the formal knowledge that is the official basis for receiving a diploma. The contribution to theory is that success in college is based not only in the acquisition of formal knowledge but also in the prior or simultaneous acquisition of heuristic knowledge, which has quite different characteristics from formal knowledge, for example in terms of timing, distribution, recognized status, manner of acquisition, and use. This theoretically important finding also has implications for practice. For example, programs designed by student services specialists that aim to enhance the academic success of Hispanic students should include specific components that help the students to master the heuristic knowledge appropriate for their campus.

Conclusion

The two examples of dialogical research show that this approach can be used in developed countries in at least two ways. Among those segments of the population that have experienced a historical condition of discrimination and lack of power, dialogical research can be applied in much the same manner as in third world countries, where the method was developed to help people construct a more democratic society. In countries such as the United States, these groups might include racial, ethnic, and linguistic minorities; gender or sexual preference groups that feel discriminated against; religious groups; labor unions; and so forth. For such groups, the purpose of dialogical research would be to raise their collective understanding of their situation and to find viable alternatives for the social arrangements that have created the oppressive conditions in which they live.

The second example shows that dialogical research can be effectively combined with more traditional field research methods to gain theoretical and practical knowledge about a particular problem or social situation. By carefully constructing the research questions and the stimulus objects, the researcher can deal effectively with such important methodological considerations as bounding of the data collection (Miles & Huberman, 1984) and saturation of grounded concepts (Glaser & Strauss, 1967). Moreover, because dialogue has a powerful conditioning effect on the subjects, dialogical research also can be used as a direct way to change the knowledge, attitudes, and behavior of the subjects. This is a very potent feature of the method that can have general applicability to any group or organization that has a problematic situation that needs changing.

11

Focus Group Research
on Sensitive Topics

Setting the Agenda Without Setting the Agenda

RICHARD A. ZELLER

Every research design contains both opportunities and risks. The effective user of a research design finds ways simultaneously to capitalize on the opportunities and to avoid or mitigate the risks. One of the major opportunities of focus group research is the exploration of sensitive topics. A major risk in such research is that participants will respond to the situation in ways that lack fidelity to their actual opinions, attitudes, values, orientations, and behaviors. The burden of setting an agenda which will both capitalize on the opportunity and mitigate the risk falls on the moderator. The purpose of this chapter is to discuss the options available to the moderator and the impact of employing these various options.

A focus group researcher can use a variety of tools for setting the agenda of a focus group on sensitive topics. This needs to be done without producing excessively socially desirable responses. These tools include the screener questionnaire, the introductory comments before the focus group session, and reactions to participants' comments during the focus group session. The thesis of this chapter is that each of these activities should be conducted so as to enhance the capacity of the focus group to elicit sensitive information from participants while minimizing socially desirable responses.

A researcher can use a variety of tools for setting the agenda of focus groups on sensitive topics without producing excessively socially desirable responses. These tools have purposes. The effective researcher will use the tools to capitalize on known principles of social behavior to achieve the research objectives. In this chapter, I shall argue that the effective researcher should:

1. Capitalize on the methodological principle of reactivity in the screener questionnaire;
2. Capitalize on the communications principle of self-disclosure in the introductory comments;
3. Capitalize on the social psychological principle of legitimation in reactions to participants' comments.

The Screener Questionnaire: Capitalizing on Reactivity

Reactivity refers to the phenomenon that the very process of measurement can induce change in the phenomenon itself. Ever since Star and Hughes (1949-1950) demonstrated that people who get asked political questions at time 1 are more knowledgeable about political issues at time 2 than people who do not get asked political questions at time 1, methodologists have warned researchers about the negative effects of reactivity. These testing effects are often presented as competing hypotheses to the substantive hypotheses concerning group differences.

In focus group research the principle of reactivity can and should be converted from a liability into an asset. If the participants in a focus group have to spent some time thinking about the topic to be discussed before the focus group, the conversation will be more informative and lively. Therefore, it is in the interest of the researcher to find finesseful ways to get the participants to mull over the topic before the focus group session. Reactivity can be used to accomplish this objective.

Ordinarily, participants are recruited for participation into a focus group using a screener questionnaire. Items on this questionnaire are designed to ensure that the participants meet the demographic and behavioral criteria that have been established for focus group participation. These items usually are presented in a qualification format. If the potential participant answers a question in one way, the questionnaire continues; if he or she answers the question in another way, the questioning is ended and the person is not invited to participate in the focus group.

Often times, in deference to the negative connotation usually associated with reactivity, researchers will scrupulously avoid asking any questions about the topics to be discussed in the focus group. They wish to avoid biasing or prejudicing the participants. This does not, of course, mean that the participants do not have any expectations about what is going to occur at the soon-to-occur focus group. It only means that the participants make up their own definition of what will occur.

One thesis of this chapter is that, in addition to using it for participant selection, the screener questionnaire should also be used to sensitize the participants to the topics to be discussed in the focus group. In addition to participant selection items, questions relevant to the topics to be discussed should be asked. For example, if one is conducting a focus group on adolescent sexual activity, a screener questionnaire should ascertain qualification for such groups (age, gender, etc.). In addition, questions should be asked about sexual activity, frequency and variety of partners, appropriate level of commitment to partners, use of contraceptives, sexually transmitted disease considerations, etc.

The principle of reactivity suggests that the asking of such sensitive questions will alert the participants to those topics. While such awareness might threaten the validity of a survey or experiment, it is here argued that it enhances the value of the participants' comments in a focus group. This enhancement occurs because the time and attention that the participant devotes to the focus group is not only the 2 hours in the discussion but also the days or weeks before the focus group during which the participant is mulling over the issues raised reactively in the screener questionnaire. Participants are going to mull over what they say before they say it. The issue is whether they have the opportunity to mull it over for minutes or days. Hence, I am challenging the classic: "Say the first think that comes into your mind" ideology of researchers such as McClelland (1961). Instead, I am arguing that our information about their reflected self-appraisal will have more fidelity to what they really think if they have some time to put their thoughts together. This is more likely to occur when participants are sensitized to the topics to be discussed in a focus group days or weeks in advance than when they discover what topics are to be discussed as the discussion unfolds.

Introductory Comments:
Capitalizing on Self-Disclosure

Self-disclosure is a communication in which one person tells another something that he or she does not tell just anyone (Hybels & Weaver, 1989, p. 145). A major principle of interpersonal communication is that a relationship is enhanced by providing enough but not too much personal, private information about oneself to an other; either too little or too much revelation undermines the relationship. There is a range of acceptable self disclosure.

Figure 11.1 presents a schematic representation of the relationship between the level of self-disclosure and the acceptability of the disclosure by the other. An examination of Figure 11.1 reveals the curvilinear nature of this relationship. Self's disclosure is unacceptable to the other when it is inadequate (too low, or below 6); the acceptability curve between letters *a* and *e* is below the line of marginal acceptability. Self's disclosure is also unacceptable to the other when it is excessive (too high, or above 12); the acceptability curve between letters *k* and *o* is below the line of marginal acceptability. An appropriate level of self-disclosure is between 6 and 12; the acceptability curve between letters *e* and *k* is above the line of marginal acceptability. Optimal self-disclosure is at point 9 represented by the letter *h*.

Inadequate Self-Disclosure

Self's disclosure to an acquaintance other is inadequate in the following conversation:

Self: Good morning.

Other: Hi, how are you?

Self: What makes you want to know?

Other's "Hi, how are you?" was a greeting. However, self's reaction to other's greeting was that self was not going to reveal the slightest detail of her condition. Self was playing her cards too close to the vest. An appropriate response of modest self-disclosure would have been, "I'm fine, how are you." Indeed, self may have responded in this fashion even if she was not feeling well at all. Such a response in such a condition is a socially desirable response designed to foster a comfortable interac-

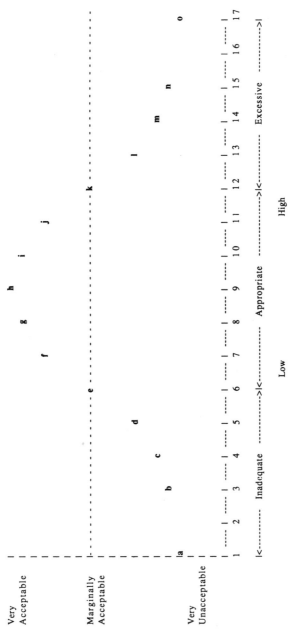

Figure 11.1 A Schematic Representation of the Relationship Between Level of Self-Disclosure and the Acceptability of the Self-Disclosure by the Other

tion even when it does not have fidelity with how self actually feels. In Figure 11.1, location *d* above point 5 is approximately the location of self's response to other as described above. This conversation could be transformed into the acceptable range (i.e., location *f* above point 7) if it were to continue as follows:

Other: I was just interested.

Self: Okay. I'm fine.

The modest increase in self-disclosure has moved self's behavior into the acceptable range.

People often use inadequate self-disclosure as a means of punishing others. The person who refuses to talk to his or her spouse because of a disagreement about the disciplining of the children is using an inadequate level of self-disclosure to indicate displeasure with the spouse's position with respect to the issue at hand. The dunkard practice of shunning, in which nobody will talk to the person who has broken the rules of the order, is also in the tradition. The negative impact of this inadequate level of self-disclosure is represented by location *a* above point 1 in Figure 11.1.

Excessive Self-Disclosure

Self's disclosure to an acquaintance, other, is excessive in the following conversation:

Self: Good morning.

Other: Hi, how are you?

Self: I'm just rotten. I'm having my period and the cramps are awful. Thank God! I thought I was pregnant by Charlie, the jerk. I just broke up with him, and boy did I tell him off. Did you know that while he was going with me, he was screwing Barbara? He had the gall to start describing their sex, like in graphic detail, all his techniques for giving her oral sex and everything! I don't know how he could have gotten me pregnant, he couldn't even cum! Can you believe his gall?

Whether self's self-disclosure was excessive depends on the kind of relationship self has with other. If they were casual friends, self's reaction to other's greeting provided grossly excessive detail concerning her private, personal life. In this situation, self's disclosure was at location *o* above point 17 in Figure 11.1.

If self and other had a close and intimate relationship, self's comments may have been excessive but would be handled within the relationship. In this situation, self's disclosure was at location *l* above point 13 in the figure.

A more appropriate level of self-disclosure is illustrated in the following conversation:

Self: Good morning.

Other: Hi, how are you?

Self: I've felt better. I just broke up with Charlie. That's a bummer.

In this conversation, self is indeed responding to other's question. Her response on this occasion provides appropriate, perhaps high, but not excessive information about self's condition. The door has been left open to either further exploration of what happened (i.e., other might ask, "Do you want to talk about it?") or not. In this situation, self's disclosure was at location *j* above point 11. Thus the appropriateness of the level of self-disclosure depends on the circumstances surrounding the interaction and who is participating in it.

Finesseful use of self-disclosure can alter the intimacy of a continuing relationship. That is, self can use disclosure as a Goffmanesque impression-management tool to make the relationship with other more or less intimate (Goffman, 1959). Assuming that self wants the relationship to continue but in an altered form, all self-disclosure should be within the span of appropriateness (between points 6 and 12). To make a continuing relationship less intimate, the self-disclosure should move from location *h* to location *e;* to make a continuing relationship more intimate, self-disclosure should move from location *h* to location *k*. To terminate a relationship, self-disclosure should be moved to either below location *e* or to above location *k*.

Use of Self-Disclosure to Enhance
Focus Group Discussions

The second thesis of this chapter is that an optimal option for setting the agenda of focus groups on sensitive topics is the finesseful use of an appropriate level of self-disclosure by the moderator. Consider the outcomes of the focus group desired by the moderator. The moderator, a stranger to the participants, wants them to discuss a sensitive, intimate, and personal topic. To do this, the moderator needs to establish substantial interpersonal rapport. However, the moderator ordinarily has no more than 15 to 30 minutes to establish rapport. The goal of moderation during these first 15 to 30 minutes is to create a social climate in which the participants feel free to discuss the sensitive topics on the moderator's topic outline guide.

To achieve this goal, the moderator needs simultaneously to put the participants at ease about the new and potentially threatening situation presented by the focus group and to create a setting within which they will reveal intimate aspects of their private, personal lives. Self-disclosure can be used to achieve these goals. The general principle is that self-disclosure must be appropriate but higher than optimal. In Figure 11.1, the level of self-disclosure by the moderator should be between optimal and excessive at location j or k. The moderator is attempting, within 2 hours, to entice the participants into revealing information about themselves that they would not reveal in the vast majority of interaction situations. Hence, a relatively high (but not excessive) level of self-disclosure by the moderator will accelerate the willingness of the participants to disclose private, personal information about themselves.

The introductory remarks by the moderator can be used to establish this high but not excessive level of self-disclosure. After the welcome and an explanation to the participants about the focus group procedures, taping, one-way mirror, and so on, the moderator's attention turns to the question of getting the discussion started. The participants' suspicion, based on the questions asked in the screener questionnaire, was that the focus group would concentrate on sexual decision making. It is argued here that sexual decision making is, indeed, a sensitive topic for which a high but not excessive level of self-disclosure will create a social climate within which participants will be comfortable talking.

As an illustration, the following verbatim transcription was taken from a focus group of 18- to 19-year-old women in a focus group moderated by a 45-year-old man. The challenge for the moderator was to convey to the opposite-sex, different-age participants an openness about their own private behaviors. The moderator's story followed by initial interaction among the participants was as follows:

Moderator: The discussion is on sexual decision making and interpersonal relationships between those of the female and those of male arrangements. Tomorrow night, we are talking to the guys to see what their view of this thing is.

Participant: I'd like to listen to that. *[laughter]*

Moderator: There is every reason to believe that . . .

Participant: [Like] Oprah Winfrey! *[laughter]*

Moderator: There is every reason to believe that girls and guys see sex differently.

Participant: I can tell you that right now. *[laughter]*

Moderator: What I would like to do for openers is to go around the table and have each of you introduce yourselves and provide us with some tidbit that applies to somebody you know . . . a circumstance that involves some sort of sexual decision making.

The laughter and cryptic comments by participants during the introductory remarks were encouraged by the moderator and aided in the establishment of rapport. Moreover, the moderator encouraged participants to talk about somebody they knew (rather than themselves). In this way, the self-disclosure expected of the participants was moderated. Ultimately, however, the results of the focus group would be enhanced if the participants did engage in substantial self-disclosure. Hence, the introductory story by the moderator reflected substantial self-disclosure

Moderator: Let me start, for openers, with myself. I should warn you that, you know, when you are on the dark side of 40, it's a different game. *[laughter]* This story is about when I was a freshman in college in 1962. A few years have rolled off the clock since then. I had been in college about 3 weeks and here was this relatively good-looking girl. She wasn't a knockout, but she was very nice. It was a weekend when we were going to go out to the desert. This was in southern California, where I lived. It was about a 2-hour drive to Joshua Tree National Monument. If you've never been there, it's really nice. It's about half an hour north of Palm Springs. There are great rock formations, and you can climb all over the place. We had a group of about 50 of us so we took 10 or 12 cars, and we all piled in the cars and went sailing out there. There were 6 of us in our car, 4 in the backseat and the driver and his date in the front seat.

We are driving along the freeway trying to get out of the southern California smog, and, you know, she and I were sort of, uh, getting to know each other. We had not been in the car for more than a half an hour when the following conversation took place:
She said, "I need to tell you something."
I asked, "What?"
She said, "I'm a diabetic."
I responded, "Okay." I thought, What does that have to do with me?
She said, "Some times I have seizures."
I asked, "What is involved in having a seizure?"
She said, "I sometimes absolutely lose control. I'll bend over. I'll start shaking. When I have a seizure, I need insulin."
I asked, "Do you have any insulin with you?"
She answered, "Yes. As a matter of fact, if I have a seizure, you have to inject the insulin into me."
I said, "Okay."
Her comments threw me a little bit because the dates that I had been on had not started like this before. So I said, "Do you want to walk me through this thing?"
She gets out of her purse this little kit. It has a syringe and a vile of insulin. I am supposed to stick the syringe into the vile in insulin and then pull the little plunger out so that the insulin goes into the syringe. And then, I'm supposed to undo her pants, take them down, and put that thing into her rear end and shoot it into her. I had never, in my life, been on a date where, after 30 minutes, my date had told me how to take her pants off! [laughter] This was no laughing matter, because, in point of fact, from her perspective, her life was seriously in jeopardy. Anyone she went out with . . . anyone she spent time with, needed to be prepared to save her life. So it wasn't a trivial kind of thing. So I said, "Okay."
We went on out to the desert. We went out to Joshua Tree and we all got together. We had all these rules of what we were going to do out there. You have to hike in pairs because if you hike alone, you can get lost. In the low desert of southern California in September, it can get hotter than the blazes, and you can die. So you have to have some guidelines as to how you behave. So we went through these guidelines and off we went into some of the most exciting rock climbing. We all headed off in our various directions. She and I went off and we were having a very good time.

And all of a sudden, you know what happens in those kinds of circumstances . . . there were lots of little coves and nooks and crannies where you can . . . be. [*nervous laughter from participants*] And we got into one of those little nooks and crannies and . . . all of a sudden, . . . she was all over me. [*more nervous laughter*] She was fairly sexually assertive. I tried to keep up my end of the bargain as well as I could, but I was not the most experienced person in the world. We had a *very* good time. . . . Nothing *serious* happened, but we had a lot of fun. [*more nervous laughter*] After we were finished with that, we hiked for a while. Then we got back at the appointed time. We had a big fire and ate hot dogs and went back to town. We had a wonderful time.

The vibes were not there for us to continue the relationship. She was far more interested in finding a husband than I was in being one at the time. Within the next 6 months, she found one, dropped out of school. The last I heard from her was about a year after that when she had a baby and had started her life. Let's see, her baby was born in 1963 so, let's see now, the kid is now 26 . . . older than most of you, I suppose. I went on to school and had lots of other, uh, interesting experiences, but that is the one that I thought I would share with you.

This story was longer than the usual introductory comments, which often include only one's name, age and place of residence. Moreover, the comments involved sufficient self-disclosure to elicit nervous laughter on a number of occasions. Indeed, the nervous laughter occurred when the self-disclosure was substantial and approached being excessive (location k). However, it is argued here that such self-disclosure sets the stage for the participants to talk about their own experiences with the sensitive topic of sex in this research setting. The experience in this group appeared to bear out this hunch.

The purpose of high but not excessive self-disclosure is to increase the range of appropriate self-disclosure upward. The moderator's goal in the introductory comments is to increase the appropriate level of self-disclosure. Although the lower bound of acceptable self-disclosure need not be increased, the upper bound must be increased if the focus group is going to accomplish its objective of exploring sensitive topics—because a sensitive topic is a topic on which participants are hesitant to engage in discussion. Consequently, by definition, a moderator who successfully addresses a sensitive topic must find a way to increase the upper bound of acceptable self-disclosure. So that focus groups on sensitive topics can be productive, the appropriate range of self-disclosure needs to be increased quickly and substantially.

In Figure 11.1, a successful focus group will occur only if the upper bound of appropriate self-disclosure is increased from 12 to about 18 or 20. This is because *participants must be willing to say things in the focus group that are very unacceptable and clearly excessive self-disclosure in ordinary conversation if the endeavor is going to explore successfully sensitive topics.* The moderator's goal is clear. The moderator must either change the definition of appropriate self-disclosure or fail to explore fully the sensitive topic; both cannot be simultaneously accomplished within one interaction setting.

Encouraging Diversity:
Capitalizing on Legitimation

At this juncture in the focus group, the moderator must shift the conversation to the participants themselves. In focus groups on sensitive topics, this shift should be done in such a way that two potentially contradictory goals should be met:

1. The participants should carry the conversation.
2. Excessive pressure should not placed on participants who are shy about contributing.

To achieve these two goals simultaneously, the shift in the conversation must be prefaced with legitimation of nonparticipation along with the desire for participation. The transcript continued:

Moderator [*to the participant sitting on his right*]:   Do you want to tell us of some experience that you or some friends have had with . . . what I am looking for is situations that you find yourself in where you have to make decisions. You may want to use, as an example, friends.

Participant: I can't think of any.

Moderator: You can't think of any. Do you want to pass?

Participant: At the moment.

Moderator: Okay. We'll come back to you. [*laughter*] As the session gets going, it [the conversation] will drift back and forth.

Next Participant: I'm trying to think. . . .

Because this is a sensitive topic, the first two participants were hedging their bets. They did not want to make fools out of themselves, but they were clearly enamored and excited about the impending discussion. The moderator should, in my view, legitimate not contributing (i.e., "Do you want to pass for now?") and was not pushy in attempting to elicit comments. At the same time, the moderator encouraged participants to be thinking about experiences that they might wish to share. Incidentally, the first participant, who could not think of anything to say, ultimately had the most to say of any participant in this active focus group.

Once a participant begins to tell a story, the conversation will, at least initially, be between the participant and the moderator, rather than among participants. This is illustrated below as the transcription continues:

Participant: The thing that keeps coming to mind is something that happened to my friend. . . . I can say her name because she doesn't go to school here.

Moderator: Nobody knows her, probably.

Participant: She was supposed to go here. Her name is Donna. This was about 2 years ago, no maybe a year ago, maybe a year and a half. She had been going out with her boyfriend for probably 2 years.

Moderator: So had they been going steady?

Participant: Oh yea, they were real serious. [*confused talk*] They wanted to get married and all this stuff. So every chance they could get, they would go somewhere so they could have . . . sex, you know. [*laughter*] They took every opportunity to . . . [*long pause*]

Moderator: They were sexually active?

Participant: Very! [*laughter*] And, uh, I guess, a lot of times on Sunday's he would come over and her family would go to church and then her parents would go to the country club and take her little brothers and sisters and go out for brunch. And he would come over, like, right after they left.

Moderator: Uh, huh.

Participant: And she would not go with them [her family] and then he [her boyfriend] would come as soon as they left.

Moderator: Right.

Participant: I guess they did this a bunch of times. One of the times that they did this, he came over, and they were in her room, and they had the door shut, and, you know, and they were, uh, . . . [*long pause*]

Moderator: Enjoying one another?

Participant: Yes, they were having fun. And . . . [*laughter*] her father came in to get his tennis racket. [*much laughter*]

Moderator: Were they doing this surreptitiously. That is, the parents were presumably unaware of the sexual involvement.

Participant: Oh, Yea! He [the father] came back to get something by himself, and they were, uh, enjoying themselves, and he saw the car there and he was, like, "Oh, I didn't know Jim was here."

Moderator: Oh, yea! Right! [*laughter*]

Participant: He came upstairs and he heard something and . . . [*laughter*] and he opened the door and . . .

Another Participant: Surprise! [*laughter*]

Participant: She did not really get too detailed about it. [*laughter*] But they were quite surprised! [Her boyfriend] grabbed his things and ran out the door. . . . Her dad was just screaming, like, "Get out of here." He ran out of the house with no clothes on. [*laughter*]

Moderator: Was the father angry at him?

Participant: Oh, yea! He didn't talk to him for about 2 months after that, I think, but . . .

Moderator: He didn't talk to the daughter's boyfriend.

Participant: Right. But Jim still kept coming over just like he always did. Like, he and the father didn't talk. It was a little uncomfortable.

Another Participant: Are those two still going out?

Participant: No, they're not. She has another boyfriend now that she's just as serious about. She wants to get married too. She was supposed to go here this year, but she didn't because she wants to stay home near her boyfriend. He's a senior in high school.

Moderator: So, now is she working?

Participant: Yea.

Moderator: We'll come back to you after a while.

In my judgment, the best focus group discussion occurs when the participants talk to each other, not to the moderator. However, when a moderator is introducing a sensitive topic, it will often be useful for an initial conversation to occur between the participant who is telling the story and the moderator. The above transcription illustrates this. Except for two cryptic comments by other participants and group laughter, the entire conversation took place between the storyteller and the moderator.

The moderator encouraged the storyteller, sought clarification, and probed for interpretational context. The moderator also got the story-teller off the hook when the telling of the story involved a particularly sensitive topic for which the mere mention of its name was potentially intimidating. In the above transcription, the euphemism *enjoying one another* came to describe the act of sexual intercourse. The use of such a euphemism allowed the participants to talk about sexual intercourse without having to say *sexual intercourse*. This had a calming effect. Indeed, the storyteller came to the place in the story where she wished to indicate that Donna and Jim were engaging in sexual intercourse, but she hemmed and hawed around. At this juncture, the moderator was able to get her off the hook by inquiring whether the couple was enjoying itself. The storyteller quickly and enthusiastically endorsed that euphemism and avoided the crude and uncomfortable "he stuck his penis into her vagina" description.

At the conclusion of the next participant's story, the conversation diver-sified around the table. Virtually every participant had an opinion about the appropriateness of the behavior of those described in the story and they all wanted to make their comments. One challenge for the moderator at this time was to ensure that every participant had the opportunity to make his or her comments. This challenge was handled by assigning an order to the comments. A second challenge for the moderator was to avoid expres-sions of surprise, astonishment, or admonition in reacting to what the participants said. In any event, the focus group for the remaining 2 hours was spontaneous, enthusiastic, articulate, and informative. The job of setting the agenda without setting the agenda had been achieved. It was as if the participants had gathered together for a dorm gab session, and short of the organizational and clarification comments, the moderator was irrelevant.

Discussion

The focus group technique has substantial potential for providing information that is simultaneously relevant to sociological investigations and is difficult to obtain using other techniques (i.e., surveys, experiments, etc.). It offers the promise of providing definitions of the situation that would not otherwise be available to the researcher. In particular, the focus group can provide information on sensitive topics about which respondents are usually reticent to talk. To capitalize on this promise, the researcher needs to employ those interaction principles that will foster and encourage conversation about these sensitive topics.

In this chapter, I defined three such principles and illustrated how those principles may be employed in service to this objective. Specifically,

1. The methodological principle of reactivity should be used on the screener questionnaire to stimulate the thinking of the participants for the days before the focus group on the sensitive topics to be discussed in the session itself.
2. The communications principle of self-disclosure should be used by the moderator to increase the acceptable range of self-disclosure on the part of the participants.
3. The social psychological principle of legitimation should be used to ensure that a wide diversity of thoughts, opinions, and descriptions are seen by the participants as acceptable within the context of the group discussion.

The use of these principles requires substantial interpersonal skill. To ensure maximum success, each principle needs to be sufficiently but not excessively employed. If each principle is inadequately used, the results will be disappointing because the opportunity for focus groups to provide insight into the processes will not have been established. If each principle is excessively used, the results will be disappointing because the participants will become spooked and will avoid discussion of the topic of interest.

Thus using these principles to encourage discussion of sensitive topics is both simple and awesome. Concerning reactivity, moderators need to select screener questions that will get future participants to think about the topics of interest but not select questions that will motivate these individuals to skip the sessions. Concerning self-disclosure, moderators need to self-disclose enough to encourage self-disclosure from the participants but not so much that the participants are put off by the moderator's comments. Concerning legitimation, moderators need to provide enough legitimation to ensure that the range of comments from socially desirable to socially undesirable are aired but not to provide so much legitimation for one position that those holding other positions feel that their comments would not be well received.

These principles are simple in that it is relatively simple for someone to describe them on paper, such as I did. These principles are awesome in that there is substantial challenge in employing them effectively. In practice, use of these principles demands that moderators make quick and accurate decisions about the effects of their dramaturgical actions on their role opposites, the participants. The desired effect is that the moderator's behavior will encourage the participants to discuss the sensitive topics with a fidelity to their attitudes, opinions, values, and behaviors. The dramaturgical challenge is to make the moderator's presentation of self produce this reaction without stimulating erroneous or misleading comments from the participants. Consistent with the theme of this chapter, the moderator wants to set the agenda without setting the agenda. To do so, focus group moderators are encouraged to follow the dictum made famous by country singer Kenny Rogers when he sang, "You've got to know when to hold and know when to fold."

12

Focus Group Interviewing With Low-Income Minority Populations

A Research Experience

ROBIN L. JARRETT

What's the Problem?
Introduction to Research Issues

This chapter examines the use of focus group interviewing with a sample of low-income African-American women. As a qualitative method for generating data through group interaction, focus group interviews are widely used for marketing purposes, generally with white middle-class samples (Morgan, 1988). Increasingly however, they are being used by social scientists to study a variety of issues, including those related to low- income minority populations (Glasser & Glasser, 1970; Goodwin,

AUTHOR'S NOTE: The research reported here was funded by a Rockefeller Minority Group Post-Doctoral Award and a Small Grant Award from the Spencer Foundation. The author thanks Richard Taub and the department of human services staff who supported the research. Saadia Adell, Margaret Breslau, Deanne Orput, Chris Schiller, and Pat Summers provided valuable assistance in transcribing, coding, and organizing the data. Anna Marie Muskelly offered helpful editorial advice. Special appreciation goes to the women whose enthusiastic participation made this study possible. Earlier versions of this paper were presented at the annual meetings of the American Sociological Association (1988) and the American Sociological Association Problems of the Discipline Conference (October 1990).

1983; Hudgins, Holmes, & Locke, 1991; Jarrett, 1991; Lengua, Roosa, Schupak- Neuberg, Michaels, Berg, & Weschler, 1992).[1] Although these studies offer valuable substantive insights, they provide relatively little information on the methodological dilemmas of focus group interviewing. Many ethnographic field studies explicitly address the general strengths and limitations of qualitative methods. In particular, they identify the methodological challenges of conducting qualitative research with low-income and/or ethnic and racial group minorities (Baca Zinn, 1979; Cannon, Higginbotham, & Leung, 1988; Hannerz, 1969; Liebow, 1967; Rainwater & Pittman, 1967; Sawyer, 1973; Stack, 1974; Yancey & Rainwater, 1970; see also Becker, 1970; Berk & Adams, 1970). A fundamental observation derived from field studies is that group characteristics affect research strategies and, ultimately, the nature and quality of the data collected. Influenced by insights from ethnographic studies, this chapter also examines the methodological implications of conducting focus group interviews with low-income African-American women.

The chapter is organized into four sections. In the first section, an overview of the study is provided. Here, I discuss the substantive issues guiding the research, sample characteristics, and research methods. In the next two sections, the focus is on the specific issues of group dynamics that are raised by the study. The discussion concentrates on the interactional dynamics that characterize both the recruitment process and the group discussion itself. Although I do not systematically report on the study's findings—these are reported elsewhere (Jarrett, 1991, 1992)—verbatim excerpts from the interviews are used to illustrate key points in both sections. In the fourth section, based on issues raised earlier in the chapter, group dynamics that typify focus group interviewing in general and those that distinguish this particular sample as well as their broader implications are discussed.

Beginning at the Beginning:
The Evolution of the Study

The research project, which began in late 1987, was an exploration of topics raised in the underclass debate. Concerned with increasing impoverishment among some segments of the African-American population, social scientists have directed their attention to issues of female headship, nonmarital male-female unions, adolescent child bearing, and welfare use. Most of these studies are based on quantitative data sets (for an overview see Cook & Curtin, 1987; McGeary & Lynn, 1988). Despite a rich tradition of ethnographic studies that provide a holistic understanding of poor African-American families and elaborate on quantitative findings, recent qualitative data, with some exceptions, make few contributions to the debate.

Guided by issues raised in the underclass debate, I proposed a two-step study to explore contemporary patterns of family life among low-income African-American women. In phase one, the study would consist of a series of exploratory focus group interviews and, in phase two, detailed interviews and participant observation with a smaller subsample of focus group participants and their families.

As a method for gathering qualitative data through group interaction, the focus group interview is concerned with subjective perceptions, opinions, attitudes, values, and feelings. An interviewer or moderator convenes a homogeneous group of respondents to discuss a particular topic. Focus group interviews are particularly useful for exploring the range and patterns of subjective perspectives in a relatively short period of time (Calder, 1977; Downs, Smeyak, & Martin, 1980; Hedges, 1985; Merton, Fiske, & Kendall, 1956; Morgan, 1988; Smith, 1972).

A total of 82 low-income African-American women, interviewed between January and July 1988, comprised 10 focus groups. The purposive sample was drawn from Chicago-wide Head Start programs. Based on profiles of women hypothesized to be at risk for long-term poverty, relevant criteria for selection were established: never-married mothers who received Aid to Families with Dependent Children (AFDC) at the time of the interviews and who lived in low-income or economically transitional neighborhoods throughout the city of Chicago. The focus group study differed from the usual research emphasis on adolescents, although many of the women began their child-bearing careers as teenagers. Instead, it concentrated on women in their early to mid-twenties.

Strangers and Friends:
The Interaction Between Respondents and the Researcher

Touched by Human Hands: The Recruitment Process

Existing literature on focus group participation presents a straightforward approach to recruitment. Generally using a random sample, each respondent is invited to participate by telephone and sent a follow-up letter to confirm participation. Hard-to-reach groups—a category that may include racial minorities—are often oversampled to reach the desired numbers.

My past research experience with low-income African-American families clearly indicated that impersonal strategies, while successful in other settings, would be inappropriate for this study. Because of the nature of many studies, informants hold realistic concerns about participating in such research (Baca Zinn, 1979; Berk & Adams, 1970; Rainwater & Pittman, 1967; Sawyer, 1973; Yancey & Rainwater, 1970; see also Cannon, Higginbotham, & Leung, 1988).

The concern with nonnormative issues and behaviors is one of the most salient aspects of research on low-income minority populations. Welfare use, nonmarital child bearing, alternative family living arrangements, and underground and informal economies—areas that are labeled social problems by the larger society—often constitute such studies (Anderson, 1989; Aschenbrenner, 1975; Edin, 1991; Stack, 1974; Sullivan, 1985, 1989; Valentine, 1978). In its substantive focus, this study was no different.

Given the nature of the study, no attempt was made to recruit respondents through impersonal means; instead, I drew on personalistic strategies often associated with more intensive qualitative methods. I visited each Head Start site, usually on days and at times when parent activities were scheduled. I viewed the introduction of the study not as a formal presentation—although clearly this format characterized and was expected in the initial interactions with administrators—but as the initial establishment of a relationship between the researcher and the respondents.

The study was presented in general terms. I explained to the women that I was interested in their views on family life; their own experiences as companions, mothers, daughters, and community members. Although some researchers speculated about what families were like, many had not talked to family members firsthand. I also described the format of the interview. The interview would entail women discussing these issues within a group context, which would be conversational and somewhat free-flowing in nature, much like a conversation between friends.

Despite its informality and conversational style, the focus group discussion maintained the fundamental purpose of a data-gathering method through the use of a topical outline. The outline—flexible enough to discuss issues in the language of the women and in directions that were meaningful to them yet structured enough to allow for intergroup comparisons—circumscribed the conversation.

For some women, the focus group discussion had the feel of a rap session. A conversational gathering of friends where one could let one's hair down. This view was not inconsistent with the aims of the interview. Yet other women had conceptions of the study that were less consonant. At one site, where researchers had taped husband-wife interactions, a woman asked, "Are we going to be on camera?" At another site where counseling sessions took place, another woman queried, "Are these therapy groups?"

Women who participated in the husband-wife interviews were excluded because of their previous research involvement but also because as married women they did not fit the recruitment criteria. The site where therapy sessions had been held was excluded from the study altogether. Both examples underscore the ways in which past experiences or preconceptions influence how respondents view researchers and their studies. Such conceptions affect the kinds of roles that researchers negotiate with respondents or informants and, ultimately, the type and quality of the data collected (McCall & Simmons, 1969; Yancey & Rainwater, 1970).

In addition to the manifest purpose of generating the sample, the site visits were opportunities for women to scrutinize me, ask questions, and determine if they wished to participate. Informants generally participate in qualitative field studies because of their relationship with the researcher. Although there was little time to establish a relationship within the context of a one-time focus group interview, participants found enough cues in our initial meeting to suggest a modicum of acceptance. This, I believe, derived in part because I am a relatively youthful looking African-American woman.

I am not suggesting that race was the decisive factor; it only indicated an initial commonality (on the strengths and limitations of insider research, see Baca Zinn, 1979; Sawyer, 1973; Yancey & Rainwater, 1970). Nor am I suggesting that I was a peer in the true sense of the word, because my life chances obviously differed from those of the women studied. Rather, I sought to convey that I was genuinely interested in hearing about their lives on their own terms. Unlike the usual helping professionals who entered their lives, I was there to listen, not to advise.

In the initial interactions, potential respondents were getting a preview of my moderating role. I perceived my role as that of facilitator, there to guide the discussion around issues in the topical outline as well as pursue any promising leads that deviated from the outline. But the attention would be on the women themselves. As a moderator I was uninvested in particular viewpoints or positions, as a human being I responded to the group dynamic. In some cases my response took the form of humor; in other instances it took the form of empathy. Two examples illustrate (pseudonyms are used throughout).

Example One

Dee Dee: Well, I want a man that's gonna just provide for me and my children, be a good provider. . . . I want a real man, somebody that's gonna take care of home first.

I: So, a real man?

Rowena: A real man is like, Dee Dee was sayin.' [He] takes care of the family.

I: Do we have any other views on what a real man is?

Aisha: I'm still tryin' to figure out what is a real man. [*laughter*] Hey, I don't know. When they said, Mr. Right, ain't no such thing as Mr. Right.

I: We're going to assume that it's no Mr. Right, maybe a Mr. Reasonable. [*laughter from the group*]

Example Two

Katrina [*spoken with strong emotion*]:   My mama . . . treats my son real bad. Like for Christmas or somethin' . . . she'll buy my little brother this and that and then she'll pick up somethin' for my nephew. . . . She never does that [for my son].

I: This must be a difficult situation.

Women were also told that they would be paid $15 for their participation. The money was provided as a token of appreciation for their time. Although I assumed that payment would be an added incentive to participation, I do not believe it was a critical factor in inducing general participation. It is unlikely that women with strong reservations about the study would have participated, irrespective of the payment. Furthermore, after each focus group session, women were asked if they were willing to participate in the fieldwork phase of the study. Respondents were explicitly told that they would not be paid for this aspect of the study. Yet most of the women agreed to participate further.

After my introduction of the study, a short screening questionnaire was distributed and used to determine eligibility. With the information from the questionnaire—demographic characteristics, willingness to participate, and availability—I later telephoned each woman who fit the sample profile to invite her personally to the focus group session. I informed her of the proposed time and the availability of additional child care at the Head Start sites where the sessions would be held. Each group ranged in size from 8 to 10 respondents.

Telephoning each parent was extremely time-consuming and, in some instances, problematic. Not knowing the women's schedules, I telephoned at various times in an effort to reach them. For women without telephones, messages were left with neighbors, relatives, and Head Start personnel.

Quite often households used various strategies to screen calls. For example, in some cases, children exclusively answered the telephone and asked for caller identification before releasing the telephone to the designated recipient. Sometimes adults could be heard in the background coaching the children with questions to ask.

In other instances, an adult family member routinely monitored all calls. He or she indicated that the requested individual was unavailable until it was established that the purposes of the caller were benign. Consequently, to distinguish myself from formal agencies and their representatives, such as bill collectors, I asked for each woman by her first name and used only my first name.

The telephone calls, irrespective of the investment of time, were instructive. They provided an opportunity to establish contact with some of the grandmothers who were targeted for the second phase of focus group interviewing as well as the larger field study. The telephone calls also provided clues on the dynamic nature of women's living arrangements as well as a sense of who currently lived in the household.

The endorsement of key site personnel was important in facilitating women's participation. They allowed me to visit the various sites to talk to women directly, but most important, they smoothed the way for my initial contact with mothers. For example, at two sites, staff members telephoned all registered parents to advertise my meeting. Others publicized my visits through word of mouth and/or flyers.

Like the mothers in the Head Start program, staff members had their own views of the research. Although I was not always clear on the motivations of site staff for endorsing my project, our interactions provided some clues. For a few, it was a request from the main office that could be accommodated. For others, the research had personal meaning. Some older staff members were proud of my status as a professional, whereas more politically oriented staff members approved of what they perceived as my nonjudgmental view of low-income community and family life. Still others supported the research because of its perceived therapeutic functions, despite my specific refutations and emphasis on the interviews' information-gathering purposes. Irrespective of administrators' reasons for participating in the study, the manner in which I negotiated with them affected my access to and recruitment of respondents.

I ultimately enlisted the participation of 10 sites. Sometimes recruitment required two site visits to recruit women. A total of 4 sites failed to generate parents for the focus group interview. At one site, the few women who attended the recruitment meeting were from stably employed families and did not fit the sample profile. At two other sites, a few interested parents came out, but there were not enough parents to generate a group session. At the fourth site, parents seemed somewhat disinterested in, if not suspicious of, the study. Because of my limited contact at these sites, it could not be determined if and how these four sites differed from sites that participated in the study.

Woman to Woman:
The Interaction Between Respondents

For Lots of Reasons:
Identifying the Range and
Patterns of Attitudes and Behaviors

What focus group interviews lack in depth of information, they excel in the range of information generated. In a relatively short period of time, focus group interviews can thematically identify the diversity of viewpoints or the range of behavior patterns associated with particular issues. Household living arrangements are used to illustrate this point.

Demographic profiles document an increase in female headship among young, never-married African-American women. Based on women's firsthand accounts, the focus group interviews identify several push factors associated with leaving the parental (grandparental) home and forming an independent household. They include the following.

Child Care Conflict. "I can't tell my kids what to do without [my grandmother] saying don't do this or don't do that, or you whupping [spanking] them too hard, or you feeding them too slow. . . . Put a jacket on; its too cold outside. Take that jacket off; it's too hot."

Availability of AFDC Income. "With that aid check you can move out [of your parents' house]."

Overcrowding. "I'm staying with my mother now. Me, my sister, her two kids, my older sister, her child, my brother and my sisters. . . . I don't have no privacy. I'm looking for a place now."

Eviction. "My father, when he found out I was pregnant . . . told me to tell the baby's father to come get me. . . . He was trying to prove . . . that he wouldn't come. . . . And when he came, I left."

The Quest for Responsibility. "The person that's out there on their own is more responsible. You have to think about they are actually taking care of their home now. If they're paying rent, light bill, gas bill, they got to be responsible."

The range of information derived from the focus group interviews can be used to generate areas for questionnaire construction or provide leads for further exploration with intensive field methods.

Like We Were in the Same Boat: Sharing Common Experiences

Unlike the individual interview in which the most intensive interaction transpires between the informant and the researcher, in the focus group interview the primary interaction takes place between respondents (Hedges, 1985). Indeed, it is the presence of others that enhances the intensity of interaction and, ultimately, the richness of the data. The interchange—a dynamic give and take—stimulates respondents to analyze their views more intensely than in an individual interview (Calder, 1977; Hedges, 1985).

The establishment of intimacy and rapport between group members that facilitates the exchange of information derives, to some degree, from group homogeneity. A key assumption of focus group interviewing is that individuals with common concerns and experiences are more willing to share viewpoints and disclose personal information (Calder, 1977; Merton, Fiske, & Kendall, 1956; Smith, 1972). The following excerpt illustrates how the sharing of common experiences builds rapport.

Trish: Everybody in my family got kids. [The] three oldest girls, all three
    of us got kids. . . . [If] I want [something] from the store . . . [and ask
    my mother to watch the kids, she says,] "Trish do not talk to nobody.
    [*laughter in the background*] Go to that store.You come on back
    here. . . . I do not have no kids in this house. My kids are grown."

Shelly: My mother just like that, just like that! My kids, they potty
    trained. . . . Sometimes they don't be at home at all. I just bring
    them home and I say, "Mama, would you watch them 'till I come
    home from the store?" [She says,] "What store you goin' to?" [I
    say,] "I'm goin' to the store. I'm comin' right back." [She says,]
    "Take [them] with you."

Such mundane interchanges set the stage for deeper levels of disclosure.

And Then What Happened?
The Elaboration and Clarification of Viewpoints

The presence of others encouraged women to examine their views
more intensely. Often women asked each other direct questions in an
effort to understand their peers' viewpoints. In the process, they elaborated on and clarified their initial statements. Consider the following
exchanges.

Example One

Leigh: When you decided not to take your [birth control] Pills, did
    you explain that to him?

Valerie: Yeah, I was telling him. . . . I figure I was young then. I would
    like a baby. I want a little girl.

Leigh: But did you tell him you was off the Pill?

Valerie: I told him that.

Leigh: And what did he say?

Valerie: It was like, no, 'cause I'm not working. . . . He was . . . doing
    a little hustling work around the neighborhood. So, it was like,
    well, since I'm still with my mother, she can help me. I just wanted
    a little girl.

Leigh: So, since he didn't really want a baby y'all still continued to
    make love and so he did want a baby.

Kathy: Maybe he just wanted sex and not the baby. . . . No, I'm serious. You can make love without planning children because my baby was not planned. When I did find out about her I was mad. I didn't want her. And now I love her.

Shelly and Angie further elucidate.

Example Two

I: What's the difference between being at your mother's house and being at your boyfriend's house?

Shelly: If you was in my shoes you wouldn't want to stay at my mother's. [*laughter*] . . . I said, "Mama, . . . I'm goin' to Tony's house." [She said,] "Go on then." I said, "I ain't got to go if I [don't] want to, right?" She said, "No, you ain't got to go, but if you want somethin' [from me] you can go." . . . I'm ready to leave home now 'cause me and my mother we be goin' at it.

Angie: Do Tony stay with his mother?

Shelly: Well, they stay at a home. . . . His mother and father dead. Just him and his brothers.

Angie: Would you want to move in with him?

Shelly: No, I wouldn't want to move in with him. We gotta get us our own.

Talkin' Smart, Talkin' Tough: Performance-Oriented Interactions

As stated earlier, the group sessions had the feel of rap sessions with friends. The atmosphere was exuberantly boisterous and sometimes frank in language. In one session, Rita proclaimed with aplomb, "I carry my own protection [birth control], just like the commercial says, don't leave home without it!" In another session, Theresa asserted unequivocally, "The only thing a man is good for is to argue with and have sex. That's because a woman can do whatever he can do!"

Stimulated by the presence of others, an audience effect frequently occurs in focus groups. Members perform for each other. As a form of impression management, performing encouraged women in the groups to discuss issues with great license.

In their roles as companions, mothers, and daughters, women provided exaggerated accounts of themselves as strong women who decisively manage errant males, disobedient children, and meddlesome mothers. They claimed the following.

I am a woman. . . . I can be on my own. . . . My furniture and everything got stolen from me, but I climbed back up the ladder. I still did it because I'm strong.

I said [to my boyfriend], "Well, when I move I don't want you coming." Because if I want to see him, I can see him when I want to see him. . . . I would schedule [visits]. . . . Come over and . . . spend the night? Come and bring your toothbrush? None of that. . . . I don't want no man stayin' with me. Come to visit me, watch TV and whatever. Go home.

I heard Mama down there this morning. . . . I heard her [at the door]. I was too busy. I said, "I ain't going to that door!"

I can discipline [my children] myself. I have that bass in my voice. . . . I can just holler. I raise my voice and . . . they'll . . . sit down. They'll mind me.

Despite the distortion of facts, the initial posturing serves a generally unrecognized function; it facilitates rapport so vital for the disclosure of more personal information. The performances demonstrated that women are, in effect, speaking the same language and have similar issues and concerns.

The women themselves distinguished between performance-oriented accounts and serious talk. Linguistic markers, short and pithy, identified the shift between the two modes. The following phrases were typical:

But that's how it is
Truly; To be truthful; I'm gonna tell you the truth; That's the truth
I'm serious; Seriously; I have to be serious
For real, for real
I'm not gonna lie

The use of linguistic markers within the context of women's accounts are illustrated below.

Example One

Johnetta: See, I'm gonna tell the truth. I was 18 when I had my first [child] . . . I was grown. I should have thought about it too, just like he should have. I was on the Pill and I got off it. . . . I gave him a chance. I thought maybe we was gonna be married because we did talk about it.

Example Two

Melanie: As far as working, I have to be serious. I don't have any skills. . . . I wouldn't want to work and lose the little public aid that I do have because the medical card means a lot and the food stamps mean a lot. . . . You have to do like this until you can afford to do better. I wouldn't take a $3.50 an hour job because you would lose that security until you can get on your feet. . . . I know this sounds cold, but that's how it is.

Not surprisingly, when women shifted from the performance-oriented mode, serious accounts were sometimes less dramatic, women's lives were often less heroic. They made the following statements.

I had a hard struggle. I had to ask my mama for a lot of help. . . . I needed help for food, . . . to go to school, . . . help to watch my kids. So, far as I'm concerned . . . taking care of my two kids is very hard.

You just got to accept [a man] the way he is. You can't change him. But all you can do is just adjust.

My mother lives on the next block. . . . So you can really say, I'm still at home. . . . She comes down to my house and finds something [to say]. "Why didn't you come down the street yesterday?" . . . Now I got to give an explanation.

My child is 2, and I can whup [spank] him. . . . But I don't be wantin' to whup him all the time. I tell him I love him . . . and I be tryin' to talk to him. . . . But he makes me laugh when I get ready to whup him. . . . That's why he don't take me serious. . . . So I don't know. I tell my mother I don't know what I'm gonna do with this boy.

Performance-oriented accounts, although exaggerated, should not be ignored. They suggest stress points in women's lives. Furthermore, by presenting themselves as decisive, strong individuals who are in charge of their lives, women describe important subcultural values (Aschenbrenner, 1975; Ladner, 1971; Stack, 1974).

Telling It Like It Is:
Diffusing Idealized Accounts

Women in this study, like other poor people, are well aware of how their lives differ from those of the mainstream. Consequently, in the presence of outsiders, particularly researchers, there are strong pressures to present idealized versions of their lives. These are perspectives on the way things should be and not always the way they are.

Two particular group dynamics discourage the exclusive focus on highly idealized accounts. They include individuals who, with little prompting, are willing to discuss themselves in particularly candid ways and the presence of individuals who are willing to challenge idealized views. In tandem, they set the tone for deeper and more reality-based discussions. The following comments are from women who were unusually forthright in discussing their lives.

Example One

Ella: I don't have no patience with no kids. . . . I didn't want my daughter. . . . I wasn't ready for no kids and I knew I wasn't 'cause I was still partyin' and runnin' the streets. . . . I had a daughter . . . but I don't regret it though. But I wasn't ready for no kids, 'cause . . . I was gonna go off to [college] and I was ready to get real wild.

Example Two

Sheryl: I can't stand bein' on aid. . . . I heard my auntie. She was talkin' . . . on me behind my back. She made me feel so bad. . . . Talkin' about I don't never buy nothin' for the house. I don't have no money. She works. . . . I don't have no money to get what I want. . . . I give my son Pampers and clothes. Shoot, what do I have to give myself?

Peers who are aware of the "real deal" and who are willing to "tell it like it is" (Rainwater, 1970) provide another check on exclusively idealized accounts. These respondents challenge, both directly and indirectly, women to discuss issues as if they were strictly among peers. An underlying assumption is that everybody knows what's happening anyway. The following excerpts elucidate this point.

Example One

Adrian: I'm not ready to get out on my own. I don't have a job. . . . I'm not going to try to move on welfare. . . . So when I get me a job and all of that, I'll be ready.

Karen: That sounds good; but sometime that's not the situation. When you got a lot of people bunched up together . . . you gonna get out there with that welfare check and make it the best way you can.

Example Two

Rochelle: My two boys, if they grow up and they get a girl pregnant, I'll be damned if they not gonna marry 'em. I would take they asses to the altar and make them marry 'em. . . . I'm gonna make them do what's right.

Marcella: I understand everything you sayin' Rochelle. . . . I don't think that situation will be any better if [they] were married. . . . Sometimes marriage is not always the answer. It's good . . . to be married to the children's father. But marriage is not always the answer.

Pam: A lotta time you can't get along with the children's father. I have a daughter, she's 3 years old. . . . But [marriage] is not the answer all the time. Me and Carmen's father could not get along. . . . [It] wasn't the money. It's not 'cause I didn't have a father; he had a father. We came from good homes. We just could not get along. We don't even know how we made the baby. [*laughter*]

The unsolicited candor of individual group members indicates that such revelations, aside from their positive influence on group dynamics, satisfy personal needs. Sometimes women's comments were delivered with anger; other times they were delivered with conflict and ambiguity. These examples suggest that their disclosures provide personal catharsis and clarification.

The Interaction Is the Method: Discussion and Implications

This chapter described the dynamics that characterized a series of focus group interviews. Based on a sample of low-income African-

American women, the discussion explored the interactions characterizing the recruitment process—interactions that transpired between the researcher and the respondents—and the dynamics characterizing the group discussions—dynamics that transpired primarily between respondents. The generation of range and diversity, the establishment of rapport, the intensive examination of viewpoints, the presence of performing, and the diffusion of idealized accounts are interactions typically found in all focus group interviews. Other processes, however, were unique to this sample.

Focus group interviewing with low-income racial group members generates distinct dynamics. The research focus on nonnormative research topics poses a particular barrier to participation. It also encourages some respondents to emphasize aspirational perspectives rather than those that are related to what they actually do. While the focus group literature offers general methodological strategies to deal with recruitment issues and intergroup dynamics, particularistic concerns and processes such as those that emerged in this study remain unexplored. To address the unique features of focus group interviewing with low-income African-American women, this study employed personalized recruitment strategies and encouraged behaviorally based discussions of what women actually do.

Generally, moderators have no prior contact with respondents for fear of contaminating the study. Although care was taken not to preview the topics to be explored in the interview sessions, impersonal recruitment strategies were inappropriate for this sample. The intensive time and effort invested in meeting with administrators and women at the local sites and later telephoning each woman individually were critical in gaining access, generating the sample, and facilitating group rapport. Without these preliminary efforts, it is unlikely that the women would have agreed to participate in the first place or to participate as enthusiastically as they did. Although these observations derive from this specific study, they also suggest that other researchers using focus group interviews should closely examine the impact of recruitment strategies on the nature and outcomes of their studies.

The presentation of idealized accounts undoubtedly can be found in other focus group interviews. However, there is a distinct aspect to this issue for low-income respondents. The poor are well aware that they are publicly denigrated because their behavior diverges from mainstream patterns. While indicating that poor people normatively share mainstream values, idealized accounts tell us little about what people actually do or, more important from the perspective of focus group interviewing, what people think about what they actually do. The presence of particularly candid group members encouraged women to talk more specifically about how such perceptions were related to behavior. Apart from general group dynamics, there were specific group pressures for women to talk candidly about nonnormative issues. Observations from past ethnographic studies indicate that topics such as female headship, nonmarital child bearing, and alternative forms of male-female relationships are discussed routinely in poor African-American women's daily conversations (Abrahams, 1976; Aschenbrenner, 1975; Hannerz, 1969; Liebow, 1967; Rainwater, 1970; Stack, 1974). The normative ambiguity engendered by the disjunction between values and behaviors encourages these topics to be singled out for more intense discussion (Hannerz, 1969). These observations underscore the importance of understanding the sociocultural milieu of racial and ethnic minority groups before conducting focus group interviews.

Would other researchers using focus group interviews with low-income African-American women report similar group dynamics as this study? Would researchers using focus group interviews with low-income Asian, Hispanic, Native American, or white women report different interactions from those in this study? In light of the paucity of methodological discussions, the answers remain unclear. The ethnographic literature, however, suggests that there are tangible subcultural differences between ethnic and racial group minorities of the same socioeconomic level (Jarrett, 1990). Consequently, these subcultures may influence what various groups consider appropriate interaction conventions and conversational idioms within the context of focus groups. More research is clearly needed.

The existing literature on the "how-to" of focus group interviewing is particularly useful for discussing general issues. Although concentrating on more affluent samples, some of these discussions allude to hard-to-reach groups, a category that may include racial and ethnic minorities. Yet little systematic attention has been given to focus group interviewing with low-income and/or ethnic and racial minorities. As social scientists increasingly conduct focus group interviews with these populations, it becomes critical that they explicitly address the methodological challenges that such research engenders. This chapter begins the discussion.

Note

1. Group interviews in naturalistic settings have been used as part of ethnographic studies of low-income African-Americans (Anderson, 1976; Ladner, 1971; Liebow, 1967; Macleod, 1987; Martin & Martin, 1978). Yet here too, there is little formal discussion of this research strategy. Brief discussions can be found in Bodgan and Taylor (1975) and Burgess (1984). See also Bellah (1986), Goodwin (1983), Irwin (1972), James (1972), Kanter (1977), and Myerhoff (1978) for other examples of group interviewing in sociological and ethnographic studies.

13

Focus Groups and Community Mobilization

A Case Study From Rural North Carolina

THOMAS PLAUT
SUZANNE LANDIS
JUNE TREVOR

In July 1989, the Community Oriented Primary Care (COPC) project was initiated by a multiple agency consortium in Madison County, North Carolina. COPC involves both professionals and lay community residents in a process of health needs assessment, project design, and implementation. This chapter describes the role focus groups played in developing data that enabled the community to undertake a variety of health-related projects while improving networking between medical providers, service agencies, and community groups.

The Project Site

Located along western North Carolina's mountainous border with Tennessee, Madison County consists of a 456-mile^2 area with a population of 16,953, living in some 6,488 households. The population is virtually all white (98.8%) and 79% of the population is rural. Almost half of its labor force is employed in agriculture. Madison is a part of the 398-county federally designated Appalachian Region.

Historically, Madison has been a county of family farms where burley tobacco has been the major cash crop. But in the 1980s, major tobacco companies turned to cheaper overseas suppliers, while demand for tobacco also dropped. The number of farms in the county decreased 11.8% between 1982 and 1987. Of the remaining 1305 farms, 1142 (87.5%) had incomes less than $10,000, indicating that for most people farming has become a second source of revenue behind what county folk call "public work" in commerce, industry, and government (North Carolina State Data Center, 1989). Madison County's mean family income in 1989 was $11,072, ranking it close to the bottom (98th) of North Carolina's 100 counties; a quarter (25.8%) of its population has an income below the poverty level. About 40% of its elderly live below the poverty line as do more than 38% of its 4161 children under 18 (North Carolina Department of Environment, Health, and Natural Resources, 1989, 1991).

Almost 18% of the county (51,524 acres) is part of the National Forest system. The county's isolated and mountainous terrain has seriously limited the development of a manufacturing industry and it "took a pummeling in 1986 when a shoe factory closed, with 435 jobs lost—nearly 40% of the county's total" (McCarthy, 1990). The lack of economic opportunity has led to flight of the working-age population leaving a high percentage (14.4%) of people over 65 (the state average is 10.2%).

Health Services Development and Community Organization

In the late 1960s, two nurses traveling through the area conducting health fair screening programs were sufficiently impressed by a lack of access to primary medical care in the county to return in 1971 to establish the Hot Springs Health Program, a home nursing service and clinic in Hot Springs, one of the county's three towns. The nurses obtained federal funds the following year, hired more staff and established two other small clinics in the nearby communities of Walnut and Laurel. By 1992, the Hot Springs Health Program had grown to four medical centers staffed by eight physicians, two mid-level practitioners, a dentist, a pharmacist, and 10 nurses. In addition to primary care in its medical centers, it provides hospice; home health nursing; and clinical, dental, and pharmaceutical services. It also provides home chore services for the developmentally disabled and physician and mid-level support for the county Health Department, the college infirmary, and two nursing homes. Its physicians also serve as county medical examiners. The program's staff logs some 36,000 patient encounters annually.

The county's ability to organize its limited resources has been demonstrated not only in the building of four medical centers but also in a Habitat for Humanity housing program, a hospice, counseling and crisis services for battered women and victims of sexual assault, volunteer fire departments and community development clubs. A privately funded service called Neighbors in Need provides funds, food, and other emergency assistance to people in crisis. The networking of these organizations with public services (schools, mental health centers, emergency medical services, the county Health Department and the Department of Social Services) was a primary reason the W. K. Kellogg Foundation chose to fund the 4-year Madison Community Health Project.

Community Oriented Primary Care

COPC begins with an assessment of the health needs of the population of a defined geographic area—in this case Madison County—and then involves both professional and laypeople in designing, implementing, and monitoring projects fashioned to meet the needs identified in the assessment. The concept of community is at the core of COPC theory and practice. The community, not outside experts, medical providers, or other professionals, defines needs and realities. The community—in dialogue with medical and human services professionals—consequently plays a major role in determining health-related interventions. If the professionals take too strong a leadership role, they lose the community support and the interventions fail or their impact is greatly reduced (Cancian & Armstead, 1990; Maguire, 1987). COPC was developed by two physicians, Sidney and Emily Kark, while they were working among the Zulu in South Africa in the 1940s. They defined four stages:

1. Identifying the community—meaning the total population, not just users of the medical center; studying the community, including its social institutions, structure and patterns of relationships, traditional healing methods, diet, and nutrition and economy
2. Identifying community health problems
3. Involving the community in determining priorities in health needs

4. Constant monitoring of projects to evaluate their effectiveness and enable their ongoing modification (Kark, 1981; Nutting, 1990; Overall & Williamson, 1989; Trostle, 1986).

Applying the COPC Concept to Madison County

The Idea of Community

COPC begins with the community assessment, a task co-directed in the Madison County project by a sociologist, who had worked in the county for more than a decade, and an epidemiologist. The first goal of the assessment was to understand what people in Madison County meant by the word *community*. The county's three postmasters were asked to map communities within their ZIP Code areas. Their maps were then validated and refined by local informants. Communities were defined as small social groups based on traditional kinship ties and land holdings. A total of 72 units were identified, and 350 community helpers (defined as people whom residents of a specific community would call if they needed advice or assistance) were also identified. Thus for many residents, the county is not as much their community as is the traditional, kinship-based neighborhood of the mountain cove. Such strong identification with local place and relationships would shape COPC projects; specific communities and their own trusted networks and organizations became the base for action.

Employing Focus Groups as a Primary
Means of Assessment

One of the county representatives on the project's seven-member executive board insisted that individual surveys not be employed in the project's community assessment. "These people have been surveyed to death," he said. "They're tired of being asked if they're poor." This aversion to surveys was subsequently confirmed by other county residents. How could data be obtained from residents? There were the aggregate statistics from county agencies such as the Department of Social Services, the Health Department, schools, and the Hot Springs Health Program. Both the Delphi method and nominal group techniques were suggested as ways of eliciting opinions of country residents (Abramson, 1984, pp. 60-164) The Delphi method was thought to be too complicated. Nominal group techniques were not used for data gathering, but employed later in the COPC process to assist community representatives determine priorities among the felt needs articulated in focus group interviews. Focus groups were chosen as a nonthreatening and effective means of obtaining community perceptions of health, health-related behaviors, and services delivery. Focus groups had previously been employed to evaluate Hot Springs Health Program staff relationships (Plaut 1988). The Madison Community Health Project staff designed the community assessment methodology for local conditions and project goals. The fragmentation of the county by its mountainous geography, its 72 subjectively defined communities, its various agencies and schools, and the project goal of community-based change required that as many groups as possible be included in the research process. Consequently, 40 focus groups were conducted: 7 with teachers; 8 with social services, mental health, and community support personnel (the sheriff's office, Extension Service, and day care and congregate meal site staff); 11 with medical providers and 14 with community groups.

The focus groups were conducted between August and December 1989, involving 416 county residents. The setting for each group was its own turf, be it a school, a fire department garage, a church, or an office. The size of each group was determined by interest and its membership; the median was 7 and mean was 10.4, the skew being created by two large outlier groups, one having 33 and the other 37 participants. The range in group size (3 to 37) exceeded the optimal 4 to 12 individuals, and the number of groups seemed excessive to the research staff in that after only a few interviews the responses became predictable (Morgan, 1988 pp. 41-48). However, the focus groups were not only a source of data, but a process for resident involvement in and legitimation of the project and its interventions.

Given the technical difficulties presented by some locations and the discomfort created by initial uncertainty of a number of groups about the nature and purpose of the focus groups, audio taping was considered to be more problematic than helpful. Consequently, a two-person facilitation team was used, most often made up of a male and female, although two women worked as facilitators on three occasions. The facilitators alternated roles of note taking and facilitating from session to session, often taking into account the nature of the group. (For example, it was uncomfortable for a woman to facilitate an interview with an all-male volunteer fire department.) The questions presented to each of the 40 focus groups were the following.

1. What personal health problems or physical complaints appear to be most commonly mentioned by people in the community?
2. What barriers to health care or medically related issues do people in the community talk about?
3. What in this group's opinion are the serious health problems in the county? What are the causes of these serious health problems? What in this group's opinion are the serious barriers to health care?
4. What needs to be done to alleviate these problems?
5. Do you feel that there is any group of the population not receiving adequate medical care? Why not?
6. Who do people call in this community when they need help or advice? (This final question was asked only of community groups, such as volunteer fire departments and community development clubs.)

Focus group participants were given a copy of the questions to provide an opportunity for individual written responses. This proved significant for cases in which a respondent noted either an issue passed over in the discussion or something he or she felt was too sensitive to be mentioned in the group. For example, one teacher felt she could not discuss indications of family violence among her students for fear of offending people from the community in her group, but she was able to write her concern on the question sheet as well as discuss it with the facilitators privately after the meeting.

Madison County Focus Group Results

Each focus group session was written up in narrative form by both facilitators within 24 hours. These accounts were then compared and consolidated into a single report. The reports were subjected to a content analysis to transform the qualitative data into a quantified form. Some 230 diseases, causes of pathology, perceived barriers to health care, and so forth were coded on a scale of 0 to 2: 0 meant no mention of a particular topic, 1 indicated that the issue had been raised but did not have apparent group consensus (which enabled the entry of written as well as verbal responses), and 2 indicated apparent group consensus.

Apparent consensus is obviously a soft measure. Responses were scored as such only in cases where both staff members of the research staff felt that everybody in the group clearly agreed on a particular response. When such agreement was evidenced, the facilitator asked "Does everyone agree with this?" Individual written reservations, or verbal ones shared with staff after a group interview, reduced scores from 2 to 1 on several occasions. Scores were totaled and variables ranked according to score and fed back to the project's Community Advisory Board to assist in the design of interventions.

For question 1, the complaints most heard in the community related to pain, which was associated with arthritis-rheumatism and backache, allergies, and heart disease. When focus group members were asked for their own opinion of serious health problems in the county, diseases related to aging and the frail elderly topped the list (Alzheimer's disease, circulatory problems, cardiovascular disease, and getting old).

For questions 2 and 3, the highest score in the groups' own views of serious illness was alcohol abuse. This was a surprise to the facilitators, who had not seen its significance in their own notes; the quantitative analysis revealed consistency in the perception of the alcohol problem in all but the community-based groups. (In reviewing the data, some have suggested that community pride, the taboo on alcohol use created by religious fundamentalism, concern over family embarrassment and privacy, and/or fear of recrimination may have prevented the alcohol issue from being raised in the 10 community-based groups.)

Stress-related symptoms such as headaches and stomach aches were ranked second to alcohol. A number of informants talked about the stress felt by farmers, who must produce to make payments on farm equipment and land taxes before they can provide food, shelter, and medical care for their families. The harsh demands of life for many county residents caused depression to be scored within the top five ranked health problems. Teachers said that family problems caused stress-related illness in children and depression especially among high school students who see little opportunity after graduation: "They want to stay in the area, but have to leave if they are going to find jobs."

The causes of health problems cited were lack of preventive health care, lack of care of self in the early stages of an illness or injury, poor diet, poor parenting, poor hygiene, and abuse and neglect. The following examples of causes cited are taken from focus groups with teachers.

The [children's] stress comes from just trying to survive. [The children] are always hearing about how hard it is to get by from their parents. Many [children] work in the tobacco fields and in tomatoes.

Kids don't sleep at night. They just come in here and put their heads down on the desk—and we let them sleep. They can't learn anything when they're that tired. We just let them sleep. Some of them stay up because they're working—in tobacco in the evening or digging nightcrawlers to sell to tourists.

Some stay up all night watching television. There's nobody there to set limits . . . nobody there to parent.

[Due to the combination of the timing of factory shifts and single parenting] some children as young as the third grade are preparing their own meals. Some as young as the third grade have to dress and feed their younger brothers and sisters before school.

Kids are affected by alcohol abuse—both in terms of witnessing heavy drinking and by being victims or witnesses of physical abuse accompanied by drinking.

The kids get knocked around at home, so they do it to each other at school.

We can't teach as much now as we did 10 years ago—we spend much more time now . . . trying to control their behavior.

In my first 10 years, I never made a report to the Department of Social Services for suspected abuse. Now we have to report four or five cases every year in this one school alone.

The teachers said that difficult conditions at home had serious consequences for children's health.

Fifty percent of the kids at this school do not get taken to the doctor.

Mothers work now. They send sick kids to school. Single parents can't afford to lose a day's work and stay home with a sick child.

[About] 15 out of the 25 kids in my classroom have never seen a dentist.

Dental care is a big problem. How do I know? Just look in their mouths—you can see the cavities.

One boy has a large cavity in a front tooth and he always tries to hide it by holding his lip down over his tooth.

Teacher's comments relating to neglect were echoed by others working with youth. A Girl Scout leader said that "of the 250 Girl Scouts in

our troops we referred 16 to [the Department of Social Services']
Protective Services last year." Such comments played a major role in a
Community Advisory Board decision to create the project for parents
of newborn children described below. The economics of medical care
topped the list of perceived barriers to health care. The expense of visits
to medical facilities, especially for people on fixed incomes, and the
costs of medicines, insurance, and transportation were ranked high.
Consequently, the groups seen as not having access to adequate medical
care were the elderly; working people who are unable to afford the high
costs of private medical insurance and yet are ineligible for Medicaid
assistance; and children and teenagers whose parents cannot get them
to the medical centers because they can't afford it, don't have a car to
transport them, or are at work.

The next questions concerned what should be done to alleviate the
problems of poor health and inaccessible health care. Although there
was general discussion about the need for a federal response to the
health-care crisis in the United States, the focus groups were encouraged
by the facilitators to center their answers on what could be done locally.
Consequently, preventive health education scored highest among needed
solutions, followed by transportation for the elderly and children; education on how to use existing health-care services, preventive care, parenting, and nutrition; expanded home care services for the frail elderly;
and development of support groups for parents.

The groups noted as not receiving adequate care were the elderly,
people unable to qualify for publicly assisted care and unable to afford
private insurance, people who feel they can't afford medical care,
children, people without means of transportation, and people not educated to access health care.

Other Sources of Data

The focus group data were developed alongside epidemiological
statistics on mortality and morbidity and on demographic, economic,
and social data provided by both federal and state agencies. The county
death rate in 1986 was 9.04/1,000, compared with a state rate of
8.62/1,000. Heart disease was the leading cause of death and had a rate
of 317 per 100,000: the state rate was 306 (North Carolina State Center
for Health Statistics, 1987). Perhaps the most interesting finding in the
epidemiological data was that Madison County is not atypical—its

overall health is no better and no worse than other American counties. What appeared to be a problem with a high rate of strokes (92.17/100,000 compared with a national average of 62.5/100,000) disappeared when seen in terms of years of life lost, a measure that subtracts an age at death from 75. There were virtually no years of life lost to stroke in Madison County, indicating that people die of stroke after the age of 75. Elevated rates for death from diabetes indicated a need for more attention to medical care, monitoring, and diet. The elevated pneumonia-influenza rate (51.84/100,000 compared with a national 29/100,000) suggested greater attention be paid to respiratory illness and preventive measures such as influenza and pneumococcal vaccinations. Data on dental caries (27% to 63% of kindergarten to eighth grade students in the county's eight schools), indicated a serious need for dental hygiene and preventive care.

It is important to note, however, that epidemiological data based on rates of illness were found to be problematic in the COPC community assessment, because the incidences are so small at the community level. One death from sudden infant death syndrome (SIDS) from 1988 to 1990 gave the county a SIDS death rate of 20.60/1,000, compared with a North Carolina state rate of 8.94/1,000 (North Carolina Department of Environment, Health, and Natural Resources, 1991).

The county's annual child abuse rate, as reported by the North Carolina Department of Human Resources, Division of Social Services, for the years 1985 to 1988, proved to be a cause for concern. The abuse report rate per 1000 for the entire state averaged 5.7 to 5.9. The range in Madison County was 8 to 10. Neighboring counties with similar socioeconomic and demographic characteristics had rates of 3 per 1000. Madison's substantiated abuse rate was also higher. Focus group interviews with teachers, social workers, and scout leaders confirmed these findings. A privately funded Rape Crisis Center, established in the county in 1986, served 174 clients in 1988.

Turning Data into Action

Challenging Agencies

Facilitators had promised the focus groups to refer insights and complaints to the appropriate agency. Consequently, the Hot Springs Health Program was told it suffered from the image of being a "poor person's clinic." This image, which stemmed from earlier years when it received federal funds, is far from the current reality; it is a private group medical practice. The poor person's clinic view had also contributed to the idea that its physicians were "not good enough to be in private practice," despite their training and credentials. The program's administrators and physicians also were told of complaints about scheduling and long waiting periods, and cold receptionists at one of the offices. The complaints were addressed, at least partially, by the computerization of appointment schedules and medical records. A workshop for the receptionists and clinical assistants enabled them to share their frustrations about doctors' behavior during a meeting with the physicians and led to the establishment of a regular biweekly meeting to focus on stress and office problems. A public relations campaign emphasizing staff skill and the range of services was developed, using local media and explanatory posters in waiting rooms, to counter the image problem.

Community Mobilization

Community mobilization around health issues is an important outcome of the COPC process. Once the assessment data are in, community members must decide what they mean and, consequently, what interventions or action are required. In the process of applying for the grant that funded the Madison Community Health Project, the researchers invited representatives of county agencies and community organizations to luncheons to elicit ideas and support. Once funded, this advisory group became the project's Community Advisory Board (CAB). Within two years it grew from 25 to 40 people representing most county public and private service agencies as well as community groups. In the winter of 1990, project staff used nominal group techniques with the Community Advisory Board to develop a consensus on the three most serious health problems in the county, three causes of the problems, the groups affected by them, agencies already working on them, and finally, what interventions consequently should be undertaken. The resulting interventions are described below.

Oral Health Program. To address community concerns about children's caries, an oral health program was started in the fall of 1990. Free dental sealants were made available to all second graders in the county schools. Public health dentists visited each school and screened 166 students and placed sealants in 118 of them. Dental health education was included for both students and their parents. Dental health information also was distributed to the community at large via the CAB weekly column in the county newspaper.

Programs for Senior Citizens. In the fall of 1990, grant funds were used to purchase flu and pneumococcal vaccine so that the Madison County Health Department could offer free vaccinations to people aged 65 and older. Clinics were offered at the Health Department, congregate meal sites, churches, volunteer fire departments, and community development club sites, with the help of community volunteers. More than 560 of the some 2600 people over 65 in the county received flu and/or pneumonia shots the first year. In October 1991, a health fair for senior citizens was attended by more than 500 people. The fair included dental and other physical screenings, free consultations with volunteer physicians, free flu, pneumonia, and tetanus vaccinations, a series of lectures on health-related topics, some 30 information booths, and lunch. A total of 396 people received vaccinations at the fair, and another 270 seniors were given vaccinations at the Health Department, congregate meal sites, and through the Home Health Service of the Hot Springs Health Program.

Infants and Parents: The Laurel PTA Parent Team Program. The Community Advisory Board decided that an efficient way to help children was to assist parents of newborn children. It found a local community organization, the Laurel School District PTA, willing to recruit volunteer women who were then trained by project and agency personnel to be lay helpers (Service & Salber, 1979). The trained women went into the homes of referred newborns in the Laurel School District with a home safety and infant care kit (designed in consultation with the lay helpers), the CAB-produced *Parents Resources Guide,* and other information. Through periodic visits they were to ensure that infants received immunizations and appropriate medical and home care. Similar materials were provided to parents of newborns in a neighboring school district, but without the lay helper assistance; this control group provides a comparative measure of effectiveness of the lay helper approach.

Programs for Teenagers. The original focus group data concerning school-age children led the CAB to initiate a high school project. Although a student self-report survey was blocked by school board members troubled by questions about depression and sexual behavior (two major causes of morbidity and mortality among teens), project staff was able to conduct interviews with several classes and a group of peer counselors. These interviews revealed student concern over stress, a sense of isolation from both parents and peers, and lack of assistance and direction from adults. Concern about drug use (especially alcohol) and sexually transmitted diseases was also evidenced. As a result, several forums were held for high school seniors on AIDS and stress and time management. A program to match successful college students as one-on-one peer counselors with high school students is in the planning stage.

Health Education. Health education for the public at large was provided in the weekly "Healthwise" column in the county newspaper. CAB member agencies rotated responsibility for writing the column, which has provided information on everything from AIDS, depression, and dental hygiene to programs such as the Senior Health Fair.

The Process of Community Empowerment:
The Metamorphosis From
Advisory Board to Health Coalition

The experience of evaluating focus group data and designing and implementing community projects gave the Community Advisory Board members a shared history of achievement and a new collective identity. An outside evaluator reported that

> 93% of the members responded that they are almost always or often enthusiastic about being a part of the CAB . . . over 85% . . . signified that the COPC project had helped them make use of community resources . . . 63.3% rated the CAB as *very productive,* while the remaining 36.7% indicated it as *somewhat productive.*

The high morale of the CAB was indicated in the study by comments like "meetings are informal and members feel free to express their opinions" and members have "freedom to share ideas" (Shaler, 1992a, p. 48).

By spring 1992, the Community Advisory Board had grown beyond the Kellogg COPC project it had been created to advise. It applied to other foundations to fund new interventions. The board was renamed the Madison Community Health Consortium and was defined by its new mission statement as "a partnership that seeks to improve the overall health of Madison County citizens by networking community agencies and groups in the on-going process of needs assessment and project development, implementation and evaluation."

The Efficacy of Focus Group Methods

Project staff were particularly impressed by the ability of focus groups to gather information not readily accessible via other research methodologies. An example of such ability is found in the comments and feelings expressed in a meeting with farm, factory, and service workers who also served in a volunteer fire department. A total of 18 men gathered at the volunteer fire department's garage for the interview. They appeared very uncomfortable; our field notes report that the session "started with silence," which eventually was broken by the following comments:

> We're really not the ones to ask about this.
> Basically, we're a pretty healthy county.
> We're the only county without an AIDS patient.

It took nearly an hour for the level of trust required for the men to begin to share the insights, feelings, and worldviews usually held within their group. For example, in response to questions about barriers to health care, they told a series of stories that demonstrated their sense of physician insensitivity.

> That boy's body lay in a ditch for 3 hours before a medical examiner (a job rotated by local physicians) would let us move him.

> It took them 1 hour and 45 minutes for a medical examiner to move K's body to the funeral home. We had to sit there and watch the "ooh-ahh crowd" stand there and stare at the body.

> That doctor charged me $35 and then told me, "you have to stay out of the dust for a while. Now I'm a farmer. How am I going to stay away from the dust?"

The interview process enabled a degree of informality, which permitted the venting of frustration and anger: One participant broke his evening-long silence with, "We're plain tired of being shit on." When asked what might be done to improve the medical services, one respondent evoked cheers from his fellows by suggesting we "nail the doctors' feet to the floor and burn the place!"

This catharsis led to further reflection of the men's place in a county suffering the demise of farming and loss of its limited industrial base, while an increase in services brought in new kinds of people with different life-styles and value systems. As for the doctors: "They're hippies. They don't dress right" and "They're not what we're accustomed to. They ought to look like doctors."

Once such feelings had been vented, the men were able to discuss the condition of the elderly poor in the county and make recommendations to ease their plight. The data reveal significant problems of class, worldview, and workplace: Many of the volunteer firemen and ambulance drivers worked jobs in service and industry that require a clean uniform; they resent people who appear to sidestep such decorum. Second, the comments indicate a significant difference between traditional, rural and local values and those imported by newcomers such as medical providers and the strong feelings generated by that difference. These focus group-generated insights now are used to sensitize medical and public health students training in the county medical centers.

Accessing deep feelings of anger and resentment would be highly unlikely in a one-on-one survey; the group process created the safe space in which feelings could be expressed. Social research has not done well in reaching people who are isolated by the daily, exhausting struggles for survival, services, and dignity—people who will not respond to surveys or whose experiences, insights, and feelings lie outside the range of data survey methods. These people also are uncomfortable with individual interviews. We found that almost all elements of the community could be accessed in the safe and familiar context of their own turf, relations, and organizations through focus groups. Only long-term participant observation has a similar capacity for such disclosure, but it is expensive and is most effective with small groups (Gans 1982; Liebow 1967; Whyte 1981).

Summary

The use of focus groups in the Madison County Health Project allowed community residents to define their health needs and take consequent action. The vigor of their response suggests the utility of the focus group, not only as a research instrument but as a means whereby a community can recognize its needs within the framework of its own language and contexts, and mobilize accordingly. As one observer (who criticizes American COPC projects for being too physician directed) put it, "The Madison Community Health Project has utilized community participation, unlike many other COPC projects. In essence, the Madison Community Health Project has put the 'community' back in COPC" (Shaler, 1992b, p. 49). Focus group methods made such community involvement possible.

Appendix: Scored and Ranked Responses
to Focus Group Questions

Question 1. What personal health problems or physical complaints appear to be most commonly mentioned by people in the community? (Highest possible score: 80.)

Score	Rank	Code	Description
53	1	P.	Arthritis/rheumatism
45	2	A.	Backache/references to back
39	3	L.	Allergies/sinus
39	3	T.	Heart disease/references to heart
38	4	R.	Blood pressure
33	5	B.	Headache/references to head
27	6	C.	Stomach ache/references to stomach
27	6	M.	Sore throats/colds
27	6	U.	Cancer
22	7	JJ.	Virus, flu
22	7	K.	Ear infections/problems

Question 2. What in this group's opinion are the serious health problems in Madison County?

Score	Rank	Code	Description
38	1	F.	Alcohol abuse
27	2	J.	Stress-related physical symptoms: headaches and stomach aches
22	3	EE.	Cancer
21	3	I.	Aging: nonspecific references to chronic diseases and problems associated with aging; if we add in the scores for Alzheimer's disease (V.), circulatory problems (MM.), and cardiovascular disease (S.), the total score for age-related disease would be 51, indicating its primary significance in the eyes of county residents
20	4	K.	Depression
20	4	W.	Dental problems

Question 3. What is this group's opinion of causes of serious health problems?

Score	Rank	Code	Description
51	1	B.	Lack of preventive care and self-care, refers to lack of screening and follow-up to screening or lack of knowledge of preventive care or self-care when mentioned in terms of leading to serious health problems or illnesses
50	2	C.	Poor diet (home and school)
46	3	A.	Poor parenting (supervision)/poor hygiene
30	4	Q.	Abuse, neglect
22	5	P.	Geographic isolation
21	6	D.	Smoking/tobacco use
20	7	R.	Poverty/financial difficulty
20	7	N.	Family stress, related to single parenting, marital discord, low income, alcohol, and drugs

Question 3a. What in this group's opinion are the serious barriers to health care?

Community Groups' Views

Score	Rank	Code	Description
20	1	C.	Cost of insurance
20	1	D.	Lack of transportation
19	2	A.	Cost of medical visits
19	2	B.	Cost of medicines
12	3	O.	Lack of insurance
12	3	W.	Lack of preventative care or adequate exercise
11	4	L1.	Patient perception of having received poor care
10	5	X.	Physical distance and isolation from medical services
10	5	L4.	Concern over scheduling at medical centers

Summary of Professional Focus Groups' Views

Score	Rank	Code	Description
41	1	D.	Lack of transportation
41	1	O.	Lack of insurance
35	2	A.	Cost of medical visits
30	3	Z.	People delaying seeking medical treatment
30	3	B.	Cost of medicines
30	3	C.	Cost of insurance
29	4	W.	Lack of preventative care or adequate exercise
25	5	T.	Poverty
20	6	H.	Pride/self-reliance
19	7	Q.	Lack of basic education and basic skills
18	8	G.	Lack of in-home care for the elderly
17	9	S.	Abuse/neglect
16	10	X.	Physical distance and isolation from medical services

Question 4. What needs to be done to handle these problems?

Score	Rank	Code	Description
52	1	A.	Preventative health education
48	2	E.	Transportation services for the elderly and schoolchildren
44	3	A1.	Education on how to use health system
34	4	G.	Expand home care for the elderly
31	5	B.	Parenting education/support groups
29	6	C.	Nutrition education
24	7	T.	Fees charges adjusted for income level
19	8	M.	Better emergency services
18	9	R.	Centralized information source on local services
17	10	Y.	Educating providers to local values and culture

Question 5. Do you feel that there is any group of the population not receiving adequate medical care? Why not?

Score	Rank	Code	Description
70	1	A.	The elderly, due to cost, lack of access to medical facilities and other programs, being homebound by illness, low income, and lack of transportation
52	2	C.	People caught between public assistance and private insurance or people without insurance
44	3	H.	People who feel they are unable to afford the costs, often referred to as the poor
41	4	B.	Children and teenagers
29	5	F.	People without means of transportation
23	6	D.	People not educated to use the health care system

PART IV

Conclusions

14

Future Directions for Focus Groups

DAVID L. MORGAN

In many ways, this chapter is like a final report from the conference at Menucha that brought together most of the authors in this book (see the Preface). In particular, we devoted the final day of the conference to a series of focus groups that discussed future directions for focus groups. There is obviously a certain irony in doing focus groups with focus group researchers to discuss the future of focus groups. Still, this process was very familiar to many of us, except that we had applied it with groups of experts on other topics. What was new was delving into the insights that came from our own expertise.

We began this process in the morning, with three smaller, unstructured groups that lasted 1.5 hours. Each morning group had the goal of developing topics for an afternoon session among all the conference participants. After the three groups reported on their themes, I merged their ideas into four broad recommendations for our future directions: (1) do more research on focus groups, (2) create more links to other disciplines, (3) develop focus groups for various purposes, and (4) work on technology issues.

In the afternoon, I used these four themes to lead a focus group with all the conference participants. This group was both large (more than 15 members) and long (nearly 3 hours). It was also an unusually exciting and productive session. The success of this group came from our high level of interest in the topic and the camaraderie that we had built up over the previous 2 days. By this point in the conference, our discussions had evolved into an extended exchange among a series of newfound friends. Moderating a group this large and this long would

225

have been quite a challenge under other circumstances, but in this case it was a delight from start to finish.

The three morning sessions and the longer afternoon session together produced a total of more than 100 pages of transcripts. I began the analysis process with open coding (Strauss & Corbin, 1990), which summarized the key points in each discussion while avoiding interpretations. I then integrated and organized this summary material, relying most heavily on the discussions in the afternoon group in which everyone had participated. As a final step, I went back over the summaries from the three morning sessions to avoid missing any important insights.

Although I have tried to stay close to our original discussions in this analysis, what follows is indeed my own handiwork; it thus contains some unavoidable elements of personal interpretation. At the very least, it implicitly reflects my interpretation of which topics were most worthy of inclusion. I have concentrated the more explicitly interpretive material in the summaries for each section and in the conclusions section, but it should be clear that I, rather than the conference participants, bear the ultimate responsibility for this report.

The format for the rest of this chapter uses a common organizational system for reports from focus group research, presenting the key points related to our four basic themes. The report itself concentrates on the content of our discussion of these four themes, with relatively few direct quotations. In part, this format represents my judgment that the purpose of this chapter is to share our thinking with the broader community of focus group researchers, rather than to provide a deeper insight into our personal perspectives. In addition, however, this format reflects the reality that there is so much material that sheer space limitations require a greater emphasis on what we said rather than on how we said it. Finally, because many of the topics that we discussed also appear in the earlier chapters, I have added notes that direct readers to this additional material.

We Need to Do More Research on Focus Groups

This was the topic that received the most discussion in our groups. In many ways, this amount of attention reflected a self-conscious realization of our historically unique position. On the one hand, we felt that it was important to recognize that we had a large amount of knowledge to share, based on our prior experience. On the other hand, we also felt that we still had a lot to learn and that research was an important way to accomplish this learning. One participant summarized our position by noting that we represented the first generation of social science researchers who had renewed the interest in focus groups. As such, our task has been largely to adapt what we found elsewhere. We now are at a point of transition; from here, we need to encourage a next generation who will be the ones to produce further research on this technique. In other words, we felt that one of the key contributions that we could make was to use our experience to point to the most crucial areas for research on focus groups.

Uses for Methodological Research

Setting Standards

There was a strong feeling that one of the best reasons for doing more research on focus groups would be to produce a set of empirically grounded standards for our procedures. We were especially concerned about this issue as part of the broader question of quality control, because the rapidly growing popularity of focus groups may well lead to a fair amount of substandard work. By generating research-based standards, we would have a solid foundation from which to respond to critics who want to blame the method for poor results that may actually be due to improper applications of the method.

In our discussions, we realized that focus groups, like any other method, will have their critics, but that doing methodological research would enable us both to respond to reasonable criticisms and to cut off unfounded attacks. The basic strategy would be to convert criticisms into empirical issues and thereby encourage the kind of research that would generate growth in our field. Ultimately, we agreed that it would be impossible to convince everyone, because there would always be some who see focus group as impure, no matter what evidence we offer. Therefore, in planning our research, we should concentrate on those willing to be convinced by seeing that we are careful and systematic about our procedures. (Chapter 5 deals extensively with questions of quality control and standards; these issues are also discussed in Chapter 1.)

In reviewing the criticisms of focus groups that were likely to come from quantitative researchers, we thought that many of the issues would fall under the traditional headings of reliability and validity. In general, we were able to convert these issues to researchable topics. The summary of these discussions appears in the next section.

We also considered a different set of criticisms that would be more likely to come from qualitative researchers. In particular, we believed that framing our research on focus groups around issues of reliability and validity might tend to alienate this constituency. As an alternative, several of the participants were attracted to Lincoln and Guba's (1985) efforts to develop alternative criteria for assessing the goodness of qualitative research—such as an emphasis on trustworthiness rather than validity and on transferability rather than generalizability. There was a general consensus that we should not overstate our claims about focus groups. In particular, there was a recognition that focus groups do not have either the generalizability of quantitative research that is based on random samples or the naturalness of qualitative research that is based on fieldwork. Thus a further advantage of setting research-based standards for our work would be to define an appropriate degree of modesty about what focus groups can and cannot do.

Defining Our Strengths and Limitations

Several aspects of our discussions touched on the idea that we need to be clear about the advantages that focus groups have to offer and thus about where they fit within a variety of different approaches to data gathering. We saw this as part of the recent tendency to accept a variety of different research procedures, so long as each is done carefully and systematically and produces results that have value. By doing research on focus groups, we would be both confirming their benefits and testing their limits. As a group, we spent more time discussing the limitations of focus groups. In part, this emphasis derived from our general consensus on the value of focus groups, and in part, it was due to our ongoing concern that focus groups not be oversold. Many of the limitations that we discussed apply to a number of different research methods, including focus groups. For example, several participants noted that focus groups have been particularly popular in cross-cultural research, but that this kind of work always demands a considerable degree of care and sensitivity to others' perspectives. Others pointed out that this caveat carries over to many settings for exploratory research, where gaining good data often depends on having at least a little insider knowledge. We also discussed the fact that focus groups rely on self-reported data, so they have limitations whenever people have a poor ability to report on a topic or have reasons to conceal things. In addition, we recognized that focus groups are a form of interview and are thus subject to demand characteristics that may lead the research participants to frame their discussions in terms of what they believe we want to hear.

We also highlighted a set of issues that are more likely to occur in focus groups, as a result of bringing multiple participants into contact with each other. Interestingly, our discussions of these issues also emphasized ways in which we could turn these problems into advantages. Thus, although we generally agreed that working with groups heightens issues of social desirability and conformity, we also felt that observing these group influences in action can provide insights into participants' normative expectations for each other. Similarly, several of our participants noted the difficulties involved in doing focus groups in conflict-ridden settings and, more generally, whenever the research calls for mixing participants across different levels of hierarchy or status. Yet we also discussed the ways that research within these settings can create opportunities for different participants to communicate their perspectives to each other. (See Chapters 1 and 9 for further discussions of the strengths and weaknesses of focus groups.)

At the broadest level, we felt that we must be aware of our limitations even as we make others aware of our strengths. At the same time, we particularly agreed that there is no need to be defensive about our limitations. Many thought that this attitude represented a considerable change from the more combative climate of the late 1970s into the 1980s, when there was often bitter debate over what was right or worthwhile. Instead, we now sensed a far greater degree of tolerance and even mutual curiosity. By using this new climate to guide our exploration of the strengths and weaknesses of focus groups, we hoped to avoid the trap of doing advocacy-oriented research and thus to provide a more forthright understanding of what focus groups can and cannot do.

Topics for Methodological Research

Group Dynamics Issues

The question of how we could best use group processes to meet our research needs kept resurfacing throughout our discussions. On a general level, we wanted to see more research on aspects of groups that either encourage or discourage the expression of diverse opinions. More specifically, we wanted to see more work on social desirability and conformity, as noted above, and also on how the homogeneity or heterogeneity of groups affected what participants are willing to say.

Another specific issue that several people mentioned was voting in groups. Several of us believed that voting should be avoided, both because of the poor quality of data that it produces and its tendency to create conformity. But where, we wondered, are the data to support this belief? Similarly, we agreed that we preferred to avoid pushing for consensual decisions in our groups, for fear of stifling diverse opinions, yet we admitted that we had relatively little data on the actual effects of pushing for consensus in focus groups. Our general conclusion was that how one handled group dynamics issues depends greatly on what one wants to learn from the group. On the one hand, if we set up our groups to push for diverse opinions, then we will learn more about individual differences. On the other hand, if we push for consensus, then we can learn more about the degree of participants' commitment to divergent views. Similarly, we may sacrifice our interest in encouraging free expression if our goal is to learn about pathways into decision making or about the role that rational and nonrational arguments play in decisions. We were also curious about strategies that begin by letting participants freely express their own views and then purposely push them in one direction or the other. From a research point of view, each of these ideas involves modifying aspects of group dynamics within the same research project to investigate how this affects the nature of participants' discussions.

Moderator Issues

We all recognized that one of the key ways that we deal with group dynamics and a number of other issues is through the moderator's control over the group. Based on our informal comparisons of the differences in how we lead discussions, we sensed a need to be more explicit about both what we are doing as moderators and why we choose to do it one way rather than another.

One dimension that differentiated our moderating styles was the level of knowledge that we claimed about the particular topic. At the extremes, there are differences between what we can learn through acting naive (thus gaining basic information through being wised up) and acting well informed (thus exploring fine details and subtle distinctions in what participants know).

A more lively discussion surrounded questions about the moderator's level of involvement in the group. We distinguished between moderating styles that emphasize a degree of separateness from the group and those that stress more self-disclosure or expressions of empathy on the part of the moderator. Our exchanges on this issue also raised the question of whether we, as researchers and moderators, belong inside the data collection process or outside it. Is neutrality really possible when the researcher is actively involved in the data collection?

Rather than trying to resolve issues that are, after all, inherent in qualitative methods, we concentrated on the possibilities for research on the effectiveness of different styles of moderating. In particular, we felt that we needed more knowledge about which kinds of groups are most sensitive to differences in moderator style, such as groups on topics that may require self-disclosures from the participants. More generally, we endorsed the need for research devoted to determining which styles of moderating work best with which kinds of groups discussing which kinds of topics. (See Chapter 11 for a discussion of issues related to self-disclosure and moderator style.)

We also considered the moderator's role in terms that were more explicitly concerned with reliability. Assuming we have made an informed choice about the overall moderator style for a particular project, the basic question is whether we should stick to it and be as consistent as possible across groups. Although it is obvious that this kind of standardization would increase certain aspects of reliability, we also felt that it would restrict our ability to adapt to the dynamics of each individual group. Thus the narrow goal of consistency in moderator style can interfere with the broader goal of allowing each group to have the same opportunity to express its views on the topic in question. One suggested solution was to run the initial portion of each group in a consistent fashion, to allow for comparability, but then to leave room for shifts in moderator style to deal with the unique aspects of each group during the latter part of the discussion.

Overall, we thought that we needed programmatic research to improve our understanding of the likely outcomes of choosing one particular approach to moderating. At the same time, we recognized that we needed to understand these choices within the context of a particular type of participants discussing a particular topic. Consequently, research on differences in moderator style will need to concentrate on both general principles and specific applications.

Validity Issues

Our conversations generated numerous suggestions for research that would assess the validity of data gathered through focus groups. Many of these ideas emphasized triangulation with other methods, such as individual depth interviews and surveys. We developed three basic advantages that can come from comparisons with results from other methods. First, we can show evidence for the validity of our own data by demonstrating how its findings overlap with those from other techniques. Second, we can demonstrate the advantages of focus groups by showing ways in which they are more effective at producing the data of interest. Finally, we can produce empirically based statements about the limits of focus groups by locating the circumstances in which other methods provide more useful data.

In considering different strategies for triangulation, we expressed considerable frustration over the lack of studies that have paired focus with individual interviews. While advocating more research in this area, we also wished to avoid the trap of using the results of individual interviews as a standard for assessing focus groups, i.e., treating them as a test of criterion validity. We shared the view that if research finds differences between the results from individual and group interviews, then the methodological goal should be to understand the sources of these differences. Several members of our group were particularly anxious to avoid the conclusion that any differences that are due to group processes represent some kind of contamination or invalidity. In particular, we pointed out that groups can provide comparisons that lead people to talk about a wider range of experiences and opinions than may occur in individual interviews. Similarly, the interactions in groups can provide challenges to overidealized statements, leading to more accurate accounts of what people actually do. (Chapter 9 considers these issues in more systematic detail.)

Although we believed that triangulation can be a major tool in assessing the validity of focus groups, we did not feel that it is a panacea. In particular, we recognized that true triangulation, in which two different methods are applied to the same research question, is an expensive and time-consuming enterprise. In this light, we felt that it is important to distinguish this kind of multimethod research from projects that used focus groups only to compensate for specific limitations in another method (e.g., to generate item wordings for surveys). We also recognized that it would be naive to expect a large degree of overlap whenever one applies two different methods to the same research question, because multiple methods can lead to multiple interpretations. (Chapter 8 considers strategies for triangulation, especially as they relate to validity issues.)

Given the limits of triangulation, we also discussed several other approaches to assessing the validity of data from focus groups. One

such technique is member checks, i.e., going back to research participants to get their reactions to the research results. One obvious design
for member checks would be to conduct a small number of individual
interviews, following the focus groups, for the express purpose of
validating what participants had said in the groups. Another approach
would be to conduct follow-up focus groups to discuss findings with
either the original participants or a fresh set of similar participants. We
also discussed audits as a different validation technique, i.e., seeking
an external review where the goal was to track research conclusions
back to the procedures that originally generated them, at each step
justifying the process that produced the conclusion.

Other Research Issues

In addition to the major research topics considered above, we also
devoted at least some attention to a large number of other possibilities,
most of which involved new procedures. For example, several people
noted that marketers use considerably more stimulus material than we
do, and argued for exploring the possibility of having participants react
to vignettes or other prepared discussion aids. Others felt that social
science researchers should pay more attention to the nonverbal aspects
of group interaction. Several people also noted that we are currently
weak on applying focus groups to longitudinal research and that we
should develop ways of using focus groups to collect data over time.

On balance, we spent rather less time on research that involves new
ways of doing focus groups, because we felt that this would be an
inevitable aspect of the growth in our field. Instead, we thought that the
more important goal for our future directions should be to encourage
reflexive research on the advantages and limitations of focus groups.
Because of the expense involved in setting up research for the sole purpose
of head-to-head comparisons of various techniques, we saw natural variation within research projects as the most likely course for our efforts. For
individual researchers, this strategy would create the possibility of publishing both substantive and methodological pieces from the same
project. We thought that this opportunity could be particularly reward-
ing for graduate students and recent doctorates, who have both the most
to gain by demonstrating methodological sophistication and the most
to lose by doing work that is too narrowly methodological.

This brought us back to the question of how best to support the next
generation of focus group researchers, and the primary topic that we

addressed here was the creation of infrastructure. Promoting publication outlets is the most obvious challenge in this regard. Holding more conferences such as this one and generating more edited collections were nominated as immediately available solutions to this problem, especially if we can broaden our outreach to a wider range of potential participants in these ventures. In the long run, however, we were anxious to locate established journals that will look favorably on this kind of work. In addition to publication opportunities, we also advocated more use of professional meetings as opportunities either to do workshops in fields where there is already clear interest or to foster interest where it is only beginning to emerge. Along with all of this activity, we also considered a number of mechanisms, such as a newsletter to maintain communication across the increasingly widespread network of people who are doing research involving focus groups.

Stepping back from all of our advocacy of more research on focus groups, it was clear that we did not see such research as an end in itself. Rather, we saw it as part of the larger goal of demonstrating the value of focus groups. Ultimately, it is our results themselves that will have to have value. Doing research that maximizes our strengths and minimizes our weaknesses is the best way to ensure the value of the results we produce with focus groups.

We Need to Create More Links to Other Disciplines

In our discussions, we were both excited by the range of researchers who are interested in focus groups and a bit nervous about what all this expansion might mean for the field. There was consensus that focus groups are attractive to many researchers who have been trained in other methods because of the practical value of focus groups as a data-collection tool. A particularly interesting view was that some positivists are attracted to focus group because they have encountered the limits of their familiar procedures. We saw this as pointing to a future in which focus groups will be used by people from a wide variety of disciplines and a wide variety of methodological stances. Thus as we develop focus groups, we must be aware of the multiple perspectives that different kinds of researchers will bring to our field.

Reciprocity Should Be a Key Element
in Our Contacts With Other Fields

A basic theme of our discussions was that operating across both disciplines and methodological paradigms will provide focus group researchers with an unusually wide range of options and resources. To take advantage of this, we advocated an orientation toward others' work that is based on reciprocity: As we carry our methods to them, we will also learn from them. The benefits of this reciprocity are an exposure to new knowledge and new approaches that will translate into better ways to accomplish our own ends and produce continued growth in our field.

Often, the issues that focus group researchers have been struggling with are familiar topics in other fields, such as group dynamics and interaction in social psychology or communication studies. Thus there is already a realm of thought and expertise that we can tap into in exchange for our own knowledge. The basic advantages of such reciprocal partnerships are to keep each field from having to reinvent the wheel and to save us from becoming locked into an overnarrow way of thinking about our procedures. In particular, we felt that contacts with new disciplines will expand our vocabulary, as we encounter both new terms that we need to understand and new ways to describe our procedures so that others can understand them from their perspective.

Of course, we also recognized that reciprocal exchanges will be easier in some fields than others. Marketing research presents a particular problem here, due to its proprietary nature. To maintain a competitive edge, marketers must both produce new knowledge and limit others' access to their most innovative techniques. Several participants felt frustrated by marketers' tendency to publish very partial accounts of their techniques. Too often, we have been drawn to the possibilities but lacked sufficient information to emulate or evaluate specific techniques, such as the use of dual moderators. In these circumstances, we have had to reinvent the wheel.

In response, we argued that the slower pace of research and dissemination in our field limited any realistic threat to marketers. Because of the time it would take before we could publish any work using techniques that we learned from others, only the most truly innovative procedures would be threatened by more open exchanges between social science practitioners and marketers. In general, we emphasized this long-run view. Thus our exchanges with other disciplines do not have to be balanced on a project by project basis; instead, over time, these partnerships will yield a mutual sharing of expertise and new ideas.

What Will Be Our Role in Interdisciplinary Work?

There was a broad consensus in our discussions that those of us with the most experience in the social science applications of focus groups have a responsibility to show leadership and promote standards. At the same time, we also recognized the reality that there will be different standards in different fields. Again, marketers provide a good example, as our world of publish or perish is very different from their standard of making a sale or convincing a client. As a general principle, we agreed that interdisciplinary work requires us to be aware of the different ways that research is conducted and used in various fields.

One set of disciplinary differences that we discussed concerned the variation between addressing audiences of qualitative or quantitative researchers. A major issue that we dealt with was distinguishing between differences in vocabulary versus more substantive disagreements. This returned us to some of the issues we had discussed under the heading of reliability and validity. In general, we concluded that these contrasting approaches to data quality do not necessarily force us into an either-or choice; instead, we agreed that we can gain a much better sense of the strengths and limitation of focus groups by considering the issues raised by each approach.

In sum, we thought that whether our role is as leaders—carrying our greater experience with focus groups to other researchers—or as learners—profiting from their experiences—we need to begin from an awareness of the perspective of others. This more open orientation to different approaches seemed to diverge from the traditional assumption that research methods have relatively universal applicability. We acknowledged that we could choose to develop focus groups along the traditional lines of treating methods merely as tools that are disassociated from the theories and disciplines that generated them. Our preference, however, was to base our contacts with other fields on a need to recognize how our own origins affect the ways in which we think about and use focus groups. Seen in this light, the need to articulate our perspective to others through interdisciplinary contacts can be an important avenue for improving our understanding of our own approaches to focus groups.

Opportunities for Interdisciplinary Work

In looking at our contacts with other disciplines, we were particularly excited about the possible contributions to our field from contacts with communication studies. (See Chapter 4.) We also foresaw more use of focus groups in education, where we can profit from the knowledge generated by that field's relatively early renewal of interest in qualitative methods. Outside the social sciences, we anticipated the increasing use of focus groups in the professions, including law, architecture, and medicine. We saw such applications already occurring in the more change-oriented professions, especially public health, and we expected them to spread. Given the often very practical interests of these professions, we felt that they would not only find many potential uses for focus groups but also uncover a wide array of new issues for us to consider.

In addition to considering opportunities for interdisciplinary contacts, we also asked ourselves just how well we had considered the issues in our home disciplines. Even though most of us came from a background in social psychology, we acknowledged that we had paid relatively little attention to such areas as attribution, token status, and self-categorization. And, under the broad umbrella of social psychology, we had tended to ignore the issues raised by symbolic interactionists.

We easily reached the conclusion that contacts with ideas in new disciplines and in our own familiar fields offer both great opportunities and substantial challenges for future applications of focus groups. In considering these possibilities, however, we realized that disciplinary differences are not the only issues that we face in developing focus groups. In particular, the real differences often seem to arise more from the purposes to which we are applying focus groups, rather than the substantive topic or disciplinary basis for our research.

We Need to Develop Focus Groups for Various Purposes

In sorting out the purposes for which social scientists use focus groups, we came up with a list that included basic research, evaluation research, change-oriented research, and policy research. Across each of these areas, we also noted a strong tendency to use focus groups whenever cross-cultural or cross-national samples are involved. Thus we saw that focus groups can span the gamut of purposes to which social science data might be applied and that they are especially valuable whenever the goal is to compare participants whose perspectives differ from those of the researcher.

Among these various uses for focus groups, several of the members of our group were particularly interested in types of research for which the goal was to produce change, including social marketing, action research, and participatory research. It was clear that focus groups can be a useful technique for reaching the goals of each of these fields, including disseminating information in ways that it will be likely to be used, finding strategies to help people to make the changes they desire, and empowering people to collect data and use them for their own purposes. (See Chapters 10 and 13 for discussions of action-oriented research.)

Considering these new uses for focus groups raised issues about our taken-for-granted assumptions in doing focus groups, especially about the relationship between the researcher and the researched. We realized that relatively little had been written about the ethical issues involved in focus groups, and we spent a considerable amount of time developing this theme. At the broadest level, we raised a number of concerns that apply to qualitative methods in general. In these areas, we reaffirmed the value of the classic human subjects' guidelines that direct our attention to the possible negative outcomes that participants may experience. At the most detailed level, we considered a number of issues that applied to unique research settings or topics. There, we felt that we should consult key informants or colleagues with a background in the particular area, so that we can begin with the kind of local, contextual information necessary to protect our participants. Beyond these general guidelines, we considered two topics that arise specifically from the group interview setting. First, there are additional privacy concerns, because participants reveal themselves to each other, not just to the researchers. Second, and tied to this, there are potential stresses associated with the intensity of the interaction in many groups. To respond to both of these concerns, we need to be particularly concerned with how the participants feel after they have left the group. Often, the open discussions in our groups are an unusual experience for our participants; if these discussions foster an overdisclosure of personal information, participants may feel threatened by what they had revealed. We acknowledged

This, in turn, facilitates comparisons of alternative codings, or readings, of the data as well as outside audits of our analysis procedures.

Another advantage of computers arises from the more interpretive goal of getting a better idea of just how much useful information there actually is in our data. In part this occurs through the systematic coding that these programs require, and in part it occurs through the more detailed reports of our coding that the programs produce. These same features of computerized analysis also make it easier to saturate concepts by first labeling transcript segments with broad code categories and then separating out the various dimensions of these concepts. We saw this kind of coding as useful because it makes you more aware of how much you know about a given concept. It can also make you more focused in your later data gathering, so that you concentrate more on the areas where you are not saturated, that is, where participants still have new things to tell you.

Turning to the negative aspects of computerized analysis, several people noted that the real problem with the current computer programs is that they were an "attractive nuisance," that is, they are too easy to misuse and they can cover up sloppy work. Others were convinced that these computer packages will affect how we did our analyses. In particular, there was concern that current packages encourage the counting of predetermined codes by making these analytic procedures not just easy but powerful, while doing little to facilitate other approaches, such as creating codes from scratch through the reading and rereading of transcripts. The fear was that this transformation of our analysis style will happen in gradual and subtle ways, so that we might not even be aware of these changes as they occur.

This led us back to discussions of the limits of quantification in analyzing focus groups. Some of us maintained that counting is useful for capturing patterns so that we can be sure about what is said in our groups. Even so, we agreed that the more important goal is typically to get at why things are said, to understand why people have the experiences and feelings that they do. Quantification in general and computer programs in particular do not answer these questions for us. What they can do is to arrange our data in ways that make it easier to see either patterns in our transcripts or areas where we need to collect more data; still, even these advantages rest on the analyst's judgment.

Stepping back from specifics, we saw that it was clear that most of us are willing to experiment with new technology, especially in terms of data analysis, but that we do so from a skeptical point of view. In considering why this might be so, one of the participants in a morning group pointed out that qualitative data can be time-consuming to deal with as well as difficult to communicate to others. This can lead to pressure for some sort of technological fix, whether through meter readings or computerized analysis. But, as one of the afternoon participants eloquently summarized, the bottom line is that machines cannot do the induction for us. Ultimately, each of us must not only reach his or her own conclusions, but we must also be prepared to defend the procedures that we use in getting there.

Conclusions

Taking a wider view of the many specific points in our discussions about future directions for focus groups, we noted that one broad theme emerges: Many of the lessons that we have learned in the past will serve us well in the future.

In regard to research issues, there was unanimity in our groups that doing research on focus groups will improve both our self-knowledge and our wider legitimacy. There was also agreement that our best strategy for the foreseeable future is to build methodological components into our ongoing research. Our discussions clearly indicated that we are ready and eager for this task, so the real challenge will not be to do this work, but to disseminate it. In considering the challenge of publishing research on focus groups, we noted that there is a clear connection with our past efforts to create acceptance for research that uses focus groups. We must now shift these efforts toward gaining acceptance for new work that does research on focus groups. Thus we must continue many of the efforts that were necessary to establish our field to further its growth through more research on focus groups.

We were also unanimous in our desire to promote links with other disciplines, and this too is an area where much of what we have already accomplished will help with our future tasks. Just as we had to reach out to others in our own disciplines to establish the initial legitimacy of focus groups, we will have to do a certain amount of work to convince those in other disciplines. And just as we have drawn on many fields within our own disciplines to gain the knowledge that we needed to do focus groups, we can draw on the additional knowledge in other fields as a way to improve our procedures. Of course, accomplishing these cross-disciplinary contacts will not always go smoothly. Some of our difficulty will just be a matter of translating each other's vocabularies, but in other cases each of us will be expressing ideas that the other has never considered before. Fortunately, it has been our willingness to deal with new ideas and to convince others of their merit that has brought us this far, so there is every reason to believe that this openness will continue to be a prominent aspect of our future directions.

In regard to developing focus groups for other purposes, we were unquestionably convinced that focus groups were a powerful technique and that they warranted our efforts both to spread their use and to improve their effectiveness. Adapting focus groups to new purposes is thus another challenge that continues the work we have done in the past, but there will be other challenges here as well. In particular, we must be highly responsive to the ethical implications of focus groups as we move from applications that seek not just to understand others' behaviors but to change them. In considering these uses of focus groups, we may well have to distinguish between efforts to help people control their own lives versus unethical manipulation. To paraphrase one of the participants, although we may think we are simply providing a tool, we are also sharpening a blade that someone else may use as a weapon. But much of the past success of focus group research has been due to our ability to operate in the real world, and this will provide good preparation for meeting the challenges posed by these new uses for focus groups.

Turning to technology issues, our discussions showed a clear interest in not losing our place on the cutting edge. Certainly we will not ignore the advances in data-gathering technology and technique created by marketers and others, nor will we remain outside the debates that qualitative researchers are pursuing in regard to data analysis. Nonetheless, we voiced distinct reservations about these newer technologies. Part of this reticence stems from the very practical nature of much of our research: Until we are convinced that new technologies will really add to the value of our results, we will remain skeptics. This skepticism is especially notable when compared to the enthusiasm with which we discussed other aspects of our future directions. Overall, this points to the conclusion that what will keep us on the cutting edge is research on focus groups, more interdisciplinary contacts, and new purposes for focus groups, rather than an emphasis on technology per se.

Finally, I would like to highlight a further strength that will benefit focus group researchers as we face the future. In reviewing the themes that we raised in our discussions, I was struck by the realization that many of the skills that we have acquired to do focus groups will aid us in the continuing development of our field. In particular, our interest in talking to people who may be different from ourselves to understand their perspectives is mirrored by our ability to carry on conversations with an unusually wide range of social science researchers. Thus it is probably no accident that focus group research has been able to cross disciplinary boundaries and span methodological orientations. Our goal should be to continue these conversations. Ultimately, our role in charting future directions for focus groups should be analogous to moderating a focus group: not to direct the discussion but to facilitate it, so that the multiple voices can both speak and respond to each other.

References

Abrahams, R. (1976). *Talking black*. Rowley, MA: Newbury House.

Abramson, J. H. (1984). *Survey methods in community medicine: An introduction to epidemiological and evaluative studies*. New York: Churchill Livingstone.

Acuña, R. (1972). *Occupied America. The Chicanos struggle toward liberation*. San Francisco: Canfield Press.

Adler, P., & Adler, P. (1987). *Membership roles in field research*. Newbury Park, CA: Sage.

Anderson, E. (1976). *A place on the corner*. Chicago: University of Chicago Press.

Anderson, E. (1989). Sex codes and family life among poor inner-city youth. *The Annals of the American Academy of Political and Social Science, 501*, 59-78.

Asch, S. E. (1952). Group forces in the modification and distortion of judgments. In *Social psychology* (chap. 16). Englewood Cliffs, NJ: Prentice-Hall.

Aschenbrenner, J. (1975). *Lifelines: Black families in Chicago*. New York: Holt, Rinehart & Winston.

Axelrod, M. (1975). Marketers get an eyeful when focus groups expose products, ideas, images, ad copy, etc. to consumers. *Marketing News, 8*, 6-7.

Babbie, E. (1989). *The practice of social research*. Belmont, CA: Wadsworth.

Baca Zinn, M. (1979). Field research in minority communities: Ethical, methodological, and political observations by an insider. *Social Problems, 27*, 209-219.

Bailey, R., & Flores, G. V. (1973). Internal colonialism and racial minorities in the U.S.: An overview. In F. Bonilla & R. Girling (Eds.). *Structures of dependency* (pp. 149-160). Palo Alto: Authors.

Baldassare, M. (1979). *Residential crowding in urban America*. Berkeley: University of California Press.

Baldassare, M. (1981). The effect of household density on subgroups. *American Sociological Review, 46*, 110-118.

Bales, R. F. (1950). *Interaction process analysis: A method for the study of small groups.* Reading, MA: Addison-Wesley.

Basch, C. E. (1987). Focus group interview: An underutilized research technique for improving theory and practice in health education. *Health Education Quarterly, 14*(4), 411-448.

Bauman, L. J., & Adair. E. G. (1992). The use of ethnographic interviewing to inform questionnaire construction. *Health Education Quarterly, 19*, 1-8.

Becker, H. S. (1970). Practitioners of vice and crime. In R. Habenstein (Ed.), *Pathways to data: Field methods for studying ongoing social organizations* (pp. 30-49). Chicago: Aldine.

Becker, M. H. (1979). Understanding patient compliance: The contributions of attitudes and other psychosocial factors. In S. J. Cohen (Ed.), *New directions in patient compliance* (pp. 1-31). Lexington, MA: Heath.

Becker, M. H., & Joseph, J. G. (1988). AIDS and behavioral change to reduce risk: A review. *American Journal of Public Health, 78*(4), 394-410.

Bellah, R. (1986). *Habits of the heart: Individualism and commitment in American life.* New York: Harper & Row.

Bellenger, D. N., Barnhardt, K. L., & Goldstucker, J. L. (1976). *Qualitative research in marketing.* Chicago: American Marketing Association.

Berk, R. A., & Adams, J. M. (1970.) Establishing rapport with deviant groups. *Social Problems, 18*, 102-117.

Bernard, R. H. (1988). *Research methods in cultural anthropology.* Newbury Park, CA: Sage.

Bloom, N. (1989). Have discussion groups had their day? *Industrial Marketing Digest, 14*, 147-153.

Blumer, H. (1969). *Symbolic interactionism: Perspective and method.* Englewood Cliffs, NJ: Prentice-Hall.

Bogardus, E. S. (1926). The group interview. *Journal of Applied Sociology, 10*, 372-382.

Bogdan, R., & Taylor, S. J. (1975). *Introduction to qualitative research methods: A phenomenological approach to the social sciences.* New York: Wiley.

Booth, A. (1976). *Urban crowding and its consequences.* New York: Praeger.

Booth, A., & Edwards, J. N. (1976). Crowding and family relations. *American Sociological Review, 41*, 110-118.

Booth, A., Johnson, D. R. & Edwards, J. N. (1980). Reply to Gove and Hughes. *American Sociological Review, 45*, 870-873.

Bormann, E. G. (1972). Fantasy and rhetorical vision: The rhetorical criticism of social reality. *Quarterly Journal of Speech, 58*, 396-407.

Bormann, E. G. (1973). The Eagleton affair: A fantasy theme analysis. *Quarterly Journal of Speech, 68*, 143-159.

Bormann, E. G. (1982). Fantasy and rhetorical vision: Ten years later. *Quarterly Journal of Speech, 68*, 288-305.

Bortree, W. H. (1986). Focus groups reduce innovation risks. *Bank Marketing, 18*, 18-24.

Bradburn, N. (1969). *The structure of psychological well-being.* Chicago: Aldine.

Brewer, J., & Hunter, A. (1989). *Multimethod research: A synthesis of styles.* Newbury Park, CA: Sage.

Briggs, C. (1986). *Learning how to ask.* Cambridge: Cambridge University Press.

Brislin, R. W. (1986). The wording and translation of research instruments. In W. J. Lohner & J. W. Berry (Eds.), *Field methods in cross-cultural research* (pp. 137-164). Beverly Hills, CA: Sage.

Brown, J., & Sime, J. (1981). A methodology for accounts. In M. Brenner (Ed.), *Social method and social life* (pp. 159-188). London: Academic Press.

Brown, R., & Levinson, S. (1978). Universals in language usage: Politeness phenomena. In E. Goody (Ed.), *Questions and politeness* (pp. 56-289). Cambridge: Cambridge University Press.

Burgess, R. G. (1984). *In the field: An introduction to field research.* Boston: Allen & Unwin.

Burgoon, M., & Ruffner, M. (1978). *Human communication.* New York: Holt Rinehart & Winston.

Burke, K. (1946). *A grammar of motives.* Englewood Cliffs, NJ: Prentice-Hall.

Byrne, D. (1971). *The attraction paradigm.* New York: Academic Press.

Calder, B. J. (1977). Focus groups and the nature of qualitative marketing research. *Journal of Marketing Research, 14,* 353-364.

Campbell, D. T., & Stanley, J. C. (1966). *Experimental and quasi-experimental designs for research.* Chicago: Rand McNally.

Cancian, F. M., & Armstead, C. (1990, August). *Participatory research: An introduction.* Paper presented at the American Sociological Association Convention, Washington, DC.

Cannon, L. W., Higginbotham, E., & Leung, M. L. A. (1988). Race and class bias in qualitative research on women. *Gender & Society, 2,* 449-462.

Cappella, J. N. (1981). Mutual influence in expressive behavior: A review of adult and infant-adult dyadic interaction. *Psychological Bulletin, 89,* 101-132.

Cappella, J. N., & Palmer, M. T. (1992). The effect of partners' conversation on the association between attitude similarity and attraction. *Communication Monographs, 59,* 180-189.

Cartwright, D. (1953). Analysis of qualitative material. In L. Festinger & D. Katz (Eds.), *Research methods in the behavioral sciences* (pp. 421-470). New York: Holt, Rinehart & Winston.

Chayovan, N., Kamnuansilpa, P., & Knodel, J. (1988). *Thailand demographic and health survey, 1987.* Bangkok: Chulalongkorn University, Institute of Population Studies.

Chesebro, J. W. (1980). Paradoxical views of "homosexuality" in the rhetoric of social scientists: A fantasy theme analysis. *Quarterly Journal of Speech, 66,* 127-139.

Cicourel, A. (1974). *Cognitive sociology.* New York: Free Press.

Connolly, T., Jessup, L. M., & Valacich, J. S. (1990). Effects of anonymity and evaluative tone on idea generation in computer mediated groups. *Management Science, 36,* 97-120.

Converse, J. M., & Presser, S. (1986). *Survey questions: Handcrafting the standardized questionnaire.* (Sage University Paper, Quantitative Research Methods Series, Vol. 63). Beverly Hills, CA: Sage.

Cook, T. C., & Campbell, D. T. (1979). *Quasi-experimentation: Design and analysis issues for field settings.* Boston: Houghton Mifflin.

Cook, T., & Curtin, T. (1987). The mainstream and the underclass: Why are the differences so salient and the similarities so unobtrusive? In J. C. Masters & W. P. Smith (Eds.), *Social comparison, social justice, and relative deprivation: Theoretical, empirical, and policy perspectives* (pp. 218-269). Hillsdale, NJ: Lawrence Erlbaum.

Crabtree, B. F., & Miller, W. L. (1991). A qualitative approach to primary care research: The long interview. *Family Medicine, 23*(2), 145-151.

Crabtree, B. F., & Miller, W. L. (1992). *Doing qualitative research.* Newbury Park, CA: Sage.

Denzin, N. (Ed.). (1970). *Sociological methods*. Chicago: Aldine.

Denzin, N. K. (1979). *Interpretive interactionism*. Newbury Park, CA: Sage.

Denzin, N. K. (1988). Postmodern social theory. *Sociological Theory, 4,* 194-204.

Denzin, N. K. (1989). *The research act*. Englewood Cliffs, NJ: Prentice-Hall.

Desvousges, W. H., & Frey, J. H. (1989). Integrating focus groups and surveys: Examples from environmental risk studies. *Journal of Official Statistics 5,* 349-363.

deVries, H., Weijts, W., Dijkstra, M., & Kok, G. (1992). The utilization of qualitative and quantitative data for health education program planning, implementation, and evaluation: A spiral approach. *Health Education Quarterly, 19,* 101-115.

Dickens, D., & Fontana, A. (Eds.). (1992.). *Postmodernism and social inquiry*. Unpublished manuscript.

Douglas, J. D. (1985). *Creative interviewing*. Beverly Hills, CA: Sage.

Downs, C., Smayak, G. P., & Martin, E. (1980). *Professional interviewing*. New York: Harper & Row.

Duffy, B. (1991). *Focus groups: An important research technique for internal evaluation units*. Unpublished manuscript.

Eadie, W. F., & Powell, R. G. (1991, February). *RHETSEN2: A new measure of rhetorical sensitivity*. Paper presented at the annual meeting of the Western States Communication Association, Phoenix.

Edin, K. (1991). Surviving the welfare system: How AFDC recipients make ends meet in Chicago. *Social Problems, 38,* 462-474.

Fedder, C. J. (1990). Biz-to-biz focus groups require a special touch. *Marketing News, 24,* 46.

Fern, E. F. (1983). Focus groups: a review of some contradictory evidence, implications, and suggestions for future research. *Advances in Consumer Research, 10,* 121-126.

Fielding, N., & Lee, R. (Eds.). (1991). *Using computers in qualitative research*. Newbury Park, CA: Sage.

Fishbein, M., & Azjen, I. (1981). Acceptance, yielding, and impact: Cognitive processes in persuasion. In R. E. Petty, T. M. Ostrom, & T. C. Brock (Eds.), *Cognitive responses in persuasion* (pp. 339-359). Hillsdale, NJ: Lawrence Erlbaum.

Fisher, J. D. (1988). Possible effects of reference group-based social influence on AIDS-risk behavior and AIDS prevention. *American Psychologist, 43*(11), 914-920.

Flores, G. V. (1973). Race and culture in the internal colony: Keeping the Chicano in his place. In F. Bonilla & R. Girling (Eds.), *Structures of dependency* (pp. 189-223). Palo Alto: Authors.

Folch-Lyon, E., & Trost, J. F. (1981). Conducting focus group sessions. *Studies in family planning, 12,* 443-449.

Fowler, F. J. (1988). *Survey research methods* (rev. ed.). Newbury Park, CA: Sage.

French, W. L., Gross, E., & Resnick, H. (1986). Effects of a budget-cut crisis on a faculty at a large state university. *Sociology and Social Research, 70,* 272-275.

Freire, P. (1970). *Pedagogy of the oppressed*. New York: Continuum.

Frey, J. H., & Carns, D. E. (1988). Job satisfaction of casino card dealers. *Sociology and Social Research, 72,* 159-164.

Frey, J. H., & Fontana, A. (1988). *Job satisfaction and work values among mature workers*. Paper presented at the American Sociological Association meetings, Atlanta, Georgia.

Gallupe, R. B., Dennis, A. R., Cooper, W. H., Valacich, J. S., Bastianutti, L. M., & Nunamaker, J. F. (1992). Electronic brainstorming and group size. *Academy of Management Journal, 35,* 350-369.

Gallupe, B., DeSanctis, G., & Dickson, G. (1988). Computer-based support for group problem solving: An experimental investigation. *MIS Quarterly, 12,* 277-299.

Gans, H. J. (1982). *The urban villagers.* New York: The Free Press.

Geertz, C. (1988). *Work and lives: The anthropologist as an author.* Stanford, CA: Stanford University Press.

Gilgun, J. F., Daly, K., & Handel, G. (1992). *Qualitative methods in family research.* Newbury Park, CA: Sage.

Glaser, B., & Strauss, A. (1967). *The discovery of grounded theory.* Chicago: Aldine.

Glasser, P. H., & Glasser, L. N. (1970). *Families in crisis.* New York: Harper & Row.

Goffman, E. (1959). *The presentation of self in everyday life.* Garden City, NY: Doubleday.

Goldman, A. E. (1962). The group depth interview. *Journal of Marketing, 26,* 61-81.

Gonsiorek, J. C., & Shernoff, M. (1991). AIDS prevention and public policy: The experience of gay males. In J. C. Gonsiorek & J. D. Weinrich (Eds.), *Homosexuality: Psychology's role in the health crisis* (pp. 230-243). Newbury Park, CA: Sage.

Goodwin, L. (1983). *The causes and cures of welfare: New evidence on the social psychology of the poor.* Lexington, MA: Lexington.

Gordon, R. L. (1975). *Interviewing: Strategy, techniques, and tactics.* Homewood, IL: Dorsey.

Gove, W. R., & Hughes, M. (1983). *Overcrowding in the household.* New York: Academic Press.

Gove, W. R., Hughes, M., & Galle, O. (1979). Overcrowding in the home: An empirical investigation of its possible pathological consequences. *American Sociological Review, 44,* 59-80.

Greenbaum, T. L. (1988). *The practical handbook and guide to focus group research.* Lexington, MA: Lexington.

Groves, R. (1989). *Survey costs and survey errors.* New York: John Wiley.

Grunig, L. A. (1990). Using focus group research in public relations. *Public Relations Review, 16,* 36-49.

Gubrium, J. (1988). *Analyzing field reality.* Newbury Park, CA: Sage.

Gustafson, D. H., Shukla, R. M., Delbecq, A. L., & Walster, G. W. (1973). A comparative study of differences in subjective estimation made by individuals, interacting groups, Delphi groups, and nominal groups. *Organizational Behavior and Human Performance, 9,* 280-291.

Guthrie, E. (1935). *The psychology of learning.* New York: Harper & Row.

Hannerz, U. (1969). *Soulside: Inquiries into ghetto culture and community.* New York: Columbia University Press.

Harmon, P., & King, D. (1985). *Expert systems.* New York: John Wiley.

Hart, R. P., & Burks, D. M. (1972). Rhetorical sensitivity and social interaction. *Speech Monographs, 39,* 76-91.

Havanon, N., Knodel, J., & Sittitrai, W. (1990). The impact of family size on wealth accumulation. Project on the socio-economic consequences of fertility decline for the Thai family (Report No. 5). Bangkok: Chulalongkorn University, Institute of Population Studies.

Hayward, W., & Rose, J. (1990). "We'll meet again . . .": Repeat attendance at focus group discussions. Does it matter? *Journal of the Market Research Society, 32,* 377-407.

Hedges, A. (1985). Group interviewing. In R. Walker (Ed.), *Applied qualitative research* (pp. 71-91). Brookfield, VT: Gower.

Hirokawa, R. Y. (1983a). Group communication and problem solving effectiveness: An investigation of group phases. *Human Communication Research, 9,* 291-305.

Hirokawa, R. Y. (1983b). Group communication and problem solving effectiveness II. *Western Journal of Speech Communication, 47*, 59-74.

Hochhauser, M. (1987, August). *Readability of AIDS educational materials.* Paper presented at the 95th annual convention of the American Psychological Association, New York.

Hooper, M. C. (1989). In crisis or calm, focus groups hit the mark. *Association Management, 41*, 116-119, 184.

Hudgins J. L., Holmes, B., & Locke, M. E. (1991). The impact of family structure variation among black families on the underenumeration of black males. Part two, Focus group research. Hampton, VA: Hampton University, Black Family Institute.

Hybels, S., & Weaver, R. L. (1989). *Communicating effectively* (2nd ed.). New York: Random House.

Hymes, D. (1972). Models of the interaction of language and social life. In J. J. Gumperz & D. Hymes (Eds.), *The ethnography of communication: Directions in sociolinguistics* (pp. 35-71). New York: Holt, Rinehart & Winston.

Hymes, D. (1974). *Foundations in sociolinguistics: An ethnographic approach.* Philadelphia: University of Pennsylvania Press.

Irwin, J. (1970). *The felon.* Englewood Cliffs, NJ: Prentice-Hall.

Irwin, J. (1972). Participant observation of criminals. In J. Douglas (Ed.), *Research on deviance* (pp. 117-138). New York: Random House.

Isenberg, D. J. (1986). Group polarization: A critical review and meta-analysis. *Journal of Personality and Social Psychology, 50*, 1141-1151.

James, J. (1972). On the block: Urban research perspectives. *Urban Anthropology, 1*, 125-140.

Janis, I. L. (1972). *Victims of groupthink.* Boston: Houghton Mifflin.

Jarrett, R. L. (1990). *A comparative examination of socialization patterns among low-income African-Americans, Chicanos, Puerto Ricans, and whites: A review of the ethnographic literature.* New York: Social Science Research Council.

Jarrett, R. L. (1991). *Gender roles among low-income, African-American women: Qualitative explorations.* Unpublished manuscript.

Jarrett, R. L. (1992). A family case study: An examination of the underclass debate. In J. Gilgun, G. Handel, & K. Daley (Eds.), *Qualitative methods in family research* (pp. 172-197). Newbury Park, CA: Sage.

Joseph, J. G., Emmons, C. A., Kessler, R. C., Wortman, C. B., O'Brien, K., Hocker, W. T., & Schaefer, C. (1984). Coping with the threat of AIDS: An approach to psychosocial assessment. *American Psychologist, 39*(11), 1297-1302.

Kahn, R. L., & Cannell, C. (1957). *The dynamics of interviewing: Theory, technique, and cases.* New York: Wiley.

Kanter, R. M. (1977). *Men and women of the corporation.* New York: Basic.

Kaplan, A. (1964). *The conduct of inquiry: Methodology for behavioral science.* San Francisco: Chandler.

Kaplan, H. B. (1989). Methodological problems in the study of psychosocial influences on the AIDS process. *Social Science and Medicine, 29*(3), 277-292.

Kark, S. (1981). *Community-oriented primary health care.* New York: Appleton-Century-Crofts.

Katz, E. (1957). The two-step flow of communication. *Public Opinion Quarterly, 21*, 61-78.

Katz, E. (1967). Diffusion III: Interpersonal influence. In D. Sills (Ed.), *International encyclopedia of the social sciences* (Vol. 4). New York: Macmillan.

Kelly, J. A., & St. Lawrence, J. S. (1988). AIDS prevention and treatment. *Clinical Psychology Review, 8,* 255-284.

Kelman, H. (1961). Processes of opinion change. *Public Opinion Quarterly, 25,* 57-78.

Kish, L. (1987). *Statistical design for research.* New York: Wiley.

Klausner, W. J. (1972). *Reflections in a log pond.* Bangkok: Suksit Siam.

Klausner, W. J. (1981). *Reflections on Thai culture.* Bangkok: Suksit Siam.

Klein, E. (1989). What you can—and can't—learn from focus groups. *D&B Reports, 37,* 26-28.

Knodel, J., Chamratrithirong, A., & Debavalya, N. (1987). *Thailand's reproductive revolution: Rapid fertility decline in a third-world setting.* Madison: University of Wisconsin Press.

Knodel, J., Havanon, N., & Pramualratana, A. (1984). Fertility transition in Thailand: A qualitative analysis. *Population and Development Review, 10*(2), 297-328.

Knodel, J., Havanon, N., & Sittitrai, W. (1990). Family size and the education of children in the context of rapid fertility decline. *Population and Development Review, 16*(1), 31-62.

Knodel, J., Podhisita, C., & Sittitrai, W. (1988). *An annotated questionnaire to explore the socio-economic consequences of family size in Thailand. Project on socio-economic consequences of fertility decline for the Thai family* (Report No. 1). Bangkok: Chulalongkorn University, Institute for Population Studies.

Knodel, J., Sittitrai, W., & Brown, T. (1990). *Focus group discussions for social science research: A practical guide with an emphasis on the topic of aging* (Population Studies Center, No. 90-3). Ann Arbor: University of Michigan.

Krueger, R. A. (1988). *Focus groups: A practical guide for applied research.* Newbury Park, CA: Sage.

Ladner, J. A. (1971). *Tomorrow's tomorrow: The Black woman.* New York: Anchor.

Lazarsfeld, P., Berelson, B., & Gaudet, H. (1948). *The people's choice.* New York: Columbia University Press.

Lengua L. J., Roosa, M. W., Schupak-Neuberg, E., Michaels, M. L.,Berg, C. N., & Weschler, L. F. (1992). Using focus groups to guide the development of a parenting program for difficult-to-reach, high-risk families. *Family Relations, 41,* 163-168.

Lewin, K. (1951). *Field theory in social science: Selected theoretical papers* (Dorwin Cartwight, Ed.). New York, Harper.

Liebow, E. (1967). *Tally's corner: A study of Negro streetcorner men.* Boston: Little, Brown.

Lincoln, Y. S., & Guba, E. G. (1985). *Naturalistic inquiry.* Beverly Hills, CA: Sage.

Littlejohn, S. W. (1989). *Theories of human communication.* Belmont, CA: Wadsworth.

Lofland, J. (1971). *Analyzing social settings: A guide to qualitative observation and analysis.* Belmont, CA: Wadsworth.

Lofland, J., & Lofland, L. H. (1984). *Analyzing social settings* (2nd ed.). Belmont, CA: Wadsworth.

Loo, C., & Ong, P. (1984). Crowding perceptions, attitudes, and consequences among the Chinese. *Environment and Behavior 16,* 55-87.

Lown, E., Winkler, K., Fullilove, R. E., & Fullilove, M. T. (1991). *Tossin' and tweakin': Women's consciousness in the crack culture.* Unpublished manuscript, University of California at San Francisco and HIV Center for Clinical and Behavioral Studies, New York.

Lyng, S. G., & Snow, D. A. (1986). Vocabularies of motive and high-risk behavior: The case of skydiving. *Advances in Group Processes, 3,* 157-179.

Macleod, J. (1987). *Ain't no makin' it: Leveled aspirations in a low-income community.* Boulder, CO: Westview.

Maguire, P. (1987). *Doing participatory research: A feminist approach.* Amherst, MA: University of Massachusetts, School of Education, The Center for International Education.

Malinowski, B. (1967). *A diary in the strict sense of the term.* New York: Harcourt, Brace, & World.

Marcus, G., & Fischer, M. (Eds.). (1986). *Anthropology as cultural critique: An experimental moment in the human sciences.* Chicago: University of Chicago Press.

Mariampolski, H. (1989). Probing correctly uncovers truth behind answers in focus group. *Marketing News, 22,* 22-26.

Martin, E., & Martln, J. M. (1978). *The black extended family.* Chicago: University of Chicago Press.

Martin, W. (1977, February). The Baptists want you! *Texas Monthly,* pp. 83-87, 149-157.

McCall, G. J., & Simmons, J. L. (Eds.). (1969). *Issues in participant observation: A text and reader.* Menlo Park, CA: Addison-Wesley.

McCarthy, C. (1990, June 2). A very profitable medical practice. *Washington Post,* p. A19.

McClelland, D. C. (1961). *The achieving society.* Princeton, NJ: Van Nostrand.

McCracken, G. (1988). *The long interview.* Beverly Hills, CA: Sage.

McDonald, W. J., & Topper, G. E. (1988). Focus groups with children: A structural approach. *Applied Marketing Research, 28,* 3-11.

McGeary M. G., & Lynn, L. E. (Eds.). (1988). *Urban change and poverty.* Washington, DC: National Academy Press.

McHenry, N. (1992). Who do you ask? What do you ask? And how? Polling the community for CRA. *Bank Marketing, 24,* 30-31.

Merton, R. K. (1987). The focused interview and focus groups. *Public Opinion Quarterly. 51,* 550-566.

Merton, R. K., Fiske, M., & Kendall, P. L. (1956). *The focused interview.* Glencoe, IL: Free Press.

Merton, R. K., Fiske, M., & Kendall, P. L. (1990). *The focused interview.* New York: Free Press.

Miles, M. B., & Huberman, A. M. (1984). *Qualitative data analysis: A sourcebook of new methods.* Beverly Hills, CA: Sage.

Miller, C. (1991). Respondents project, let psyches go crazy. *Marketing News, 25,* 1-19.

Miller, G. R., & Steinberg, M. (1975). *Between people: A new analysis of interpersonal communication.* Chicago: Science Research Associates.

Miller, W. L., & Crabtree, B. F. (1992a). Depth interviewing: The long interview approach. In M. Stewart, F. Tudiver, M. J. Bass, E. V. Dunn, & P. G. Norton (Eds.), *Tools for primary care research* (pp. 3-30). Newbury Park, CA: Sage.

Miller, W. L., & Crabtree, B. F. (1992b). Primary care research: A multimethod typology and qualitative road map. In B. F. Crabtree & W. L. Miller (Eds.), *Doing qualitative research.* Newbury Park, CA: Sage.

Miller, W. L., & Crabtree, B. F. (in press). Clinical research. In N. Denzin & Y. Lincoln (Eds.), *Handbook of qualitative research.* Newbury Park, CA: Sage.

Mishler, E. G. (1986). *The discourse of medicine: Dialectics of medical interviews.* Norwood, NJ: Ablex.

Moeller, G. H., Mescher, M. A., More, T. A., & Shafter, E. L. (1980). The informal interview as a technique for recreation research. *Journal of Leisure Research, 12,* 174-182.

Montano, D. E. (1986). Predicting and understanding influenza vaccination behavior: Alternatives to the health belief model. *Medical Care, 25,* 438-453.

Morgan, D. L. (1988). *Focus groups as qualitative research.* Newbury Park, CA: Sage.

Morgan, D. L. (1990, August). *Designing focus group research.* Paper presented at the American Sociological Association Conference, Washington, DC.

Morgan, D. L. (1992). Designing focus group research. In M. Stewart, F. Tudiver, M. J. Bass, E. V. Dunn, & P. G. Norton (Eds.), *Tools for primary care research* (pp. 194-208). Newbury Park, CA: Sage.

Morgan, D. L. & Spanish, M. T. (1984). Focus groups: A new tool for qualitative research. *Qualitative Sociology, 7,* 253-270.

Morse, J. M. (Ed.). (1989). *Qualitative nursing research: A contemporary dialogue.* Rockville, MD: Aspen.

Moses, L. E. (1952). Non-parametric statistics for psychological research. *Psychological Bulletin, 49,* 122-143.

Myerhoff, B. (1978). *Number our days.* New York: Simon & Schuster.

North Carolina Department of Environment, Health, and Natural Resources. (1989). *Community Diagnosis: County Data Book for Madison County.* Raleigh: North Carolina Department of Environment, Health, and Natural Resources.

North Carolina Department of Environment, Health, and Natural Resources (1991). *Community Diagnosis: County Data Book for Madison County.* Raleigh: North Carolina Department of Environment, Health, and Natural Resources.

North Carolina State Data Center. (1986). *1986 Profile: North Carolina counties.* Raleigh, NC: Office of Budget and Management.

North Carolina State Center for Health Statistics. (1987). *Leading causes of mortality: North Carolina vital statistics, 1986,* vol. 2. Raleigh: North Carolina Department of Environment, Health, and Natural Resources.

North Carolina State Data Center. (1989). *LINK computer data base of 1987.* U.S. Census of Agriculture, Advance State Report for North Carolina. Report number AC87-A-37(A). Washington: Government Printing Office.

Nutting, P. (1990). *Community-oriented primary care: From principle to practice.* Albuquerque: University of New Mexico Press.

O'Brien, K. (1989). *The Portland Men's Study: A report to the community on progress and plans* (Respondent Report). Portland, OR: Portland State University, Department of Psychology.

O'Connor, P. J., Crabtree, B. F, & Abourizk, N. N. (1992). Longitudinal study of a diabetes education and care intervention: Predictors of improved glycemic control. *Journal of American Board Family Practice, 5*(4), 381-387.

Ogbu, J. U. (1978). *Minority education and caste: The American system in cross-cultural perspective.* New York: Academic Press.

Overall, N. A., & Williamson, J. (1989). *Community oriented primary care in action: A practice manual for primary care settings.* Berkeley: University of California, School of Public Health.

Packer, M. J., & Addison, R. B. (Eds.). (1989). *Entering the circle: Hermeneutic investigation in psychology.* Albany: State University of New York Press.

Pagnucco, D. J., & Quinn, R. P. (1988). "Natural group" interviews: Alternative to focus group. *Marketing News, 22,* 44.

Patton, M. Q. (1990). *Qualitative evaluation and research methods.* Newbury Park, CA: Sage.

Plaut, T. (1988). Cross-cultural conflict between providers and clients and staff members. In S. E. Keefe (Ed.), *Appalachian mental health.* Lexington: University Press of Kentucky.

Podhisita, C., Havanon, N., Knodel, J., & Sittitrai, W. (1990). Women's work and family size in rural Thailand. *Asia-Pacific Population Journal, 5*(2), 31-52.

Potts, D. (1990). Bias lurks in all phases of qualitative research. *Marketing News, 24,* 12-13.

Putnam, L. L., Van Hoeven, S. A., & Bullis, C. A. (1991). The role of rituals and fantasy themes in teachers' bargaining. *Western Journal of Speech Communication, 55,* 85-103.

Rainwater, L. (1970). *Behind ghetto walls: Black families in a federal slum.* Chicago: Aldine.

Rainwater, L., & Pittman, D. J. (1967). Ethical problems in studying a politically sensitive and deviant community. *Social Problems, 14,* 357-366.

Richards, L., & Richards, T. (1991). Computing in qualitative analysis: A healthy development? *Qualitative Health Research, 1*(2), 234-262.

Rigler, E. (1987). Focus on focus groups. *ABA Banking Journal, 79,* 96-100.

Rogers, E. M., & Shoemaker, F. F. (1971). *Communication of innovations: A cross-cultural approach.* New York: Free Press.

Roller, M. (1992). Employee research aids productivity and morale. *Marketing News, 26,* 14.

Rosenberg, M. (1965). *Society and the adolescent self-image.* Princeton, NJ: Princeton University Press.

Sawyer, E. (1973). Methodological problems in studying so-called "deviant" communities. In J. Ladner, (Ed.), *The death of white sociology* (pp. 361-379). New York: Random House.

Schatzman, L., & Strauss, A. L. (1973). *Field research: Strategies for a natural sociology.* Englewood Cliffs, NJ: Prentice-Hall.

Schutz, A. (1967). *The phenomenology of the social world.* Evanston, IL: Northwestern University Press.

Schwartz, R. M. (1991). Attention to details keeps clients coming back. *Marketing News, 25,* 6-7.

Seibold, D. R., & Roper, R. E. (1979). Psychological determinants of health care intentions: Test of the Triandis and Fishbein models. In D. Nimmo (Ed.), *Communication yearbook 3* (pp. 625-643). New Brunswick, NJ: Transaction Books.

Seidel, J. V., & Clark, J. A. (1984). The ethnograph: A computer program for the analysis of qualitative data. *Qualitative Sociology 7*(1/2), 110-125.

Seidel, J. V., Kjolseth, R., & Seymour, E. (1988). *The ethnograph: A user's guide.* Littleton, CO: Qualis Research Associates.

Service, C., & Salber, E. J. (1979). *Community health education: The lay advisor approach.* Durham, NC: Duke University, Health Systems Inc.

Shaler, G. (19912a). *An assessment of the Madison County Community Oriented Primary Care Project's Community Advisory Board.* Chapel Hill: University of North Carolina, Health Behavior and Health Education Department.

Shaler, G. (1992b). *Putting the community back in COPC-Madison community health project.* Unpublished master's paper, University of North Carolina, Chapel Hill.

Shaw, M. (1981). *Group dynamics: The psychology of small group behavior.* New York: McGraw-Hill.

Siegel, S., & Castellan, N. J. (1988). *Nonparametric statistics for the behavioral sciences* (2nd ed.). New York: McGraw-Hill.

Simon, M. (1987). Physician focus groups require special techniques. *Marketing News, 21*, 21-22.

Sink, D. W. (1991). Focus groups as an approach to outcome assessment. *American Review of Public Administration, 21*, 197-204.

Sittitrai, W., Wolff, B., Knodel, J., Havanon, N., & Podhisita, C. (1991). *Family size and family well being: The views of Thai villagers* (Project on Socio-Economic Consequences of Fertility Decline for the Thai Family, Report No. 5). Bangkok: Chulalongkorn University, Institute of Population Studies.

Smith, J. M. (1972). *Interviewing in market and social research.* Boston: Routledge & Kegan Paul.

Smith, M. J. (1988). *Contemporary communication research methods.* Belmont, CA: Wadsworth.

Socarides, C. W. (1970). Homosexuality and medicine. *Journal of the American Medical Association, 212*, 1199-1202.

Spethman, B. (1992). Focus groups key to researching kids: These aren't pint sized adults, so interaction counts as much as the question. *Advertising Age, 63*, S1-S24.

Spradley, J. P. (1979). *The ethnographic interview.* New York: Holt, Rinehart, & Winston.

Stack, C. B. (1974). *All our kin: Strategies for survival in a Black community.* New York: Harper & Row.

Stall, R. D., Coates, T. J., & Hoff, C. (1988). Behavioral risk reduction for HIV infection among gay and bisexual men: A review of results from the United States. *American Psychologist, 43*(11), 878-885.

Star, S. A., & Hughes, H. M. (1949-1950). Report on an educational campaign: The Cincinnati plan for the United Nations. *American Journal of Sociology, 55*, 389.

Steckler, A., McLeroy, K. R., Goodman, R. M., Bird, S. T., & McCormick, L. (1992). Toward integrating qualitative and quantitative methods: An introduction. *Health Education Quarterly, 19*, 1-8.

Steiner, I. D. (1972). *Group process and productivity.* New York: Academic Press.

Stewart, D. W., Shamdasani, P. N. (1990). *Focus groups: Theory and practice.* Newbury Park, CA: Sage.

Stone, L., & Campbell, G. (1984). The use and misuse of surveys in international development: An experiment from Nepal. *Human Organization 43*, 27-37.

Strauss, A., & Corbin, J. (1990). *Basics of qualitative research: Gounded theory procedures and techniques.* Newbury Park, CA: Sage.

Sullivan, M. (1985). *Teen fathers in the inner-city.* New York: Ford Foundation.

Sullivan, M. (1989). *Getting paid: Youth crime and work in the inner-city.* Ithaca, NY: Cornell University Press.

Sunnafrank, M., & Miller, G. R. (1981). The role of initial conversations in determining attraction to similar and dissimilar strangers. *Human Communication Research, 8*, 16-25.

Taylor, S. J., & Bogdan, R. (1984). *Introduction to qualitative research methods: The search for meanings* (2nd ed). New York: Wiley.

Tesch, R. (1990). *Qualitative research: Analysis types and software tools.* New York: Falmer.

Thompson, J. D., & Demerath, N. J. (1952). Some experiences with the group interview. *Social Forces, 31*, 148-154.

Tinto, V. (1987). *Leaving college: Rethinking the causes and cures of student attrition.* Chicago: University of Chicago Press.

Triandis, H. C. (1980). Values, attitudes, and interpersonal behavior. In H. E. How (Ed.), *Nebraska symposium on motivation* (Vol. 27, pp. 195-259). Lincoln: University of Nebraska Press.

Trostle, J. (1986). Anthropology and epidemiology in the twentieth century: A selective history of the collaborative projects and theoretical affinities. In C. R. Janes, R. Stall, & S. M. Gifford (Eds.). *Anthropology and epidemiology.* Boston: D. Reidel.

U.S. Department of Health and Human Services. (1986). *Surgeon General's report on acquired immune deficiency syndrome.* Washington, DC: Author.

Valentine, B. L. (1978). *Hustling and other hard work: Life styles of the ghetto.* New York: Free Press.

Van de Ven, A. H., & Delbecq, A. L. (1971). Nominal vs interacting group processes for committee decision making effectiveness. *Academy of Management Journal, 14,* 203-212.

VanGundy, A. B. (1988). *Techniques of structured problem solving* (2nd ed.). New York: Van Nostrand Reinhold.

Van Maanen, J. (1988). *Tales of the field.* Chicago: University of Chicago Press.

Walter, D. (1985). New foundation will survey nation's gay voting patterns. *Advocate, 424,* 16.

Ward, V. M., Bertrand, J. T., & Brown, L. F. (1991). The comparability of focus group and survey results. *Evaluation Review 15,* 266-283.

Webb, E. J., Campbell, D. T., Schwartz, R. D., & Sechrest, L. (1965). *Unobtrusive measures.* Chicago: Rand McNally.

Weber, R. P. (1985). *Basic content analysis.* Beverly Hills, CA: Sage.

Wells, W. D. (1979). Group interviewing. In J. B. Higgenbotham & K. K. Cox (Eds.), *Focus group interviews: A reader* (pp. 2-12). Chicago: American Marketing Association.

Whyte, W. F. (1981). *Street corner society.* Chicago: University of Chicago Press.

Wilson, E. O. (1975). *Sociobiology: The new synthesis.* Cambridge, MA: Belknap.

Winski, J. M. (1992). "Addicted" to research, Nick shows strong kids' lure: Agency exec says net hits the hot button. *Advertising Age, 63,* S2, S22.

Woolridge, P. M. (1991). Focus group respondents deserve a little empathy. *Marketing News, 25,* 6-7.

Yancey, W. L., & Rainwater, L. (1970). Problems in the ethnography of the urban underclass. In R. Habenstein (Ed.), *Pathways to data: Field methods for studying ongoing social organizations* (pp. 245-269). Chicago: Aldine.

Yin, R. K. (1989). *Case studies research* (2nd Ed.). Newbury Park, CA: Sage.

Yovovich, B. G. (1991). Focusing on customers' needs and motivations. *Business Marketing, 76,* 41-43.

Zucker, L. (1966). Mental health and homosexuality. *Journal of Sex Research, 2,* 111-125.

Zuckerman, H. (1972). Interviewing an ultra-elite. *Public Opinion Quarterly. 36,* 159-175.

Author Index

Subject Index

About the Contributors

Terrance L. Albrecht received her Ph.D. in 1978 from Michigan State University. She is currently Professor of Communication and Chair of the Department of Communication at the University of South Florida. She has used focus groups to conduct studies on mixed status relationships in health care contexts. She has conducted numerous studies on the role of social support in health and well-being and the influence of personal relationships on organizational innovation. Her recent articles have appeared in *Human Communication Research, Communication Monographs, Journal of Social and Personal Relationships,* and *Communication Research.* She was lead author of *Communicating Social Support* and is co-editing two books in progress, *Contemporary Communication Theory* and *The Communication of Social Support: Messages, Interactions, Relationships, and Community.*

Benjamin F. Crabtree, Ph.D., is a medical anthropologist in the Department of Family Practice, University of Nebraska Medical Center, where he is an Associate Professor and Director of Research. He has contributed numerous articles and chapters on both qualitative and quantitative methods, covering topics ranging from time series analysis and log-linear models to in-depth interviewing and qualitative analysis strategies. He is a co-editor of *Doing Qualitative Research.* His work has been published in the *Journal of Clinical Epidemiology, Public Health Reports,* and *Family Medicine.*

John N. Edwards is Professor of Sociology at Virginia Polytechnic Institute and State University. He received his Master's and Ph.D. degrees from the University of Nebraska. His primary research interests concern issues related to marriage and the family. He is currently a co-investigator on a U.S. longitudinal project dealing with marital change and instability over the life course. He has written several books and numerous journal articles.

Andrea Fontana is a Professor of Sociology at University of Nevada at Las Vegas. He has published articles on Sartre, Goffman, Pareto, and existential sociology as well as articles on various aspects of aging. He is the current editor of *Symbolic Interaction.* He has authored and edited various books, including *Existential Self in Society.* His current research is exploring the application of postmodernism to sociology.

James H. Frey is Professor of Sociology and Director of the Center for Survey Research at the University of Nevada at Las Vegas. He is the author of *Survey Research by Telephone* and *An Organizational Analysis of University Environment Relations,* editor of *The Governance of Intercollegiate Athletics* and co-editor of *Government and Sport.* He has published articles on postretirement workers, sport sociology, deviant behavior, and research methodology. His current research is in the areas of organization deviance, question-order response effects, and sport socialization.

Theodore D. Fuller is Associate Professor of Sociology at Virginia Polytechnic Institute and State University. He received his Master's and Ph.D. degrees from the University of Michigan. Since 1974, he has worked extensively in Thailand, primarily in the area of rural-to-urban migration. He has published one book, several chapters, and numerous articles based on his research in Thailand.

Robin L. Jarrett received her Ph.D. in Sociology from the University of Chicago. Her specialties include family and socialization, qualitative methods, and urban poverty. She has received grants and fellowships from the American Sociological Association, National Science Foundation, Rockefeller Foundation, Social Science Research Council, and the

Spencer Foundation to study low-income families. She is a member of the American Sociological Association, National Council on Family Relations, and the Social Science Research Council's Working Group on Communities and Neighborhoods, Family Processes and Individual Development. She is an Assistant Professor at Loyola University in Chicago and currently is on leave as a Visiting Scholar at the Russell Sage Foundation. She has received a 5-year W. T. Grant Faculty Scholar award to conduct ethnographic research on the relationship between family life, community context, and social mobility outcomes among poor youth.

Gerianne M. Johnson received her Ph.D. from the University of Washington. She is currently an Assistant Professor of Speech and Communication Studies at San Francisco State University. Her research interests include communication network influences on organizational empowerment among disabled employees, social support, and organizational innovation.

John Knodel is Professor of Sociology and Research Associate at the Population Studies Center of the University of Michigan. He received his Ph.D. from Princeton University. He has used focus groups in the field of social demography since 1982 in connection with several research projects in Thailand dealing with fertility decline, consequences of family size for family well-being, and the transition from primary to secondary school. He is currently engaged in a comparative focus group study dealing with the position and support of the elderly in four Asian countries. His publications include articles in numerous demographic and sociological journals as well as several monographs including Thailand's *Reproductive Revolution: Rapid Fertility Decline in a Third World Setting* and *Demographic Behavior in the Past: German Village Populations in the 18th and 19th Centuries.*

Richard A. Krueger received his Ph.D. from the University of Minnesota in Educational Policy Studies. In his role as Professor and Program Evaluation Leader with the University of Minnesota Extension Service, he assists university faculty in evaluating their educational programs. In addition, he teaches graduate courses in Program Evaluation in the College of Education, for which he serves as Adjunct Professor. His areas of research interest are focus group interviewing and program evaluation. He is the author of *Focus Groups: A Practical Guide for Applied*

Research. He regularly conducts workshops on focus group interviewing, speaks at conferences, and consults on the uses of focus group interviews.

Suzanne Landis, M.D., M.P.H., is the Madison Community Health Project Director. She is a Diplomate of the American Board of Internal Medicine and the American Board of Preventive Medicine. She balances a medical practice with teaching in the Mountain Area Health Education Center Family Practice Residency Program in Asheville, North Carolina, and is also a Clinical Associate Professor in the Department of Medicine of the University of North Carolina at Chapel Hill. She received her medical degree from the University of Pennsylvania Medical School.

David L. Morgan, Ph.D., is an Associate Professor in the Institute of Aging at Portland State University where he is also affiliated with the departments of Urban Studies and Sociology. His research interests center on the role that social networks and personal relationships play in coping with major transitions across the life course, such as widowhood and caregiving. In addition to his book *Focus Groups as Qualitative Research,* his articles have appeared in such journals as *American Journal of Sociology, The Gerontologist, Journal of Health and Social Behavior,* and the *Journal of Social and Personal Relationships.*

William L. Miller, M.D., M.A., a Family Physician Anthropologist in the Department of Family Medicine at the University of Connecticut, is active in an effort to make qualitative research more accessible to health-care researchers. He has contributed book chapters and articles detailing step-by-step applications of qualitative methods, including the book *Doing Qualitative Research,* which he co-edited. His research interests center on the role of the patient-physician relationship in health care, on physician and patient understanding of pain and pain management, and on hypertension.

Kerth O'Brien received her Ph.D. from the University of Michigan and is now a member of the faculty in the Department of Psychology at Portland State University. She is a social psychologist whose research interests lie in the effects of social relationships—especially, major role-related relationships—on health-related behaviors and on psychological health.

Patrick J. O'Connor, M.D., M.P.H., is a Family Physician and Epidemiologist in the Department of Family Medicine at the University of Connecticut. His research and teaching focuses on practical ways to improve diabetes and chronic disease care, especially in minority populations. He has published a series of articles that elucidate social and medical predictors of clinical outcomes, including metabolic control, quality of life, hospitalizations, and mortality. His research includes the use of both qualitative and quantitative methods.

Raymond V. Padilla received his Ph.D. in Higher Education from the University of California at Berkeley. His career experiences include Latino Education Coordinator for the Michigan Department of Education, Director of the Bilingual Bicultural Teacher Education Programs at Eastern Michigan University, and Director of the Hispanic Research Center at Arizona State University. He is currently a Professor in the Division of Educational Leadership and Policy Studies and a Research Professor at the Hispanic Research Center, both at Arizona State University. His research interests include bilingual education and Hispanics in higher education. He is the inventor of *HyperQual,* a program for qualitative data analysis on the Macintosh. He also invented *HyperFocus,* which is specifically designed for focus group data analysis.

Thomas Plaut, Ph.D. became involved in the Madison Community Health Project in the grant-writing stage and lately was asked to coordinate its community assessment process. He previously had helped organize hospice, victim assistance, and housing programs in the county. He has published articles on the nature of community and social change in Appalachia and on interactional problems between medical and social service providers and rural clients. A Professor of Sociology at Mars Hill College, he received his Ph.D. from the Union Institute.

Santhat Sermsri is Associate Professor of Sociology and the former Dean of the Faculty of Social Sciences and Humanities, Mahidol University, Bangkok, Thailand. He received his Ph.D. from Brown University with concentrations in Demography and Medical Sociology. His research interests include health care use and the impact of urbanization on health. He is the author of numerous articles, chapters, and technical reports.

Werasit Sittitrai earned his Ph.D. in Political Science and Anthropology from the University of Hawaii. He is a faculty member of the Institute of Population Studies at Chulaongakorn University and Deputy Director of the Thai Red Cross Society's Program on AIDS. He is also a current member of the World Health Organization's Steering Committee on Social and Behavioral Research on AIDS. He has conducted quantitative and qualitative research on a variety of topics, including family planning; socioeconomic consequences of fertility decline; the Thai elderly; sexual behavior; and operations research on condom use and risk of HIV infection among sex workers, adolescents, factory workers, and hill tribe populations. Among his publications is a manual on focus group discussions in sexual behavior research.

June Trevor has been the Project Coordinator for the Madison Community Health Project since 1989. Before that, she spent 7 years directing community-based Adult Development Activity Programs (ADAP) in Madison County. She previously conducted surveys in the areas of health, housing and education for the Research Triangle Institute, Raleigh, North Carolina. She also has worked as a Vista Volunteer Community Organizer.

Sairudee Vorakitphokatorn is Assistant Professor of Psychology at the Institute of Population and Social Research, Mahidol University, Bangkok, Thailand. She received her Ph.D. from the University of Illinois. Her primary research interests are in the area of child development. She has also recently conducted several research projects on AIDS. She is the author of numerous papers and reports.

Joseph B. Walther received his Ph.D. from the University of Arizona. He is currently Assistant Professor of Communication Studies at Northwestern University. He has directed focus groups for Tucson Newspapers, Inc. and conducted marketing research for the Survey Research Center in Dallas. His current research interests include social cognition and relational management and nonverbal and computer mediated communication. His work has been published in *Communication Research, Human Communication Research, The Journal of Nonverbal Behavior, The Journal of Business Communication,* and the *Journal of Social and Personal Relationships.* He is also the recipient of a software grant from Collaborative Group Technologies Corporation to study group interaction using decision support technology.

Brent Wolff is a doctoral candidate in Sociology at the University of Michigan and a Student Affiliate of the Population Studies Center. He is the co-author of *Child Survival: Risks and the Road to Health,* which reviews child health issues in developing countries. He is devoting his dissertation research to the study of social factors in access to maternal and child health care in various African settings. He was a co-analyst of the focus group transcripts at the Institute of Population Studies at Chulalongkorn University.

M. Kim Yanoshik, M.S., is a doctoral candidate in Sociology at the University of Connecticut and part-time Instructor at the University Health Center and Medical School. She is interested in bringing patient-centered health care to medical education and medical practice. Her research areas include patient and provider models of health and illness and women's health issues and contraceptive changes and challenges during the 1990s. She is co-editor and contributor to the book *Healing Technology: Feminist Perspectives.*

Richard A. Zeller received his Ph.D. in Sociology from the University of Wisconsin at Madison. He is a Professor of Sociology at Bowling Green State University, Bowling Green, Ohio. He is also International Consultant to the Augustine/Zeller Group. His substantive interests are in social psychology, human sexuality, statistics, research methodology, and applied research. He has published three books, manuals, and numerous professional articles and has made many professional presentations. He has conducted research for a variety of manufacturing, financial, medical, political, philanthropic, social service, and governmental organizations. He has served as Consultant to the National Institute of Mental Health, the National Science Foundation, and the International Development Research Centre. He has received numerous professional and instructional honors and awards.